THE LITURGY AND THE WORD OF GOD

THE LITURGY AND THE WORD OF GOD

Martimort

Jounel

Danielou

von Balthasar

Bouyer

Roquet

Gelineau

Coudreau

Moeller

Lecuyer

Spuelbeck

THE LITURGICAL PRESS

St. John's Abbey Collegeville, Minnesota

THE LITURGY AND THE WORD OF GOD—

Papers given at the Third National Congress of the *Centre de Pastorale Liturgique,* Strasbourg, France, 1958, first published under the title *Parole de Dieu et Liturgie*, Lex Orandi Series, Ed. du Cerf.

Nihil obstat: John Eidenschink, O.S.B., J.C.D., *Censor deputatus. Imprimi potest*: ✠ Baldwin Dworschak, O.S.B., Abbot of St. John's Abbey. *Imprimatur*: ✠ Peter W. Bartholome, D.D., Bishop of St. Cloud. October 20, 1959.

CONCLUSIONS FORMULATED BY THE STRASBOURG CONGRESS

1. *No liturgy without the Bible.*

The liturgy draws on the Bible for its readings and chants. Further, it is interwoven with echoes of the Bible, and in its hymns and prayers it makes use of words which are those of the Bible. Thus the Church prays throughout the whole world, and she has always done so.

It is not enough to say that the Bible occupies a privileged place in the liturgical celebration. It plays such a fundamental role that without the Bible there would be no liturgy.

We cannot enter profoundly into the liturgical celebration if we ignore sacred history. No liturgical progress is possible without the Biblical education of clergy and faithful alike.

2. *The Church reads the Bible in the liturgical assembly.*

Here we see the continuity between the Old Testament and the Church: the Word of God of old was addressed to the people assembled in the desert, gathered together by Moses. The Church always addresses the people as an assembly.

The liturgical assembly is the privileged site of the proclamation of the Word of God.

3. *The Church reads the whole Bible.*

The whole text of the Bible is not found in the books of the Roman liturgy. But four remarks must be made in this connection:

a) Every year, some pages of the majority of the holy Books have a place in the Breviary, as an invitation to read and meditate on the whole Book. The private reading of the Bible is the effect and fruit of the liturgical celebration.

b) If there are special passages to which the Church frequently refers, it is because these pages are the summits of sacred history. But these are understood the more fully the more one knows the whole of the Bible.

c) The Missal is more and more, for the faithful, the starting-point of Biblical culture.

d) Initiation into the Bible starting from the Missal allows us to avoid a subjective interpretation of the Biblical texts. It removes the danger of illuminism. It causes us to be the more fully aware of the fact that the Bible is given us by the Church. It emphasizes, furthermore, the profound bond which unites the Word of God and the sacrament.

4. *The whole Mass proclaims the Word of God.*

The first part of the Mass is, properly speaking, neither a Foremass nor a catechism lesson, but a liturgy of the Word of God. As the *Directoire* reminds us, "The Word of God is a proclamation in the Church of the mystery of salvation which is realized in the Eucharist" (*Directoire*, n. 1).

At the consecration, the Word of God (which was pronounced before being written) becomes the living, efficacious, saving and sanctifying Word.

5. *In the liturgy God speaks to us today.*

The Word of God gathered up in the Bible is not presented to us as a collection of archives, but as a Word addressed to us today by the living God.

To the man who reads the Bible without faith, the Book is a witness to the past; to the Christian who hears the text proclaimed in the liturgical assembly, the Word is present, of today; it reaches the depths of his being and causes him to communicate in the present action of God in the world.

6. *The liturgy carries out here and now what the Bible proclaims.*

The Bible tells and sings of the great works of God. Throughout the whole of the Old and the New Testaments God creates, judges, delivers His people, makes a covenant with them, is present in their midst to sanctify them.

In the Church the sacraments carry on in our midst the works of God, those of the Old and the New Testament. The same God acts in an analogous manner yesterday and today, to create, judge, save, make covenant with, dwell with His people and sanctify them.

The liturgy causes us to enter into the history of salvation. We are *in* sacred history. There is a rigorous continuity between Scripture and the Church.

7. *The sacraments are Biblical signs.*

Instituted by the Lord as signs of the New Covenant, the sacraments have a pre-history which is rooted in the whole Old Testament. This is why in the course of their celebration the Church evokes the most ancient pages of the Bible (Abel, Abraham, Melchisedech in the Canon of the Mass; Sara, Rebecca, Rachel in marriage; paradise, the flood, the exodus in the consecration of the baptismal water, etc.)

It is a fact of tradition that in her liturgy the Church establishes analogies between the sacraments of the New Covenant and the works of God under the Old Law. She does not call up a kind of play of serviceable images; she goes straight to the religious content of these accounts. The liturgy (in its most authentic elements) reunites us with the soul of the Bible: God continues to act and to intervene in human history as He began to do long ago.

And this is why, at the same time as it refers to the Biblical past, the liturgy, faithful to the spirit of the Bible, announces the future toward which we are tending. It announces that God will in the future perform analogous and still greater works.

8. *Even though the use of the Missal is more and more widespread, it is with their ears that the faithful should hear the Word of God.*

If the Bible is the Word of God addressed to men, they ought to *listen to it.* They ought to hear it with their ears; a lector is, then, indispensable. We cannot insist too much on the following:

a) before speaking to the faithful, the lector should wait until they have finished sitting down (for ordinary readings) or standing up (for the Gospel);

b) the reading must be carried out slowly enough and loudly enough to be heard;

c) pausing at appropriate places facilitates the understanding of the text;

d) before proclaiming a text, it is essential to have read it and understood it.

This technique is to serve a life of faith: the Word which we are to make heard is the Word of God. And, therefore, it is to be regretted that so often the reading in the mother tongue is carried out less carefully and that a less respectful attitude is maintained during it than when the proclamation is made in Latin.

9. *The faithful must understand the Word of God.*

For this we need a translation that is at once faithful and well phrased. Yet the attempt should never be made to render the text understandable by modifying it. The Bible is the Word of God; it is not man's business to soften it.

On the other hand, it is possible by means of a short comment given before the reading to remove textual difficulties. Finally, and above all, the proclamation of the Word should be followed by the homily which aids the actual congregation present to enter into the understanding of the Word of God. To be understood, the Bible demands a constant effort on our part. This effort must be made in order to allow the humblest of the faithful to receive the Word of God.

The homily is, furthermore, not simply an explanation; it is itself a glad proclamation. It echoes the Word of God. It should lead the hearer to adore that Word and to praise it.

10. *God has spoken a human language.*

This is the simple fact: the Bible is written with human words. The progress of the various Biblical sciences, far from lessening our admiration for the Bible, can only increase it, for they allow us to enter more deeply into the divine pedagogy here laid out.

For men of today, there are many stepping-stones leading to an understanding of the Bible. Modern man, like Biblical man, has a sense of the concrete and of history, a sense of solidarity, of love for the persecuted; he is rediscovering his sense of symbolism.

Because it speaks a human language, the Bible is rich in human resonances.

11. *The Church replies to God by the Word of God.*

God awaits a response to the Word that He addresses to us. The Word of salvation requires a dialogue.

God Himself, in the psalms and Biblical canticles, and in the *Our Father,* has given us the key-words of our response.

The liturgy takes up the psalms as being a prayer continually new and always springing up from the meeting between God and man.

When the Church prays, it is always in reference to what God has done for His people in the past, in hope that He will do the same for us today. The prayer of the Church is born of the Word of God and supports itself on it.

12. *The pedagogy of the faith of the child and the adolescent is bound up with presenting the Bible in the liturgy.*

The role of the Bible in the formation of Christians and particularly in the pedagogy of the faith of children and adolescents is primary. This fact is being rediscovered more and more clearly today.

But this formation would be misleading if the Bible or Biblical history were made to seem simply a memory exercise or matter for examination.

The Bible should cause the child to enter into the life of the people of God. This is why no catechesis is fully Biblical if it is not liturgical.

Participation in the Mass, attention to the liturgical cycle, celebrations of the Word that are carried out as part of catechesis are essential in order that the student may enter into the mystery of the people of God.

13. *The work of the Word of God goes beyond the limits of the liturgical celebration.*

Before coming to the sacramental life of the Church, man must be evangelized by the proclamation of the Word of God.

And when this Word is received in the liturgical assembly, it has not completed its course.

The believer is to keep this Word, it is to germinate in him, and little by little introduce him into a wisdom which is that of the children of God. It is fulfilled in prayer, in thanksgiving, in charity, in an apostolate. It wishes to transform the world and to establish in it the kingdom of God.

"And as the rain and the snow come down from heaven, and return no more thither, but soak the earth, and water it, and make it to spring, and give seed to the sower, and bread to the eater, so shall My Word be, which shall go forth from My mouth: it shall not return to Me void, but it shall do whatsoever I please, and shall prosper in the things for which I sent it" (Is. 55:10-11).

CONTENTS

Canon A. G. Martimort

INTRODUCTION

This book, as its title indicates, is a result of the meeting of two movements characteristic of Catholicism today: the liturgical and the Biblical. To begin with, then, let us briefly trace the paths taken by these two movements up to this point of confluence.

The liturgical movement came to realize in the course of its own interior development that it must become Biblical, that it could be neither authentic nor profound unless it were accompanied by a discovery of the Scriptures. Pope Pius XII, in his discourse closing the Assisi Congress, dated the beginning of the liturgical activity of the papacy in our times from the year 1913 and the publication of the Motu Proprio *Abhinc duos annos.* And this, of course, was, following the Bull *Divino Afflatu,* a return to the psalms in the Divine Office and some restoration of primacy to the Sunday and the economy of salvation.

At the time when these pontifical documents were appearing in Rome, Dom Lambert Beauduin in Belgium had just inaugurated the memorable and fruitful campaign of which we are the fortunate beneficiaries and heirs. Putting aside the grandiloquent prayer-formulas of the eighteenth and nineteenth centuries, educated Catholics began to nourish their piety on the texts of the Missal, its prayers, its psalm verses set to Gregorian melodies, in the spirit of the various liturgical seasons. And such Catholics were numerous indeed, if one can judge from the success enjoyed by the Missal of Dom Lefebvre between the two wars.

But this first discovery of the liturgy immediately led to others, the first being that of the popular character of the liturgical celebration. Far from being meant to be savored in solitude, the liturgy is communal by nature, and the liturgical community is not composed of a restricted élite but of uneducated and simple people also: the poor have had the Gospel preached to them.

From 1943 on, therefore, when Abbé Godin posed the question: "Is France a mission country?", the liturgical movement has been striving to distribute *to the little ones this bread that they crave;* we have been in anguish at the sight of the *sheep of Christ going hungry,* to use the words of the Council of Trent.

It was at the very moment when the effort began to gain momentum towards the popular diffusion of the liturgical message that we abruptly encountered the problem of its Biblical form. In translating the texts of the Ordinary of the Mass, the nuptial blessing, baptism, the Easter Vigil, certain members of the apostolate to the people balked at the idea of evoking all these ancient patriarchs, these primitive images, these prayer-formulas taken from the Pentateuch or the Psalter. But just when these well-intentioned apostles had begun to yield to the temptation to do away with this Biblical language which they declared to be out of the reach of the ordinary man, the yearly studies of the *Centre de Pastorale Liturgique,* founded in 1943, began to reveal, and with continually greater force, the importance of the Bible in the liturgy.

Far from being an external ornament, the Bible was found to be the very speech of the liturgy; the sacramental signs are Scriptural signs; the sacred realities presented in Christian worship are those of the economy of salvation revealed by sacred history and continuing it. As in 1946 we studied the Mass, in 1947 the Lord's Day, in 1948 the liturgy of the sick, and in 1949 that of the dead, in 1951 solemn Communion and confirmation, in 1952 baptism, and holy Orders and marriage in recent years, the decisive study in each case clearly was that of the Scriptural data, clarified by the rites themselves and set out by the Fathers in their catecheses.

But why should I call this work of ours a "study"? It was rather the joyful contemplation of the Mystery, of the perfect unity of the economy of salvation, of the Christian sense of history, of the struggles of man on this earth, of the divine pedagogy of the faith. It was the awareness that meditation begun under the impulse of the Biblical message contains indefinable harmonies. This door, seemingly closed, from which the people were turning away, actually opens on a kingdom. In the liturgy God speaks by the Bible.

We have come to realize, therefore, that no liturgical progress is possible without the Biblical education of Christians, since without the Bible there is no liturgy.

Now, in God's Providence, the liturgical movement can benefit from the Biblical studies carried out during the same period. It seemed at first, it is true, that Scripture scholars and liturgists were following parallel paths destined never to meet. At about the time when Dom Beauduin was launching the liturgical movement in the French language, Father Lagrange, who in 1890 had founded the School of Biblical

Studies in Jerusalem, wrote the first of his commentaries on the Gospel, commentaries which are still not outmoded after fifty years.

Against the modernist and liberal offensive, and in the face of the discoveries of historical criticism, Catholic scholars, following the lead of Father Lagrange, studied the composition and the pre-history of the sacred Books, the archeology and comparative literature of the Orient; they devoted themselves to textual criticism, apparently an austere and arid task. This work seemed calculated to discourage the reading of the holy Books for spiritual nourishment and refreshment, yet it has, on the contrary, finally served to develop it.

Abruptly, in 1943, the encyclical *Divino afflante Spiritu* gave public support to these scholars, who up to that time had appeared suspect. After so much research of a seemingly negative trend, the Bible now appeared as being essentially the history, slow and progressive, of revelation and salvation. After the aridities of philology, literary history could at last begin to flourish.

A new era of Biblical study opened out: that of research into the Biblical themes traced out, defined, purified, interwoven, spiritualized from the beginning of revelation to the end. To the surprise of the exegetes themselves, the analysis of these themes rehabilitated, to a great extent, the use made of the Bible by the liturgy and the Fathers. It is true that discrimination has to be exercised in this regard; nevertheless, the continuity between piety and scholarship has been rediscovered; and thus the last obstacles to the Christian reading of Scripture have been removed.

The difference between the style of the notes given in Bibles published in France before the war and those of recent years is significant here; the success of the latter is a proof of the interest of the faithful in the sacred Books. Above all, we have been shown in recent years the fact of the universal appeal of the psalms – they are prayed by lay people in books of Hours or Breviaries, they are sung to popular melodies in Christian gatherings. The Bible has ceased to be the private possession of the few and has once more become the book of every Christian. And thus the way has been prepared for this present confluence of the Biblical and liturgical movements, a confluence which, we pray, will still further extend and strengthen their effectiveness.

Rev. Pierre Jounel

CHAPTER 1

THE BIBLE IN THE LITURGY

My task is, at the outset of our studies, to make an inventory of the Biblical riches contained in the liturgical books – the Missal, the Ritual, the Pontifical, and the Breviary of the Divine Office – texts that become life, the Word of God and the Word of the Church of Christ, in their actual sacramental celebration.

One cannot celebrate the liturgy without encountering the Bible at every step. This fact is obvious, both on the plane of the official texts which the Church places in our hands for the celebration and on the plane of the celebration itself. We shall, therefore, first present the place of the Bible, the inspired Book, in the liturgical formularies; and secondly, the place of the Word of God in the liturgical action, the celebration.

THE BIBLE IN THE LITURGICAL FORMULARIES

At first sight there would appear to be a great difference between the psalmody of the Hours, the celebration of the Mass, and the administration of a sacrament. But, as we know, a comparative study – and especially one made in the converging lights given by the different rites of the East and the West — reveals a fundamental identity of structure, a design in three parts: reading, chant, and prayer. The Church inherited this pattern from the morning Office of the synagogue,[1] and, as Jungmann has shown, it is "neither arbitrary nor fortuitous, but corresponds to the very nature of the economy of salvation. Salvation comes from God, whose revelation we receive when we read His Word. This Word touches our hearts and awakens in them the echo of the chant. And, finally, the prayers of the assembled faithful are gathered together and offered to God by the priest."[2]

Now, we meet the Bible in each of the three parts of this fundamental liturgical pattern, equally in the liturgy of the Mass, in the celebration of the other sacraments, and in the Divine Office.

IN THE MASS

The whole liturgy of the Mass is filled with holy Scripture, both in the celebration of the Lord's Supper and in that of the Word of God.

The readings of the Mass are almost exclusively taken from Scripture.[3] But the arrangement of these readings differs considerably from one rite to another, and within each rite the method of reading is not necessarily uniform.

The arrangement of the readings in the various rites has only one common characteristic: the fact that the liturgy of the Word always culminates in the proclamation of the Gospel.

Arrangement of the Readings in the Western Rites

Rome ordinarily has only two readings: the Gospel is always preceded by a preliminary reading. But while this first reading is in the majority of cases taken from St. Paul, any other reading from the New Testament or the Old may be substituted. The ferial Masses of Lent have no reading of an Epistle in the strict sense of the word; a pericope from the Old Testament always takes its place. Even though certain Masses, those of the Ember Wednesdays and of the Wednesday of the Great Scrutiny, have three readings, they still have no Epistle, since the first two readings are taken from the Old Testament.

The Masses of the Ember Saturdays have, by way of exception, five readings from the Old Testament before the Epistle; but this distribution is not a primitive one — the old Roman lectionaries have either four or six readings;[4] the reading from Daniel and the Canticle of the

[1] A. Baumstark, *Comparative Liturgy* (Westminster, Md.: Newman Press, 1955), p. 45.

[2] J. A. Jungmann, *Des lois de la célébration liturgique* (Paris: Ed. du Cerf, 1956), p. 103.

[3] The Gallican and Spanish liturgies often reserved the first reading of the Mass for the *Passiones* of the martyrs. The lectionary of Luxeuil witnesses to this usage for the feast of the apostles Peter and Paul (edition by Dom Salmon, Rome, 1944, p. 181). See the article by de Gaiffier, "La lecture des Actes des Martyrs dans la prière liturgique en Occident," *Analecta Bollandiana,* 1954, pp. 134-166.

[4] According to the witness of the *Comes* of Würzburg (end of the sixth century),

Three Young Men is a Gallican addition. In reducing the number of the readings from twelve to four, the new Ordo of the Easter Vigil has re-established the practice of the time of Gregory the Great,[5] causing us to read, according to the best tradition, first the Law and the Prophets, and then the Apostle and the Gospel.

In the rites of *Milan* and *Toledo* there are usually three readings, as in the ancient Gallican liturgy. St. Ambrose indicates the traditional order: "First the Prophet is read, and the Apostle, and then the Gospel."[6] Various indications, in particular the number of Collects given in the early substrate of the Gelasian Sacramentary, allow us to presume that this was also the practice of the Roman Church before St. Gregory the Great. If this is the case, then the liturgies of Milan and Toledo are the guardians of the universal tradition of the West.[7] Any liturgical reform should be aware of the weight of this testimony.

In the Oriental Rites

The Oriental rites are divided into two great families, that of Antioch and that of Alexandria.

The *Syrian tradition* has been maintained in all its purity by the *Syrians of the Oriental rite,* who always have four readings, taken from the Law, the Prophets, the Apostle and the Gospel, according to the ordinance given in the fourth century by the *Apostolic Constitutions.*[8] Here we are in contact with a tradition which may go back to the apostolic age, since the twofold reading of the Law and the Prophets formed part of the meetings in the synagogue on Sabbath mornings (Luke 4:16-31; Acts 13:15; 15:21). The *Western Syrians* and the *Maronites,* having once had the four readings of the primitive arrangement, have now fixed the number at six (Law, Prophets, Wisdom, Acts, Apostles, Gospel), although in practice they ordinarily hold only to the last two. The *Armenians* read a passage from the Old Testament, then from the Apostle and the Gospel. The *Byzantines* read only the Apostle, followed by the Gospel.

The *Egyptian* tradition (the Coptic and Ethiopian rites) has remained faithful to the four readings, but it takes them all from the

published by G. Morin, "Le plus ancien *Comes* ou le lectionnaire de l'Église romaine," in *Revue benédictine,* 1910, pp. 41-74, reproduced with some errors in the DACL, 8, col. 2284-2302.

[5] The fourth reading is not that indicated in the Gregorian Sacramentary (Wilson edition, p. 55), but that given in the appendix to Ordo XXVIII (M. Andrieu, *Les ordines romani,* 3, p. 412), which is equally Roman.

[6] Ambrose of Milan, *In psalmum* CXVIII, 17, 10, PL 15, col. 1443: *Prius propheta legitur, et apostolus, et sic evangelium.* For the system of readings in use in Toledo, see G. Morin, *Liber comicus quo Toletana Ecclesia ante annos mille et ducentos utebatur* (Maredsous, 1893).

[7] Africa seems to be an exception. When St. Augustine speaks of *tres lectiones,* he includes the psalm as one of them: *Hoc de apostolica lectione percepimus, deinde cantavimus psalmum, post haec evangelica lectio, has tres lectiones pertractavimus* (Sermon 176).

[8] The best edition is to be found in Funk, *Didascalia et Constitutiones Apostolorum* (Paderborn, 1905), Vol. I.

New Testament, each one having its own name: *Apostolos* (St. Paul), *Catholicon* (Catholic Epistle), *Praxis* (Acts), *Evangelion* (Gospel).

Whatever the number of readings retained in the various rites may be, we should note the predominance given to the New Testament and the special place accorded St. Paul. But for our purposes here, the method in accordance with which the Bible is proclaimed in the assembly of the faithful is of equal importance with the arrangement of the readings.

The Method Followed in the Readings

In the liturgy of the Mass, the Bible is read either continuously or in selected pericopes.

Continuous reading was the method used in the ancient Church. The most obvious proof of this fact is to be found in the voluminous commentaries on the Old and New Testaments left us by the Fathers, for these are simply transcriptions of their homilies on the Scripture readings given in the liturgy. From the fourth century on, we see from the letters and the sermons of St. Ambrose and St. Augustine that certain Books were reserved to certain liturgical seasons: at Milan, as at Constantinople, the Books of Job and Jonas were read during Lent; in Africa, Genesis took up part of this season, and the Acts of the Apostles were read during Easter time.[9] But, even though the various Books of the Bible were attached by preference to a special period of the year, the president of the assembly was still free to determine the length of each reading.

It was in the middle of the fifth century, in Gaul, according to the twofold testimony of Sidonius Apollinarius and Gennadius of Marseilles, that the first efforts were made to determine the pericopes proper to given seasons. But the continuous reading was, naturally, interrupted by great feasts, for which were chosen the passages most appropriate to the mystery being celebrated.

In our own times, although the reading of selected passages has become the general rule, nevertheless the ancient practice of continuous reading has left more than a few traces in the various rites: among the Syrians, both Eastern and Western, the continuous and complete reading of each Book of holy Scripture has remained the normal form. In the Byzantine liturgy, the reading of the Gospel is distributed throughout the year among the Sundays of St. John (Easter time), of St. Matthew and of St. Luke, the Gospel of St. Mark being used on ferias from the twelfth week of Matthew on.[10]

In the Roman liturgy we still find important traces of the *lectio continua*, and many of us take pleasure in discovering them. For the Gospels, we can see that St. John was read from the fourth Sunday of Lent[11]

[9] References in the DACL, 5, col. 248-249. See also Baumstark, *op. cit.*

[10] N. Nilles, *Kalendarium manuale utriusque Ecclesiae* (Ratisbonne, 1897), 2, pp. 445-459.

[11] The day on which the Roman Lent probably began before the year 380. See A.

to Pentecost; then St. Luke until the sixteenth Sunday after Pentecost (eleven pericopes for sixteen Sundays); and St. Matthew up to Septuagesima (eleven pericopes for thirteen Sundays *per annum*). The plan for reading the Epistles of St. Paul is still clearer, not only in the Sundays after Epiphany (continuous reading of the twelfth and thirteenth chapters of Romans), but also from the sixteenth to the twenty-fourth Sunday after Pentecost, where the Epistles follow the exact order of the New Testament.

Both methods followed by the Church in the liturgical reading of the Bible imply a theology of Scripture. The *lectio continua* proclaims the fact that all Scripture is for our instruction, that it is the Word of God addressed, in a continual present, to the community of believers; while the selection of pericopes implies a meaningfulness in Scripture, at once a significance in relation to some present event and an internal progression of revelation itself.

Such a selection means bringing out the typology of Scripture: the account of creation and of the Exodus read during the Easter Vigil, the great images of salvation recalled during Lent (Daniel, Suzanna, the Three Young Men, Jonas) nourished the paschal faith of the primitive Christian community. These images were reproduced on the walls of the catacombs and of the houses that served as churches,[12] and later on in mosaic on the cupolas of baptistries,[13] because the Christians of early times had a living awareness of the continuity of the mystery of salvation. They knew that by baptism they themselves had set out on a new Exodus under the leadership of the new Moses, the Good Shepherd, Jesus.

The selection of pericopes also brings out the fact of a progression in revelation, and the fact that the believer must go through successive stages to arrive at the final goal. So, for example, in the Milanese rite for the Mass of the second Sunday after Pentecost the continuity of the divine plan shines out clearly: the first reading (Num. 20:2-13) shows us Moses drawing the living water from the rock; then in the Gospel (John 2:1-11) we see the water changed into wine, thus preparing us for the consecration in which this wine is transformed into the Blood of the risen Lord.

The Chants

The Bible furnishes not only the readings of the Mass; the Christian community looks to it also in most instances for the texts of the chants by which to respond in some way to God's Word. We are thinking particularly of the Gradual response and the processional chants for the

Chavasse, "La préparation de la Pâque à Rome avant le Ve. siècle," Mélanges Chaîne, pp. 67-76.

[12] At Doura-Europos, in the third-century baptistry, Adam and Eve, David and Goliath, the Good Shepherd can be seen; cf. Jean de Lassus, *Sanctuaires chrétiens en Syrie* (Paris, 1944), p. 11. This study is summarized by the author in DACL, 15, col. 1864.

[13] L. de Bruyne, "La décoration des baptistères paléochrétiens," in *Miscellanea liturgica in honorem L. Cuniberti Mohlberg* (Rome, 1948), IV, pp. 189-220.

Entrance, the Offertory, and the Communion – and with these we must also include the Alleluia chant, which, in all rites without exception, accompanies the Gospel procession.

Among the chants of the Mass, a special place must be given to the Gradual, not only because of its antiquity – which has given to the collection of all the chants of the Mass the name of *Graduale* – but because of the exceptional place that it holds in the liturgy of the Word. It is above all by this chant that the Church responds to the Word of God with the Word of God. *Legenti respondentes cantavimus,* as St. Augustine says in one of his sermons.[14] This is, as a recently published French Missal well names it, the "chant of meditation."

To understand its complete religious value, we should not think of it as sung with the lengthy neums by which monastic piety adorned it, but rather in its primitive form of psalm verses sung by a deacon or a lector,[15] with the people singing a refrain at regular intervals, often the acclamation *Alleluia.* We find Hippolytus – in the setting of the *agape,* it is true – already suggesting that psalms containing the *alleluia* should be used.[16] And the Irish Missal of Stowe (seventh to eighth century) contains as Communion chants a whole series of psalms in which the *alleluia* is repeated again and again.[17]

It may be that the Gradual had even an earlier form than this responsorial one: the simple reading of the psalm, of which we have the last vestige in the Tract of the Lenten Masses.

We have been speaking of psalmody; it is from the Psalter that, from the beginning, the Gradual was traditionally taken, and later on the processional chants as well: *Davidicum psalmum consona voce cantavimus,* St. Leo said to his assembled people.[18] The processional chants, at least the Introit and the Communion, follow one another in the Roman rite for the Sundays after Pentecost according to a kind of continuous psalmody (Ps. 12, 17, 24, 26, 27 . . . for the Introit; Ps. 9, 12, 16, 17 . . . for the Communion). But the Gradual psalm is always selected for its own sake, as Dom Hesbert has shown in his *Antiphonale Missarum.*[19] We find the Bible in the chants of the Mass, then, both in the form of *lectio continua* and in that of selected pericopes. We have already shown the significance of each method in speaking about the readings.

We should also note here the fact that, while the majority of Mass rites use varying formulas in the Communion chants, the ancient Church had only one Communion psalm, Psalm 33: *Benedicam Dominum* with

[14] St. Augustine, *Enarrationes super psalmos,* in Psalm. 40, 1.

[15] *Cantor cum cantatorio ascendit et dicit responsum* (*Ordo Primus,* n. 57, ed. Andrieu, IV, p. 86). During the paschal night it was the same lector who read in Latin both the Lesson and the Canticle before giving place to a lector in Greek. (Appendix to Ordo 28, ed. Andrieu, III, p. 412.)

[16] Hippolytus of Rome, *La tradition apostolique,* n. 26, ed. Botte, Sources chrétiennes, II (Paris: Ed. du Cerf, 1946), p. 61.

[17] G. H. Warner, The Stowe Missal (London, 1915), p. 18.

[18] Leo the Great, *Sermo 3 de Natali ipsius,* PL 54, col. 45.

[19] R. J. Hesbert, *Antiphonale Missarum sextuplex* (Brussels-Paris, 1935), p. 88.

the verse *Gustate et videte*. This is the testimony of the *Apostolic Constitutions* (fourth century) and of the Liturgy of St. James for Syria, of St. Augustine for Africa[20] and St. Cyril for Jerusalem. This same theme is developed today in the Armenian Communion chant: "Come to the Lord and be filled with His light, alleluia: taste and see how good is the Lord, alleluia."[21]

As to the Alleluia chant preceding the Gospel, this is not a kind of second Gradual, as some liturgists have thought, but an acclamation accompanying the Gospel procession. Here the witness of all the Oriental liturgies is conclusive.[22] When, in Rome, it seemed desirable to add a psalm verse to the Alleluia, this was always chosen by preference from among the royal psalms, especially from Psalm 92, *Dominus regnavit*. This was for a long time sung in Greek in remembrance of the Byzantine origin of the ceremony: it acclaimed the Christ-Basileus who, under the image of the book of the Gospels, appears, surrounded with lights and incense, in the midst of the assembled community. But however moving the rite which accompanies it may be, the Alleluia verse should never be considered equal in liturgical importance to the Gradual psalm. And still less should it be allowed to supplant it in the celebration.

The Prayers

In the prayers of the liturgy of the Mass, the place of the Bible is less immediately evident but it is no less important. It is true that the prayers of assembly or those over the offerings, the great Eucharistic prayer (the Oriental *anaphoras,* the Roman canon, the Spanish *illatio,* the Gallican *immolatio*), which are the free creations of the religious genius of a people or of a period, could have been nourished from sources other than the Bible only.

But it was the Bible that gave them their typology; it is frequently from meditation on the Scriptural event, on the conjunction between the Scriptural event of the past and its accomplishment in the New Covenant, that the prayer is spontaneously born. We need only remember the *Exsultet,* the twelve prayers of the old Easter Vigil and those of the old Pentecost Vigil, the ancient Ambrosian Prefaces—which had a place for several centuries in our Roman-French sacramentaries and which are still the glory of the Milanese Missal[23]—in order to grasp the full expressiveness of liturgical prayer nourished by Biblical typology.

But the Eucharistic prayer takes far more than its typology from the Bible. It places itself in the stream of the history of salvation,

[20] *Communion* (Rite and antiphon of), in DACL, 3, col. 2428-2429.
[21] *Liturgie de la Messe arménienne* (Venice, 1939), p. 68.
[22] The whole picture is given in A. Raes, *Introductio in liturgiam orientalem* (Rome, 1947), pp. 78-79.
[23] For example, in Alcuin's supplement to the Gregorian Sacramentary, the prefaces of the forty-day fast, of the woman of Samaria, of the man born blind, of Lazarus; in H. A. Wilson, *The Gregorian Sacramentary* (London, 1915), pp. 265-267; or in the *Liber Sacramentorum* edited by Dom Ménard, PL 78, col. 68-72.

the stages of which are described for us in the Bible.

Having sung the greatness and holiness of God the Father, the Son and the Spirit, uniting the voice of the Church with that of the angels whom Isaias heard crying the *Sanctus;* having celebrated the divine economy of the Old Covenant, God's choice of a people as His own, the epic of the Exodus and the entrance into the Promised Land, the Oriental anaphoras—and our own Roman canon in its succession of proper Prefaces and *Communicantes*—sing the mystery of the redemptive incarnation. Then they use the very words of the Gospels and St. Paul to consecrate the bread and wine and to recall the command of the Lord to celebrate His memorial until He returns.[24]

And, finally, the *prex eucharistica* places the Sacrifice of the New Covenant in the great sacrificial history of redeemed humanity, in a mighty synthesis that goes from Genesis to the Apocalypse, from the sacrifice of Abel the Just to the offering made by the hands of the angel on the golden altar of heaven.

And all this is carried out in a Biblical way, in a long prayer of blessing and thanksgiving borrowed from the Jewish ritual of the Berakha of the Table.[25] Here appear successively the song of Moses at the Exodus (Ex. 15:1-8), Nehemias' prayer of supplication (9:5-37), and the ardent thanksgiving of St. Paul at the beginning of the Epistle to the Ephesians. If the Roman canon has channeled its prayer in the stylistic forms of the ancient pagan cult of Rome, the sap that goes through them is nonetheless new. It antedates the unknown master of the fourth century who fixed its rhythms; it comes from the people of the Bible. It was when he opened the Missal at the prayer *Supra quae propitio* that Pius XI spoke that phrase which illuminates our whole liturgy and our whole religious history: "Spiritually, we are Semites."[26]

Everywhere in our Missal—in its readings, chants, prayers—we find the Bible. And the Mass, the climax of the liturgy, is not an exceptional example of the coming together of Scripture and liturgy. This is true of the celebration of the other sacraments as well.

IN THE LITURGY OF THE SACRAMENTS

To limit the scope of our report, we shall be content to indicate (1) how the prayers accompanying the sacramental rites have been built up from the Bible, taking baptism, Orders, and marriage as examples; and (2) the place given to Biblical readings by the Oriental liturgies in the celebration of the sacraments.

[24] An excellent selection of Oriental anaphoras translated into French can be found in the two works of Adalbert Hamman, *Prières des premiers chrétiens* (Paris, 1952) and *Prières eucharistiques des premiers siècles* (Paris, 1957).

[25] See O. Casel, *Le Mémorial du Seigneur* (Paris, 1945), pp. 23-50, and L. Bouyer, *Liturgical Piety* (Notre Dame University Press, 1955), pp. 118-126.

[26] Discourse addressed to pilgrims of the *Radio catholique belge,* Sept. 6, 1938. The text is given in *Documentation catholique,* Dec. 5, 1938, col. 1460, and is reprinted in A. Croegaert, *Les rites et prières du saint sacrifice de la Messe* (Malines, 1949), 3, pp. 217-218.

The Biblical Typology of the Sacramental Rites in the Roman Liturgy

The liturgy of *baptism* reveals all its riches only to the man who studies it from the viewpoint of the ordo for the baptism of adults, placing himself in the context of the Lenten liturgy and the Easter Vigil.[27] When, during the exorcisms, the priest addresses those whom he calls "children of the promise," it is in order to pray on their behalf to the God of Abraham, Isaac and Jacob, recalling the deliverance from Egypt, Mount Sinai, and the angel protecting the people on their march across the desert.[28]

But it is especially during the holy night, in the prayer consecrating the water, that the continuity of the two Covenants is clearly shown. To the primordial waters on which rested the Spirit, to the four rivers of the earthly paradise, to the waters of the flood and the water springing from the rock to quench the people's thirst, the Lord Jesus communicated a life-giving power by receiving baptism from John, by changing water into wine at Cana, by walking on the waves of the lake, by causing water and blood to flow forth from His side opened on the Cross, by sending His apostles to baptize all nations and thus to prepare the manifestation of the holy City, the heavenly Jerusalem, which will be watered, like a new paradise, by the rushing rivers of life.

What a magnificent synthesis of Biblical theology, the realism of which should not escape our notice: in baptism these are the wonderful works of God which are renewed for him who enters the ranks of the redeemed.[29]

The meaning of the sacrament of *Orders,* by which the three degrees of the sacred hierarchy are established, is revealed in the consecratory prayers for a bishop, for priests, and for deacons by a continual reference to Biblical typology: high priest of the New Covenant, leader of the new people of God, the bishop is a new Aaron and a new Moses; the fullness of the Spirit is conferred upon him by a spiritual anointing, of which the anointing of Aaron was the image, and the sumptuous vestments of the Hebrew high priest were but the symbol of the holiness of the episcopate. The image that hovers over the elect of the Lord is that of the glory of Yahweh (consecratory prayer of the bishop).

Again, as Aaron associated his two sons, Eleazar and Ithamar, in his priestly office (Num. 3:4); as Moses set apart seventy-two elders of Israel to whom God communicated His spirit to govern the people (Num. 11:16-25); as the apostles chose men to collaborate

[27] It is the Gelasian Sacramentary (Vat. Reg. 316) that presents the ancient context most faithfully, with its three Sunday scrutinies so perfectly adapted to the needs of an adult catechumenate.

[28] *Rituale Romanum,* ed. 1952, Tit. II, cap. 4, nos. 11, 17.

[29] In this whole picture of the typology of water we should not fail to include the prayer: *Sanctificare per verbum Dei unda caelestis* of the Roman *Pontificale* (Gregorian preparation of the water in the rite for the Dedication), which is common to the three Western rites and comes directly from St. Ambrose, DACL, 2, col. 693-694.

with them—so the bishop can associate with himself a college of priests of the second order, preachers of the second rank, who will be his co-workers in the divine service and in the government of the Church (consecratory prayer of priests). And finally, as in former times the Lord chose the sons of Levi to watch faithfully over the mysterious works of His house, so today the pontiff lays his hands on the men who are to be his ministers at the altar and the administrators of his own house (prayer consecrating deacons).

Thus, the hierarchy of the Church, in its three sacred Orders, is seen to arise from the depths of Exodus. The assembly in which it carries out its ministry here and now is no longer the assembly of the desert, gathered around the Tabernacle; it is the assembly of the new people of God, united around the altar to take part in the Banquet of the Lord.

Yet the Church never forgets the whole continuity in which her own history is included. To assure ourselves of this fact, we need only reread in the Roman *Pontificale* the beginning of the famous synodal admonition which may be the work of St. Caesarius of Arles: "Beloved brothers and priests of the Lord," the bishop says to those with whom he has just celebrated the Eucharist, "you are the co-workers of our Order.[30] We ourselves, in spite of our unworthiness, hold the place of Aaron; you, that of Eleazar and Ithamar. We carry on the mission of the twelve apostles; you continue that of the seventy-two disciples. We are your shepherds, and you are the shepherds of the souls that have been entrusted to you."[31]

Christian *marriage* also is placed in the context of the history of salvation, which began with the first human couple and will be completed in the wedding-feast of the Lamb. We find again in the liturgy of marriage the recalling of the Old Covenant, with Adam and Eve established in the indissoluble unity of those who are "two in one single flesh,"[32] receiving the blessing of fruitfulness which the Lord would never revoke, neither after the fall nor in the flood. And the Old Covenant is here also with the holy women of the patriarchal period, Sara, Rebecca, Rachel—types of woman as both wife and mother;[33] with Tobias and the second Sara;[34] with the great images of the nuptial love of God for His people, and of human happiness pictured in the concrete images of abundance and fruitfulness in family life.[35]

But beyond the Old Covenant, the New gives to the union of man and wife its highest dignity by making it the sign of the union

[30] Referring to the *Ordo episcoporum,* which Dom Botte presents in *Études sur le sacrament de l'Ordre* (Paris, 1957), pp. 107-118.

[31] *Pontificale Romanum, Ordo ad Synodum.* G. Morin has identified the author of the synodal admonition in the *Revue benédictine,* 1892, pp. 99-108, a study partially reproduced in DACL, 6, col. 576-579.

[32] Gospel of the Mass *pro sponsis.*

[33] Prayer of the nuptial blessing.

[34] Introit of the Mass *pro sponsis.*

[35] Gradual, Tract, Communion antiphon of the Mass *pro sponsis.*

between Christ and His Church.[36] Although it has less of a lyric quality than the liturgy of Antioch, that of Rome makes its *velatio nuptialis* a kind of Canticle of Canticles, the themes of which should echo indefinitely in Christian family life.

From baptism to holy Orders and marriage, then, the liturgy of the sacraments opens out to us their true nature: their source is the death and resurrection of Christ, and at the same time they realize a stage in the plan of God's love, which began in paradise with the creation and the fall and is being carried out all through the ages until the Lord's return.

The Biblical Readings in the Sacramental Rites of the Orient

The East has retained more than we the communal character of the liturgical celebration. This fact is obvious in the case of the Divine Office, the obligation of which is still attached to a parish or monastic community and not to individuals. It is true also of the administration of the sacraments, including that of the anointing of the sick. Many of us were deeply moved in recent years by the accounts of the death of Mar Ivanios (1953) and of Mar Severios (1955), the two great bishops of the Syro-Malabar rite, who each passed from this world to God in the midst of a true liturgical celebration in which each was the principal actor since he was still the pontiff, as in the old accounts of saintly deaths. And this communal celebration of the sacraments always takes place in the context of a true liturgy of the Word. We shall content ourselves with giving a few examples.

Christian initiation.[37] The East has remained faithful, in its liturgical texts if not always in actual practice, to the continuous rite of Christian initiation: all the rites, with the exception of the Chaldean, assume that after baptism by immersion and confirmation, the neophyte will receive the Eucharist. "If the candidate is a very little child," states the Byzantine Ordo, "he should be communicated under the species of wine only." And so it is not astonishing to find that the baptismal rites still take the place of the Mass of the Catechumens, as they did in the times of St. Justin and Hippolytus.

After the rites of the catechumenate (signation, exorcisms, renunciation of Satan, and profession of faith), everyone goes into the baptistry. There, in all the rites except the Byzantine, readings are given before the priest blesses the water.[38] In the Byzantine rite the readings take place after confirmation, in the sanctuary, immediately before the celebration of the divine Liturgy. The pericopes are taken especially from the

[36] Epistle of the Mass and prayer of the nuptial blessing.

[37] Two Oriental rituals of Christian initiation are available to the reader of French: the Byzantine ritual in *La Prière des Églises de rite byzantin* (Chevetogne, 1937), 1, pp. 323-356; the Syrian ritual of Antioch in *L'Orient syrien,* 1956, pp. 156-185.

[38] For each baptism the Oriental priest blessed the oil of catechumens and the water, as he also blesses the oil of the sick each time this sacrament is to be administered. Only the holy chrism, blessed by the patriarch, is conserved like the Eucharist.

teaching of St. Paul on baptism (Rom. 6:1-8), from the conversation of Jesus with Nicodemus (John 3:1-8), and from the commission given to the apostles to baptize all nations (Matt. 28:16-20).

Marriage.[39] Only the Armenians and the Ethiopians give the nuptial blessing during the Mass, but all the rites accompany the celebration of the espousals and of the crowning with a certain number of Biblical readings. The Byzantines content themselves with two (Eph. 5:20-23 and John 2:1-11). The Copts have a double series for Sunday and for weekdays. And the Armenians have no less than seventeen readings, the mere naming of which (although certain pericopes are repeated) could furnish the outlines of a solid Biblical theology of marriage. Here is the list:

For the espousals: Prov. 9:12-17; Cant. 8; 14; Osee 14:6-10; Is. 27:11-13; Gal. 4:2-7, 4:13; Luke 1:26-28.

For the blessing of the bride's robe: Is. 61:10 – 62:3; 1 Pet. 3:1-9; John 2:1-11.

For the crowning (the marriage properly so called): Gen. 1:26-27; Gen. 2:21-24; Is. 61:9—62: 6; Eph. 5:11-23; Matt. 19:2-9.

For the laying aside of the crowns: Osee 14:6-8; 1 Tim. 2:9-15; John 2:1-11.

The Anointing of the Sick.[40] The rite of anointing is very long. With the Syrians it lasts about two hours. In all the rites, the participation of several priests is required if possible, according to the text of St. James: "Is anyone sick among you? Let him call in the priests of the Church" (James 5:14). In the Byzantine rite the Office of the Holy Oil is entrusted to seven priests, each of whom gives an anointing. And each of these is accompanied by two readings, an Epistle and a Gospel. Here again the choice is interesting as giving a Biblical light on the theology of the anointing of the sick.

1st anointing: James 5:10-16; Luke 10:25-37 (the Good Samaritan).

2nd anointing: Rom. 16:1-7; Luke 19:1-10 (the meal with Zaccheus).

3rd anointing: 1 Cor. 12:27 – 13:8; Matt. 10:1, 5-9 (power of healing).

4th anointing: 2 Cor. 6:16 – 7:1; Matt. 8:14-23 (healing of Peter's mother-in-law).

5th anointing: 2 Cor. 1:8-11; Matt. 25:1-13 (parable of the ten virgins).

6th anointing: Gal. 5:22 – 6:2; Matt. 15:21-28 (the daughter of the Canaanite woman).

7th anointing: 1 Thess. 5:14-23; Matt. 9:9-13 (the meal with Levi).

Our own ritual of the visiting of the sick, which is so beautiful and so little used, would be still further enriched if all these texts were included, bringing their message of hope and peace.

N.B.

[39] The complete French text of all the Oriental rituals for marriage can be found in A. Raes, *Le Mariage dans les Églises d'Orient* (Chevetogne, 1958).

[40] The French text of the Byzantine Ordo is given in *La Prière des Églises de rite byzantin,* 1, pp. 417-447.

IN THE DIVINE OFFICE

Everyone knows, of course, that in all the rites the Bible furnishes the very texture of the Divine Office with its psalmody, the singing of the canticles of the Old and New Testaments, and the continuous reading of the holy Books. We shall, therefore, make only two observations here on the subject of the relationship between the Bible and the Office.

The Place of the Biblical Readings in the Office

The Roman Office is typically monastic. This is why, following the ordinance of the Rule of St. Benedict, all the readings of any length are included in the Office for the end of the night, in the nocturns of the vigil. The day Hours, including Lauds and Vespers, have only "Little Chapters" that are mere reminders.

By contrast, the Oriental Office, retaining a far more clearly marked popular structure, gives its Scripture readings at the Hours in which the people are invited to participate: Lauds in the morning; Vespers in the evening; and on the vigils of the great feasts, vigils which are days of fasting and more intense prayer, there are readings at the Hours of Prime, Terce, Sext and None, which are called on these days the "Great Hours." This, at least, is the Byzantine tradition, which is echoed to a certain extent by the liturgies of Milan and Toledo. Thus the Spanish Breviary indicates four readings for Terce and None, and one reading for Sext on each of the three days of the fast preceding Epiphany.[41]

Let us take, for example, the feast of Epiphany itself. In the Byzantine rite, the holy theophanies of our Lord are preceded by a vigil with obligatory fasting. Each of the Great Hours of the day has three readings (Prophecy, New Testament, Gospel); then in the evening come the Vespers of the feast. This includes, together with the usual psalmody and the *lucernarium,* fifteen readings (thirteen from the Old Testament, followed by St. Paul and the Gospel) and is completed by the solemn celebration of the Liturgy of St. Basil. The Liturgy itself is followed by the blessing of the water, which includes five readings.[42]

Although the Milanese liturgy does not display such profusion, somewhat overwhelming for Latins, it does possess for the evening of January 5 a Vesper Office of similar structure: the Office of the *lucernarium* is followed by four readings with their responsorial psalms, and by the Mass of the vigil, after which the psalmody of Vespers is continued.[43]

We might note that, although the Church always gives a large place in the Divine Office to the reading of the Bible, the place for this reading is not the same in all rites, and it is not self-evident that the one accorded to it in the Roman rite is the best. We could quite well conceive of its insertion at the end of the psalmody of Vespers; here it

41 *Breviarium gothicum,* PL, 86, col. 150-174.
42 The French text is given in *La Prière des Églises de rite byzantin,* 2, pp. 143-178.
43 *Liber vesperalis juxta ritum sanctae Ecclesiae Mediolanensis* (Rome, 1939), pp. 141-147, and *Missale ambrosianum* (Milan, 1902).

would afford the best form of evening prayer for the Christian community and could serve as the prelude to evening Mass.

The Biblical Inspiration of the Prayers

Unfortunately, the Roman rite has chosen a facile solution to the question of prayers in the Office, ending all the Hours except Prime and Compline with the Collect of the Mass. We are far from the wealth of the Milanese Office, which introduces up to five proper prayers into the psalmody of Vespers and has for each of the Hours of the day a prayer asking for the special grace connected with that Hour: ". . . as at the third hour Thou didst strengthen the apostles of Thy Son by the visitation of the Holy Spirit . . ."; ". . . who didst will that Thy Son should ascend the cross at the sixth hour . . ."; ". . . who didst command that the thief who professed his faith on the gibbet of the cross should at the ninth hour pass over to paradise . . . ."[44]

Our Office, however, had an earlier state in which flowered a prayer made up entirely of psalmody and the Biblical background of the Hour being celebrated. We have two important witnesses to this. First, the Psalter Collects. In accordance with the tradition of the Egyptian monks, which was accepted from the fourth century on into the practice of the Churches of the West, after each psalm came a brief pause for prayer (the *Gloria Patri* was born of this custom). Then at the end of this silent prayer the president of the assembly gathered the whole Christian substance of the psalm that had just been heard and made it into a Collect.

We still possess three series of these psalm-prayers, which have an incomparable value in giving a Christian understanding of the Psalter. For example, consider the prayer in the Roman series concluding Psalm 112, *Laudate pueri*:[45] *Laudantes benedictum nomen tuum omnipotens Deus, rogamus ut nos in sinum matris ecclesiae collocatos, caritatis tuae facias stabilitate connecti. Per. . . .* "Praising Thy blessed Name, almighty God, we pray that we who are gathered together in the bosom of our mother, the Church, may be bound together in the firm bond of Thy love. Through Christ. . . ."

With the psalm-prayers of the sixth century, we might also recall the morning and evening prayers of the sacramentaries which may date from the same period. These are the prayers with which the president of the assembly concluded the morning and evening gatherings of the faithful. Such, for example, after those of the Leonine Sacramentary, are the *orationes ad Matutinas* (3, 94), the *orationes ad Vesperum* (3, 85), and the twenty-five *orationes paschales vespertinales* (1, 56) of the Gelasian Sacramentary.

[44] *Diurnale ambrosianum* (Milan, 1862): *ut, sicut hora tertia Apostolos Filii tui visitatione Sancti Spiritus confirmasti. . .ut qui, hora diei sexta, Filium tuum crucem ascendere voluisti. . .qui, hora nona, in crucis patibulo latronem confitentem paradisi transire jussisti. . . .*

[45] L. Brou, *The Psalter Collects* (London, 1949).

All are filled with echoes of the Bible: "Efface, we pray Thee, O Lord, the notice of our guilt inscribed by the law of sin, which Thou hast made void for us in the paschal mystery by the resurrection of Thy Son. . . ." "O Lord, true Light and Author of light, we pray Thee that Thou wouldst dispel the darkness of our vices and enlighten us with the light of virtues. . . ." "Give light, we pray Thee, O Lord, to our darkness, and in Thy kindness drive away all attacks of the night."[46]

The Gregorian Sacramentary also has an analogous series of *orationes matutinales, orationes vespertinales,* and *orationes cotidianae,*[47] which have disappeared in its successors of the ninth and tenth centuries. The abandonment of these prayers at the time when the first abridgments of the Office, the first "Breviaries," were being developed has meant an impoverishment of the Roman liturgy. Here again, may we express the desire that these documents, born of the piety of the contemporaries of St. Benedict, of St. Caesarius of Arles, or of St. Isidore of Seville, may emerge from the domain of specialists and once more be used to enrich the official prayer of the Church.

We have now carried out an investigation of the liturgical books of the East and West, sufficiently extensive in both time and space: *quod semper, quod ubique.* And this has served amply to justify our initial statement: the formularies of the Catholic liturgy are taken from Biblical texts. It remains now to show, more briefly, how this sacred text, gathered from the Bible in the liturgical formularies, is welcomed as a living Word in the very act of celebration.

THE WORD OF GOD IN THE LITURGICAL CELEBRATION

The liturgical celebration manifests the mystery of the Word of God and gives it its highest degree of effectiveness. The mystery of the Word is essentially that of a living presence: the Word of God received in the Bible is not presented to us as a document taken from the archives, as would be, for instance, the testament of Richelieu or the record of the trial of St. Joan, but as a Word transmitted to us here and now by the messenger of the living God. And it is precisely in the liturgical proclamation of the Word of God that this twofold actualization takes place, of the messenger and of the message.

The Messenger as Present in our Midst

God speaks to me here and now through His messenger. This living messenger is, above all, the Apostle. In the oldest description that we possess of the liturgical assembly, that of St. Justin (about the year 150), the author says that "the recollections of the apostles or the writ-

[46] The ancient Gelasian Sacramentary (Vat. Reg. 316): *Dele, quaesumus, Domine, conscriptum peccati lege chirographum: quod in nobis Paschali mysterio per Resurrectionem tui Filii vacuasti. . . . Te lucem veram et lucis Auctorem, Domine, deprecamur: ut digneris a nobis tenebras depellere vitiorum et clarificare nos luce virtutum. . . . Illumina, quaesumus, Domine, tenebras nostras; et totius noctis insidias repelle propitius.* For the morning and evening prayers of the Leonine Sacramentary, see the edition of Mohlberg, *Sacramentarium Veronese,* nos. 587-593.

[47] Ed. Wilson, *The Gregorian Sacramentary,* l.c., pp. 126-136.

ings of the prophets are read," thus giving the first place to the apostolic message.

When we examined the organization of the readings in the different rites, we were able to establish the fact of the universality of the Gospel reading and also of the exceptional place given to the reading of the New Testament, especially of St. Paul. When the Old Testament is included in the readings, it is not read for itself or as one more sacred text; it has its place in virtue of its prophetic character and the light shed on it by the New Testament. In the non-Roman liturgies, the Old Testament readings are nearly always explicitly commented on by the apostolic reading that follows.

And all this leads us to take cognizance of the living presence of the apostle in the midst of the Christian community. "In the organization of the Church, we are connected with Christ by the apostles; and the Church, founded on them, causes us to hear their voice when she instructs us, when she repeats to us the good news they proclaimed."[48] "The apostles were, in fact, the first to break the Eucharistic bread in Christian gatherings, and their presence was replaced, when they were no longer on earth, by the reading of their writings, which were to 'bring them back,' to render them present, so to say, in the midst of the community gathered round the altar."[49]

This living presence of the apostle in the midst of the assembled community gives an increased importance to the appeal to their intercession: "May the prayer of Matthew, Mark, Luke and John be a wall of defense to our souls," sings the choir in the Chaldean liturgy;[50] after the reading of the *Catholicon*, the Copts have the following prayer· "O Lord our God, who has revealed to us by Thy holy apostles the mystery of Thy Gospel, which is the glory of Thy Christ, and who has entrusted to them, according to the infinite riches of Thy grace, the work of preaching to all nations the incomprehensible treasures of Thy mercy: we pray Thee, make us worthy to share in their lot and in their inheritance. Grant that we may always walk in their footsteps, imitate their struggles, and share in the tribulations that they underwent for the cause of justice."[51]

The living presence of the apostle – but, above all, through his mediation, the living presence of Him who sent the apostle, Christ Himself . . . To realize this we need only consider the honors paid to the Gospel.

In the Roman Rite. In the entrance procession of a pontifical Mass, the book of the Gospels is carried by the subdeacon; then the bishop places it on the altar, after he has kissed the altar itself.[52] But this is only a vestige of the ancient liturgy; then the book of Gospels was car-

[48] O. Rousseau, "Pastoral Liturgy and the Eastern Liturgies," *The Assisi Papers* (Collegeville, Minn.: Liturgical Press, 1957), p. 117.

[49] *Ibid.*

[50] *Liturgie de la sainte Messe selon le rite chaldéen* (Paris, 1937), p. 52.

[51] "Liturgie copte de saint Basil," in *Petit Paroissien des Liturgies orientales* (Harissa: Lebanon, 1941), p. 454.

[52] *Caeremoniale Episcoporum,* lib. 2., cap. 8, nos. 25, 33.

ried to the altar in a solemn entrance procession, preceding that of the bishop, by one or more acolytes wearing chasubles; when they had come into the sanctuary, a subdeacon who had accompanied them received the book and placed it on the altar: *eum desuper planeta illius suscipiens, manibus suis honorifice super altare ponat.*[53] And the book thus remained on the altar until the moment when the deacon took it up in order to sing the Gospel.

The procession to the ambo has great majesty in the description given in the Ordo of the seventh century:[54] two acolytes carry torches and three subdeacons in charge of the incensorium walk ahead of the deacon, who has kissed the book before taking it from the altar. All, of course, are standing, while the choir sings the Alleluia and a psalm verse taken from the royal psalms. Here we have, in fact, a theophany, an appearance of Christ the King, the Son of God, of one substance with the Father, in the midst of the assembly. The honors paid to Him are those that were rendered to the imperial majesty.

Catholic faith has always thus treated the book of the Gospels as the equivalent of the living Person of the Lord. This is the reason why, from the Council of Ephesus to that of the Vatican, the book of Gospels has presided over the council meetings. St. Cyril of Alexandria gives witness to this: "The holy Synod assembled together in the church gave Christ, as it were, membership in and the presidency of the Council. For the venerable Gospel was placed upon a holy throne."[55] At the end of the seventh century Pseudo-Germain of Paris wrote: "The procession of the holy Gospel comes forth like the power of Christ triumphant over death, with the aforesaid chanting and with seven lighted candles . . . going up into the opposite ambo . . . while the clergy cry out: Glory to Thee, O Lord."[56]

When the deacon has placed the book of Gospels on the desk of the ambo, the announcement that he makes of God's Word is hailed, not only by the clergy present, but by all the people: *Gloria tibi, Domine!* Nowadays, after the singing of the pericope, the book is reverently carried by the subdeacon to the celebrant for him to kiss; but in former times it was presented to all: *tenens ante pectus suum super planetum porrigit osculandum omnibus.* And the book is finally replaced carefully in its case (*deinde ponitur in capsa*), for now the liturgy of the Word is to be followed by that of the Banquet of the Lord.

In the Oriental Rites. These yield nothing to the Roman liturgy in the homage they give to the Gospel. In his day, St. Jerome admired the practice, in all the Eastern Churches, of lighting candles at the reading of the Gospel, even though the sun had already risen.[57] As we

[53] *Ordo Primus,* nos. 30-31, ed. Andrieu, I.c., p. 77.
[54] *Ibid.,* nos. 59-60.
[55] Cyril of Alexandria, *Apology to the Emperor Theodosius,* PG 76, 471. Many other references may be found in A. Croegaert, *op. cit.,* 1, p. 560.
[56] PL 72, col. 91.
[57] *Per totas Orientis ecclesias, quando legendum est evangelium, accenduntur luminaria, jam sole rutilante* (*Adversus Vigilantium*).

all know, in the Byzantine rites the book is carried solemnly to the altar in a real procession, the Byzantine "Little Entrance," which corresponds to the Great Entrance or procession with the offerings. The Syrian rite of Antioch is content to have a procession with the book around the altar, an obvious vestige of the ancient entrance procession. The procession to the ambo – or, at least, the presentation of the Gospel when it is sung directly on the threshold of the sanctuary – is, in all the rites, similar to that of the Roman: lights, incense, singing of the Alleluia.

In the majority of the rites (Coptic, Eastern and Western Syrian, Armenian) the singing of the Gospel is reserved to the celebrant, priest or bishop. The role of the deacon is to invite the people to welcome the Word of the Lord: "Silence!" says the Syrian deacon, "with fear and purity let us hear the message of the living words of the Gospel of our Lord Jesus Christ which is read in our presence."[58] In the Armenian rite, to the invitation of the deacon: *Proschume* (Be attentive), the people answer: "It is God who speaks."[59]

The Message as Given Here and Now

It is God who speaks, and it is *today* that He speaks to His people gathered together in response to His call. Here we are at the very heart of the mystery of the Word proclaimed in the liturgy. Theologians still have much to tell us concerning the mode of this *today* which is realized in the mystery of Christian worship and concerning the sacramental efficacy of the liturgical celebration affirmed so explicitly in the decree *Maxima Redemptoris;* but the fact dominating all the controversies of the various schools is the calm use that the Church has always made, throughout the entire liturgical year, in the proclamation of the Word of God and in the celebration of her mysteries, of the word *today.*

It is quite certain that in hearing the call of the Apostle on the first Sunday of Lent: "Behold, now is the acceptable time, behold, now is the day of salvation" (2 Cor. 6:2), we have no temptation to transport ourselves back nineteen hundred years; it is *today* that we are invited to begin our paschal ascent to Jerusalem, to enter into the combat with Satan, as St. Leo the Great explains to his flock gathered in the Lateran.[60] In the same way, then, when on Palm Sunday we take part in the procession after the singing of the Gospel which announces the triumphal entry of Jesus into Jerusalem, or when, at the evening Mass on Holy Thursday, the celebrant reproduces the Gospel scene by washing the feet of twelve of his brethren, this is not an evocation of the past, it is not a play – it is *today.*

Intimately connected with the proclamation of the Word of God, making but one reality with it, the priestly homily has, moreover, as its purpose to introduce us into this *today* by opening our souls to the Word we have listened to, by planting that Word in the very heart of

[58] *La liturgie syrienne, Anaphora des Douze Apôtres* (Paris, 1950), p. 35.
[59] *Liturgie de la messe arménienne* (Venice, 1939), p. 37.
[60] Leo the Great, *Sermons,* 2, Serm. 27 (Paris, 1957), p. 33.

our spiritual needs, and, frequently, by bringing to light the matrix of meaning that otherwise would seem strange to many by reason of its different cultural context. The problem of the proclamation of the Word of God in a living language has become today a most acute one in the Latin Church. But let us not forget that the problem is twofold: the problem of translation, but also the problem of preaching. The two problems are indissolubly bound up with one another in the proclamation of the Word if we desire that it be received *today* as a fruitful seed.

The efficacy and the actuality of the living Word reach their maximum degree of realization on the further side of the proclamation itself, in the sacramental action. And this is true not only because "the Word of God is the proclamation in the Church of the mystery of salvation realized in the Eucharist,"[61] but because the words of Jesus gathered up in the Gospel, announced to the people in the Epistle of Holy Thursday, are assumed anew by the Lord as His personal action when the priest pronounces over the bread and wine the words of consecration. Here the Word of God is *actio Christi,* as Pope Pius XII reminded us in his address closing the Assisi Congress.[62]

Without wishing to anticipate the chapters to come, which will bring out this fundamental relationship of the sacrament to the Word, it is, nevertheless, indispensable for us to discover the twofold climax of the evangelical liturgy and the Eucharistic liturgy in this twofold presence of Christ manifested in the proclamation of the Gospel and in the consecration of the offerings, in order to understand the internal progress of the celebration of the Mass, and the permanence of the Word of God at the very moment when it is by its means that a new mode of the presence of the risen Lord in the assembly of the faithful is to be realized.

For it is precisely here, in the sacramental actualization of the living Word of God, that the liturgy opens out to us the mystery of the Scriptures, as did the Lord to the two disciples at Emmaus at the moment when He was about to sit down with them at table and break the bread for them. As it is in the liturgy of the Word that the progressive revelation of the Old Testament receives its definitive clarification in the light cast on it by the teaching of the apostles and by that of the Lord, the celebration of baptism or the Eucharist causes us to enter into a sacred history which continues through the ages until the Lord shall return in the manifestation of His glory.

In this perspective we can easily understand the indestructible bond that the will of the Lord and the profound life of the Church have woven between Bible and liturgy, and how it is that the Biblical renewal and the liturgical renewal can make progress only if they proceed together, each referring to the other so as to bring out all its own potentialities. What kind of a liturgical celebration would that be in which the Biblical readings remained incomprehensible to the understanding of the congregation, in which the Psalter was a sealed book

[61] *Directoire pour la pastorale de la Messe,* n. 1.
[62] *The Assisi Papers* (Collegeville, Minn.: Liturgical Press, 1957), p. 229ff.

and could no longer give to the prayer of the people its richest expression, in which the Exodus meant no more than a vague memory, in which the sacred names of Jerusalem and Sion awakened no echoes in our hearts with their wealth of hope and love? There can be no authentic liturgical life without the exultant discovery of the message carried by the Book which God has put into our hands.

But, if Christian specialists in Biblical studies search the caves at Qumran, if they devote themselves to discovering the literary genre of each inspired Book, bringing out its structure, from Genesis to Apocalypse, they are well aware that they are far more than mere historians of the past, that the whole reason for the existence of the Books, which these scholars are now restoring to the Church in the freshness of their first flowering, is to be received in a community of the faithful, to be welcomed with the fervor with which the Jews heard the scribe Esdras read them the Law, to be accepted with the same *Amen* (Neh. 8:6).

Rev. Jean Danielou, S.J.

CHAPTER 2

THE SACRAMENTS AND THE HISTORY OF SALVATION

THERE ARE, of course, many aspects under which we may consider the relations between the Bible and the liturgy. First of all, as we saw in the previous chapter, there is the fact of the importance given to Biblical texts in the ceremonies of the liturgy; in particular, the first part of the Mass is a liturgy of the Word, the essential content of which is the reading of texts from the Old and New Testaments. But the liturgy is at once word and action, *logos kai ergon;* and the Bible is at once a book and a history. It is this second aspect that we are now going to consider – the relationship of the actions that make up sacred history in the Old and New Testaments to the actions that are the sacraments of the Church.

We should, first of all, recall the fact that liturgical tradition continually establishes analogies between sacramental actions and the works of God in the Old and New Testaments. Let us take some examples from baptism and the Eucharist, sacraments which the Fathers continually relate to the essential events of the Bible. In the space available here, it is, of course, impossible to go into the details of this teaching which fills the sacramental catecheses and the liturgical texts; I can only indicate the great themes.[1]

In connection with baptism, let us take the blessing of the water given in our present ritual:

O God, as Thy Spirit hovered over the waters at the very beginning of the world, so that even then by their very nature they might have the power of sanctification....

O God, as Thou didst wash away by water the crimes of the guilty world, and so by the flood didst give us an image of the new birth; for it was the same element that signified the destruction of sin and the beginning of virtue....

I bless you, O water, creature of God, by the living God, who caused you to flow from the fountain of paradise and commanded you to flow out in four rivers and water the whole earth; who changed you in the desert to a water fit to drink and caused you to flow from the rock to quench the people's thirst....

I bless you through Jesus Christ, who in the wonderful miracle at Cana changed you by His power into wine . . .; who was baptized in you by John at the Jordan; who caused you to flow from His side together with His blood....

Let us go over these analogies. The first is that of the primordial waters sanctified by the Spirit. As the Spirit of God, hovering over these waters, raised up the first creation, so the same Spirit, hovering over the baptismal waters, raises up the new creation, effects our rebirth. The Spirit of God is the creative Spirit. Christ's word refers to this aspect: "Unless a man be born again of water and the Spirit, he cannot enter the kingdom" (John 3:5). "Why are you immersed in water?" St. Ambrose asks the neophyte. "We read: *Let the waters bring forth living things* (Gen. 1:20). And things were born. This took place at the beginning of creation. But it was reserved to our own times that water should give you a new birth by grace."[2]

Here we can begin to see the dimension that is given to baptism by this analogy. Baptism is of the same order as the creation of the world, and this because to create is an action properly divine. It is the same Spirit who raised up the first creation and who will raise up the new creation. The Spirit descended on the waters of the Jordan, thence to bring forth the new creation which is that of the Man-God. And baptism is the continuation of this creative work in the era of the Church. The very context of springtime, in which baptism is administered, expresses this analogy. Spring is the yearly anniversary of the first creation and of the new creation as well.

Immediately after speaking of creation, the prayer of consecration alludes to the flood – a new act of God's power and a new symbol of water. The relationship between the flood and baptism goes back to the first Epistle of Peter, in which baptism is called the antitype of the

[1] I have given a survey of this teaching in my book, *Bible and Liturgy* (Notre Dame University Press, 1956).

[2] *De Sacramentis,* III, 3.

flood. Optatus of Milan writes in the fifth century: "The flood was a figure of baptism because the whole universe, soiled by the tide of sin, by the intervention of water was restored to its pristine purity."[3] Water is the instrument of God's judgment; it is water that destroys the sinful world. Baptism is a mystery of death. It means the destruction of the ancient man, as the flood meant the destruction of the ancient world, so that a new creature may appear, washed clean and renewed by the baptismal water.

The essential point here is the symbolism of water. Lactantius writes: "Water is the figure of death";[4] and Ambrose: "In the water is the image of death."[5] Per Lundberg has brought out the importance of this theme of the waters of death, which seems strange to us until we remember the text of St. Paul showing us that baptism is at once death with Christ and resurrection with Him. The prayer of consecration brings out the contrast between water as creative and destructive, between the creation and the flood: "It was the same element that signified the destruction of sin and the beginning of virtue." Thus the text of St. Paul refers to the baptismal rite; this is seen to be a putting to death by immersion in water and a new birth by arising from water. We rediscover the true symbolism of the rite by referring to the realities of the Old Testament.

But we have by no means exhausted the Biblical analogies of baptism. The prayer of consecration goes on to speak of the rivers of paradise. Here we enter a whole new field. In the commentaries of the Fathers no theme recurs more frequently than that of the analogy between Adam and the catechumen. Adam, after he had sinned, was driven out of paradise. Christ promised the good thief that he would be with Him in paradise. Baptism is the return to paradise, which is the Church.

From the beginning, preparation for baptism was seen as the antitype of the temptation in the garden of Eden. St. Cyril of Jerusalem calls the baptismal renunciation of Satan the breaking of the pact which, since the fall, binds man to the devil. Baptism, as we all know, is the destruction of original sin. But the image is not that of the stain that the water washes away; it is the dramatic contrast between our exclusion from paradise and our return to paradise.

This theme of baptism as a return to paradise[6] is as essential to the liturgy as is the paschal theme. Christ is the new Adam, the first to re-enter paradise; and by baptism the catechumen enters also, for the Church is paradise. De Bruyne and other scholars have shown how the symbolism of the ancient baptistries is concerned with paradise, its tree of life, its four rivers. Cyprian writes: "The

[3] *Donat.* V, 1; *PL,* 11, 1041.
[4] *Div. Inst.* II, 10; *PL,* 6, 311a.
[5] *Sp. Sanct.* I, 6, 76; *PL,* 16, 722d.
[6] See "Catéchèse pascale et retour au Paradis," *La Maison-Dieu,* 45 (1956), pp. 99-120.

Church, like paradise, contains within its walls trees loaded with fruit. These trees are watered by four rivers, by which she dispenses the grace of baptism."[7] And Ephraem adds: "It is here that each day the fruit is gathered that gives life to all."[8] No theme is more ancient in the Church than this; it is to be found in the Odes of Solomon, in the Epistle to Diognetus; Papias got it from apostolic centers.

The prayer of consecration then alludes to the rock in the desert. We have come now to the cycle of Exodus; and first we have to consider a theme not mentioned in the prayer of consecration, but in the *Exsultet.* This is one of the most important of all: that of the crossing of the Red Sea. The first Epistle to the Corinthians sees here a figure of baptism. This figure has recently been the subject of a lengthy study by Martelet.[9] I shall do no more than quote one of the most ancient patristic witnesses, Tertullian: "When the people, leaving Egypt without hindrance, escaped from the power of Pharaoh by passing across the water, the water destroyed the king and all his army. What clearer figure of baptism could we give? The nations are freed from the world; they are freed by water; they leave the devil, who once tyrannized over them, annihilated in the water."[10]

Here again we must be careful not to stop at the images but to discover the theological analogy. Tertullian points it out to us. What is the essence of the great work that God accomplished at the crossing of the Red Sea? The people were in a desperate situation, in imminent danger of destruction. By the power of God alone, a path was opened up through the sea, the people passed through and came to the further shore, there to sing the hymn of the redeemed. This was not a work of creation, nor a work of judgment, nor a work of sanctification; it was a work of redemption, in the etymological sense of the word. It was God who delivered the people, and He alone.

Now the catechumen is in an analogous situation just before he is baptized. He is still under the domination of the prince of this world and so given up to death. Then, by an act of the power of God alone, the water of the baptismal pool opens and he passes through. And when he has arrived at the other side, he also sings the canticle of the redeemed. In both cases we are in the presence of a divine act of salvation. And between the deliverance of the Red Sea and the deliverance of baptism, here again intervenes the deliverance of Christ, who made Himself the prisoner of death and who, on this same paschal night, by the power of God, broke the iron bolts and the bronze locks of death's prison and arose to become the firstborn from the dead.

[7] *Epist.* LXIII, 10.
[8] *Hymn. Par.* VI, 9.
[9] "Sacrements, figures et exhortation en 1 Cor. 10:1-11," *R.S.R.*, 44 (1956), pp. 323-359; 515-560.
[10] *Bapt.* 9.

The figure of the rock from which living water gushed forth introduces us to a new and equally essential perspective. St. Paul makes this also a figure of baptism: "Our fathers . . . all drank the same spiritual drink (for they drank from the spiritual rock which followed them, but the rock was Christ)."[11] In the Old Testament the outpouring of living water, united with the effusion of the Spirit, is a promise for the end of time, and the texts of Ezechiel and Isaias referring to this are part of our present liturgy of baptism. Now it is very probable, as Lampe has shown,[12] that the baptism of St. John referred to this prophecy, for he also connected water and the Spirit. His baptism signified the fact that the eschatological times of the outpouring of the Spirit had now come. (And we know how dear was this theme to the community at Qumran.) But John baptized only in water. It is Christ who gives water and the Spirit.

Christ said this same thing of Himself: "If anyone thirst, let him come to Me and drink. He who believes in Me, as the Scripture says, 'From within him shall flow rivers of living water.' He said this, however, of the Spirit whom they who believed in Him were to receive; for the Spirit had not yet been given" (John 7:37-39). We may, with Cullmann, discover an announcement of baptism in the texts of John concerning living water, that of the Samaritan woman in particular.[13] And certainly we must, with him and with the whole of tradition, recognize in the water and blood flowing from the side of Christ the image of water united with the Spirit, for the blood is the figure of the Spirit. And so Christ crucified is the eschatological Rock from whose pure side flows the water that refreshes us for everlasting life, the baptism that gives the Spirit.

We should notice in this connection that the gift of the Spirit is essentially connected with the outpouring of water. In the third century we find a tendency to distinguish the rite of water, which purifies, from another rite, the anointing or imposition of hands, which gives the Spirit. Gregory Dix makes use of these texts to distinguish within Christian initiation a sacrament of the Spirit, distinct from baptism, which would be confirmation. But this is contrary to primitive tradition and to tradition as a whole. It is the water, and it alone, that gives the Holy Spirit. The accompanying rites are illustrative only. Confirmation is a different sacrament, connected with spiritual growth and with participation in the ministry.

The Biblical themes that we have been considering up to this point have been concerned with water. But, once again, this is not the essence of their relationship with baptism. In a theme such as that of the return to paradise the mention of water is secondary; the emphasis is much more on the restoration of Adam to the realm of grace for which God had destined him from the beginning and

[11] 1 Cor. 10:4.
[12] *The Seal of the Spirit,* pp. 27-28.
[13] *Les sacrements dans l'Évangile johannique,"* pp. 51-55.

to which baptism restores him. Moreover, in this theme of paradise the Eucharist appears as well as baptism, and both are closely associated. In the same way, the rock of living water is related to the Eucharist and to baptism as well.

It is the theological analogy that is essential in every case. This appears also in the other Biblical themes which tradition relates to baptism and the Eucharist. For example, let us take that of the covenant. Gregory Nazianzen writes plainly: "We must call the grace of baptism a covenant, *diatheke*."[14] The covenant is the act by which God promises, in an irrevocable way, to establish communion of life between man and Himself. Christ realizes the new and eternal covenant by uniting in Himself for ever the divine nature and a human nature in such a way that they will never be separated. We should not forget the fact that "the Covenant" was one of our Lord's names in primitive Christianity, following the text of Isaias: "I have made you: Covenant of the peoples."

Baptism is our introduction into this covenant. Baptism establishes it by the pledge of God and that of man. When baptism was given in an interrogative form, this pledging formed part of the very form of baptism, which was given in faith and in water, as Justin says.

Later on this aspect was connected with the pre-baptismal profession of faith: "You also, you catechumens," writes John Chrysostom, "should learn to know the meaning of this word: I renounce Satan. For this word in fact is the covenant (*syntheke*) with the Lord."[15] This pledge is called *symbalon*, "pact," and it is from here that the term came to be applied to the profession of faith preceding baptism. John Chrysostom emphasizes the unconditional and irrevocable character of this engagement of God's: "God does not say: If this, or, If otherwise. Such were the words of Moses when he poured out the blood of the covenant. And God promises eternal life."[16]

We should take note of the allusion to the blood of the covenant poured out by Moses. The Old Covenant was sanctioned by a sacrament, by the sprinkling of the same blood on the people and on the altar, signifying and bringing about a communion of life. It is certainly in reference to this gesture of Moses' that Christ, when He took the wine and blessed it, declared: "This is My Blood, the Blood of the New Covenant," before giving it to His disciples, a sign of the communion of life brought about between them and Himself. The Eucharist is truly the new rite which succeeds the Old Covenant and which at once witnesses to and brings about the covenant made by Christ with mankind in His incarnation and His passion.

Here again we can see the irreplaceable value of the Biblical analogy. It enables us to see the full significance of Eucharistic communion as participation in the life of God, the participation that

[14] *Or. Bapt.*, 8.
[15] *Cat.*, 2; *PG* 49, 239.
[16] *Co. Col.*, 2, 6; *PG* 62, 342.

mankind has irrevocably gained in Christ Himself and that is now offered to each man. It connects the Eucharist with Scripture by showing us that the Eucharist continues, in the era of the Church, the divine actions which took place in both Testaments. It illuminates the symbolism of the sacramental rites by showing us the partaking of the Blood as being the supreme expression of communion of life, for blood is the expression of life itself.

And again, as the covenant is our bond with God, it is also our incorporation into the people of God. In the Old Covenant, this incorporation was expressed by circumcision. Cullmann, Sahlin, and many others have shown the connection of circumcision with baptism and the valuable elements which this connection brings to the theology of baptism.[17]

"The baptism of the Christian was expressed in the circumcision of the Hebrews," writes Optatus of Milevis.[18] But the Epistle to the Ephesians had already brought out the parallelism:

> Wherefore bear in mind that once you, the Gentiles in flesh, who are called 'uncircumcision' by the so-called 'circumcision' in flesh made by human hand—bear in mind that you were at that time without Christ, excluded as aliens from the community of Israel and strangers to the covenants of the promise. . . . But now in Christ Jesus you, who were once afar off, have been brought near through the blood of Christ (Eph. 2:11-13).

It is baptism itself that is the new rite of incorporation into the people of God in the Church. But, as other aspects of the sacrament are expressed by particular ceremonies, such as the clothing with a white garment and the anointing, so with this one. The expression of our incorporation into the people of God by baptism is the ceremony of the *sphragis*, the sign of the Cross marked on the forehead of the candidate.

Ezechiel had prophesied that the members of the eschatological community would wear on their foreheads the mark of the *taw*, the sign signifying Yahweh, the *Name* of Yahweh. It seems probable that the Sadocites of Damas actually bore this mark. And the Apocalypse of St. John shows us the elect as marked with the Name of Yahweh, that is, with the *taw*. It is very likely that this was the sign with which Christians were marked originally as the sign of their incorporation into the eschatological community. Now this sign is in the form of a cross. This is why, in the Greek communities which no longer understood the meaning of the Hebrew letter, it was interpreted as being the sign of the Cross of Christ. But Hermas still says: "Those who are marked with the Name."[19]

This leads us to another theme akin to that of the covenant, that of the dwelling, the *Shekinah*. Yahweh had caused His Name to

17 See "Circoncision et baptême," *Theologie in Geschichte und Gegenwart* (Mel. Schmaus), pp. 755-777.

18 *Donat.*, V, 1; *PG* 11, 1045a.

19 See *La Théologie du Judéo-christianisme* (Desclée et Cie., 1958), pp. 384-386.

dwell among His own. This is the mystery of the Tabernacle. This Presence abandoned the people of the Old Covenant when the veil of the temple was rent. Henceforth its dwelling-place is the humanity of Christ, in whom the Name has set up its tabernacle. And this dwelling-place is in our midst in the Eucharist. We have already seen the Eucharist as communion, covenant. Now we see it as presence, *Shekinah.* As the Eucharistic prayer of the *Didache* expresses it: "We give Thee thanks, O Father, for Thy holy Name which Thou hast caused to dwell in our hearts" (X, 2). Here the Name is the Word, as Peterson has pointed out. But the expression "the Name" is the older and the more fitting. For in the Old Testament it is the Name and not the Word which is connected with the dwelling.

As for the last great aspect of the Eucharist, sacrifice, which is at once adoration, thanksgiving and expiation, the liturgy of the Mass itself invites us to seek its prefiguring in the sacrifice of Abel, in that of Abraham, and in that of Melchisedech. Here again, the prophets had proclaimed that at the end of time the perfect sacrifice would be offered by the obedient Servant, the new Isaac, and the true Lamb. It is this priestly act, by which all glory is forever rendered to the Blessed Trinity, which the Eucharistic sacrifice makes perpetually present in all times and all places.

Thus we have brought out the traditional teaching. The sacraments are conceived in relation to the acts of God in the Old Testament and the New. God acts in the world; His actions are the *mirabilia,* the deeds that are His alone. God creates, judges, makes a covenant, is present, makes holy, delivers. These same acts are carried out in the different phases of the history of salvation. There is, then, a fundamental analogy between these actions. The sacraments are simply the continuation in the era of the Church of God's acts in the Old Testament and the New. This is the proper significance of the relationship between the Bible and the liturgy. The Bible is a sacred history; the liturgy is a sacred history.

The Bible is a witness given to real events; it is a sacred *history.* There is a profane history, which is that of civilizations, witnessing to the great deeds done by men. But the Bible is the history of divine actions; it witnesses to the great deeds carried out by God. It is all for the glory of God. And so it is the proper object of faith. For "to believe" does not mean only to believe that God exists, but also that He intervenes in human life. Faith is wholly concerned with these interventions of God: the covenant, the incarnation, the resurrection, the diffusion of the Spirit. And the Old Testament in particular is already essentially a sacred history.

This point needs to be emphasized today. For in Bultmann and his disciples we find a tendency to see in the Old Testament, and in Scripture in general, only a word that God addresses to us here and now. Under the pretext that the divine events are presented in a stylized form, their very historicity is questioned. Demythization has become dehistorization. But Cullmann and Eichrodt[20]—the latter precisely in connection with the problem that concerns us here, that of typology—have brought out the primacy of the event over the word, of the *ergon* over the *logos*. The object of faith is the existence of a divine plan. It is the objective reality of the divine interventions which modifies ontologically the human situation, and to the reality of which faith causes us to adhere.

This history is properly the history of the works of God which are grasped only by faith. It does not consist in reconstituting the historical and archeological context of the people of Israel or of the primitive Church. This is a part of the history of civilizations and is of a different order. Sacred history reaches, beyond the order of bodies and minds, what Pascal calls the "order of charity"—which term meant to him, good Augustinian that he was, the supernatural order. It is concerned, therefore, with the supernatural history of mankind, the most important history ultimately, since it is concerned with the final questions of the destiny of man and of mankind, the very depths of human nature.

Thus the Old Testament has as its purpose to recall to us the great deeds that God did for His people. But this represents only one aspect. It includes the Law, but it includes also the prophets. Prophecy is part of its very substance. We must give this word its true meaning; it is not merely prediction, not merely proclamation. Prophecy is the announcement of the fact that at the end of time God will accomplish works still greater than in the past. Here the movement of the Old Testament is quite different from that of natural religions. These are essentially, as Eliade and van den Leeuw have shown, the effort to defend primordial energies against the destructive action of time.

It is with the Bible that time acquires a positive content as being the setting in which the design of God is being carried out. But this orientation toward the future is an act of faith, founded on the promises of God. The great Biblical figure Abraham is quite different from the Greek hero Ulysses. The title of Homer's poem is *Nostoi*, "the returns." The outstanding characteristic of Ulysses is nostalgia, and finally after his long journeying, he returns to the place from which he set out. Time destroys itself. But Abraham leaves Ur of the Chaldees for ever and sets out on a journey to the land that God is to give him. For the man of the Bible, paradise, the state of innocence are not the point of departure; they are the end of the journey. Such a man cannot help having an eschatological attitude.

But, wonderful to say, these hoped-for future events are not unrelated to the events of the past. The promises of God remain unchanged. God said to Isaias (43:16-29): "Remember no more

[20] W. Eichrodt, "Ist die typologische Exegese sachgemasse Exegese?," *Theol. Literaturzeitung*, 81 (1956), pp. 641-653.

what is past; behold, I will make a new wonder. I will make a path through the sea."

One of the deeds of the past was the crossing of the Red Sea, the act of deliverance by which Yahweh delivered His people from their hopeless condition. The eschatological event will be a new Exodus, a new deliverance, a new redemption. And so we begin to see what is the real basis of typology—as Goppelt and Eichrodt have pointed out—the analogy between the divine deeds carried out in the different epochs of the history of salvation.

Prophecy announces to us eschatological events. The New Testament is the paradoxical affirmation that these events have taken place in Jesus Christ. We have lost sight of the importance of the expression that continually recurs in the New Testament: "so that the prophecies might be fulfilled," and this is because we have lost the understanding of what prophecy really is. It is because prophecy announces the end of time—and not some one event to come—and because Christ *is* the end of time that Christ fulfills prophecy. What is essential, then, is the fact that Christ is proclaimed to us as being the end of time. This is the meaning of John's gesture: *Ecce Agnus Dei.* Not: There is a Lamb of God. But: The Lamb of God is here.

We should remember here that the phrase, "the *end* of time," is to be taken in its full meaning: not only the end in the sense of the conclusion of time, but also in the sense of the goal of time, the definite and decisive event, that beyond which there is nothing more because there can be nothing beyond it. The paradoxical Christian affirmation is, as Cullmann has well shown, that the decisive event is already accomplished. No discovery, no revolution can ever bring about anything as important to mankind as is the resurrection of Jesus Christ. And, in fact, in the resurrection of Christ two things were accomplished beyond which nothing further is possible: God is perfectly glorified; man is perfectly united to God. We can never go beyond Jesus Christ. He is the final goal of God's design.

But did sacred history stop with Jesus Christ? This is, indeed, what we usually seem to say. And this is because we do not place the sacraments in the perspective of sacred history. We forget that, although Jesus Christ is the goal of sacred history, His coming into the world is only the inauguration of His mysteries. In the Apostles' Creed, after the mysteries of the past, we speak of a mystery still to come: *unde venturus est;* but between the two there is a mystery of the present: *sedet ad dexteram Patris.*

For Christ's enthronement at the right hand of the Father is only the definitive installation of the incarnate Word, who at His ascension entered into the heavenly Tabernacle, in His functions as King and Priest. The glorious humanity of Christ, during the whole era of the Church, causes every grace, every illumination, every sanctification, every blessing. And these divine works carried out by

Christ in glory are, above all, the works of the sacraments. These constitute the deeds properly divine being carried out in the heart of our world, the deeds by which God accomplishes our sanctification and builds up the Body of Christ. It is in their radiance that all holiness, all virtue, all ministry is developed.

Thus the nature of the sacraments is made clear to us in the perspective of the history of salvation. They are the divine acts corresponding to this particular era in the history of salvation, the era of the Church. These divine acts are the continuation of the acts of God in the Old and New Testaments, as Cullmann has already shown.[21] For the ways in which God acts are always the same: He creates, judges, saves, makes a covenant, is present. But these acts have a different modality in each era of the history of salvation.

What characterizes the era of the Church is, on the one hand, the fact that it comes *after* the essential event of sacred history, the event by which creation has attained its purpose in such a way that nothing can be added to it. The sacramental acts are, therefore, only saving actualizations of the passion and resurrection of Christ. Baptism plunges us into His death and resurrection. The Mass is not *another* sacrifice, but the *unique* sacrifice made present in the sacrament; in this sense it is true that the sacraments add nothing to Christ and that they are only the sacramental imitation of what has already been effectively accomplished in Him.

On the other hand, the era of the Church is that in which what has already been accomplished in Christ, the Head, is communicated to all men, who form the Body. The era of the Church is the time of the mission, the growth of the Church, and the sacraments are the instruments of this growth, incorporating into Christ His new members. As Gregory of Nyssa says: "Christ builds Himself up by means of those who continually join themselves to the faith" by baptism.[22] And Methodius of Olympia shows us how the sacramental life is the continual espousal of Christ and the Church.[23] We can understand why Cyril of Jerusalem made the Canticle of Canticles the sacramental text par excellence.[24]

But the last characteristic of the era of the Church is that the transformation carried out by Christ actually reaches mankind, but it is not yet made manifest: "You are now the sons of God, but it has not yet appeared what you shall be" (1 John 3:2). Thus the sacraments have a hidden aspect. They are a veil as well as a reality. *Jesu, quem velatum nunc aspicio . . . ut te revelata cernens facie . . . .*

And this shows us one more aspect of the sacraments in the history of salvation. They are not the final stage. After the mysteries of the past, there are the mysteries of the future. Prefigured by the

[21] *Les sacrements dans l'Évangile johannique,"* p. 85.
[22] *PG*, 1397c.
[23] *Conv.*, III, 8.
[24] See *Bible and Liturgy* (Notre Dame University Press, 1956).

realities of the Old Testament and the New, the sacraments are themselves prefigurations of eternal life. Baptism anticipates the Judgment; the Eucharist is the eschatological banquet already made present in mystery. And so the sacraments recapitulate the whole history of salvation: *Recolitur memoria passionis, mens impletur gratia, et futurae gloriae nobis pignus datur.*

Thus, we see the sacraments as being the acts of God in the era of the Church. As we have said, God's ways of acting are always the same. This is what finally defines the right of the Church to bring out the analogies between the sacraments and the divine events recorded in Scripture. It is here that we find the ultimate basis of what we explained in the first section of this chapter. The universe of the liturgy is a marvelous symphony in which appear the harmonies between the different eras of the history of salvation, in which we pass from the Old Testament to the sacraments, from eschatology to spirituality, from the New Testament to eschatology, in virtue of these fundamental analogies. Knowledge of these correspondences is *the* Christian wisdom as the Fathers understood it, the spiritual understanding of Scripture. And this is where the liturgy is the mistress of exegesis.

To conclude. One of the greatest difficulties for many minds is to understand the connection between Scripture and the Church. They hold to Scripture, but they do not see the need for the Church. It is of the utmost importance that such people be shown the strict continuity between Scripture and the Church. And it is precisely this continuity that appears at the climax of the history of salvation. It is here that the realities spoken of by Scripture and the realities that constitute the Church appear as being various stages of one work. And, furthermore, by employing a unique language, which is that used by the Word of God, and by causing us to discover the Scriptural categories in the sacraments, the continual reference to Scripture found in the explanation of the sacraments manifests the fact that they belong to the same universe.

Thus Bible and liturgy illuminate one another. The Bible both authorizes and clarifies the liturgy. It authorizes it by the authority of the prophets and the figures of which it is the fulfillment, and by thus placing it in the whole pattern of God's plan. It illuminates it by giving us the forms of expression by which we can understand the authentic meaning of the rites. In its turn, the liturgy illuminates the Bible. It gives us its authentic interpretation by showing us how it is a witness to the *mirabilia Dei.* And, much more, as these acts are continued in the sacraments, they actualize the Word of God by authorizing us to apply it to the present acts of God in the Church in virtue of the analogy between these acts in the different phases of history.

Rev. Hans Urs von Balthasar

CHAPTER 3

GOD HAS SPOKEN IN HUMAN LANGUAGE

BY THE LITURGY the priest reaches Catholics only, and, among them, only the practicing believers; the liturgy has become a domain seemingly reserved to an élite. Since the purpose of this book is to show the close bonds between the liturgy and the Word of God, the liturgy and preaching, the liturgy and meditation on the Bible, it might seem as if the Word, to be truly understood, must be confined within the same closed, almost esoteric limits. Since, in spite of ourselves, we adopt with regard to the liturgy something like the discipline of the *arcana* practiced by the Fathers,[1] should we not make people feel that the Word of God also creates a sacred domain, accessible only to the believer in the act of adoration?

In this conclusion, which is not entirely chimerical but corresponds to a real tendency today, there is an element of resignation which in the Christian context is quite unsound. Christianity has no tendency to limit itself, but rather to expand, to become universal. Psychologically, an esoteric attitude often contains an element of fear.

[1] Eucharius Berbuir, *Der Weg zum Glauben* (Einsiedeln: Johannesverlag, 1955).

If we are to combat this fear—which easily disguises itself as a proper reverence for the sacred—we must not be afraid to submit the data of the Christian religion, supernaturally revealed, to the examination of the anthropological sciences, such as philology, sociology, psychology. If, in Christ, God made Himself man, if He assumed a human nature into His personal and trinitarian life, He did not do so by violating human nature. If He founded a community around His incarnation, still less did He do so by violating the laws of sociology, particularly of religious sociology. From this point of view, it cannot be denied that the religion which we consider to be the only true one has an aspect which puts it sociologically on the same level as the "other" religions.

The Bible is the sacred Book par excellence, but it is also one sacred book among others, and each religion has its own.[2] And not only does each religion have its own liturgy, but it is a known fact—which corresponds to an easily understandable anthropological tendency—that the liturgy of each religion loves to justify the most minute positive prescriptions of its worship by attributing them to the revealed, formal will of the divinity. The priestly code of the Old Testament, which attributed the temple worship in all its details to an explicit institution of Moses, thanks to his supernatural vision of all the details of the sanctuary on the holy mountain (Ex. 25–31; 35–40), confirms this common law of anthropology.[3] And, in the same way, each religion has a tendency to become esoteric.

We should not be disturbed by these parallelisms, which are not vague resemblances, but are founded on a certain identity: that of the nature of man. We should rather rejoice in them, because they are a proof of the real incarnation, that is to say, the "inhumanization" of God.[4]

If God has made Himself man, then it is man as man who has become the expression, the valid and authentic translation of the divine mystery. True, man will have need of supernatural faith in order to grasp what God, supremely free in His spontaneous revelation of Himself, wills to make known to him. But, on the other hand, the divine meaning will not remain exterior and foreign to the man who is chosen to express it. God is love; but it is as man that He has demonstrated this fact; and this is why it is uniquely in Christ that the two precepts of love can be fused into one single precept.

This is equivalent to saying that God, in revealing His face to man, has also revealed to man his own proper human likeness. There

[2] J. Leipoldt and S. Morenz, *Heilige Schriften. Betrachtungen zur Religionsgeschichte der antiken Mittelmeerwelt.* (Leipzig: Harrassowitz, 1953). Günter Lanczkowski, *Heilige Schriften,* Urbanbücherei 22 (Europaverlag).

[3] We could also mention the tendency, now outgrown, to attribute all the details of the New Testament sacramental rites to a positive institution by Christ.

[4] Max Weber, who is considered by many to be one of the greatest modern German philosophers, has inaugurated in a masterly fashion the study of the sociology of religions. Up to the present time, Catholics have made very little use of his work.

was no need for God to make use of man in order to reveal Himself; but if He determined to do so, and did so by an in-humanization, then all the dimensions of human nature, known and unknown, are to be assumed and utilized to serve as means of expression for the absolute Person. And so the Christian religion, while remaining sociologically only "one" religion among others, should necessarily also coincide with total humanism, and it is only by this title that it can be recognized as fully catholic.[5]

Humanism in Christianity: here indeed is the central theme of our era. It preoccupies us all; it is of passionate concern to our lay people because of their need to communicate with their non-Christian or non-practicing brothers; it calls for a solution at once vast and courageous in the face of world unity in the making. And it is brought out also, in a striking paradox, by those very discoveries of modern Biblical studies that hold us in suspense. Let us consider for a moment this last aspect. On the one hand, our age is discovering continually clearer analogies between the religion of revelation and the cultures that surrounded it, continually clearer evidence of the influences of these cultures on that religion; many an aspect which to our ancestors seemed purely supernatural now appears to us as being part of the religious patrimony of mankind.

But it is precisely these discoveries which, in an entirely unforeseen manner, have brought us nearer to the mystery of revelation. Possibly we can understand the mystery of Israel better than could any Christian age in the past, better even than the apostolic age itself in its context of Judaism and Hellenism. The more the concrete and historical human element is precisely defined, the more the revealed truth is seen to be profound, the more it stands out clearly; this is one of the great laws opposed to gnosticism, a law of the incarnation. The more Christ is seen to be *one with* mankind in word and thought and action, the more He is also seen to be the *Unique* who comes from on high, authorized to utter (without insanity or blasphemy) those unheard-of phrases that no mere man would dare to utter: "Which of you will accuse Me of sin?"; "My words shall not pass"; "I will come on the clouds of heaven."

Let us choose the simplest way. If we are to understand how God has spoken to man in human language, we need to consider, at least briefly, the structure of human speech. To understand human speech we need to consider what it expresses, that is, human experience.

[5] We do not question this assertion, but rather confirm it when we add another: the tendency to universalism which we have just attributed to revealed religion also has its sociological aspect. Every religion (above all, if it claims to be revealed) must necessarily tend toward totality and toward unity. We shall never succeed in distinguishing the divine and supernatural unity in the religion of Christ from this universality that includes at the same time every human universal, "abstract" as well as numerical.

We shall, therefore, first consider human experience; next, human speech; and finally, the eternal Word incarnating Himself in man and in his speech in order to transform it into God's language.

What is the specific form of human experience?[6] Man is essentially an *historic* being: his spirit perfects itself in time,[7] in the course of a unique and irreversible journey that leads him through successive stages—childhood, adolescence, maturity, old age—in such a way that the achievement of each one of these stages in no way assures the realization of the one that follows. There is an existential logic in this series of stages, even though, for St. Paul, it is bound up with an illogical element—death. Time seen as a descent toward a final catastrophe implies an element of futility and nothingness, but this element is inserted in a superior logic of grace, since God has abased Himself to this abyss made by the creature, not the Creator.

This fact only accentuates the devouring stress of our existence: each age of life, each situation requires that we abandon it and that we go beyond it; yet each means for us a gift never to be given again, a mirror of the absolute and of the duration of eternity.

Maturity can never replace or even preserve that first vision of a world fundamentally new, innocent, like paradise, filled with marvels of nature and supernature; everything is possible, everything is close to God. The incurable nostalgia of childhood is not mere romanticism; it can have, as with Péguy and Bernanos, profoundly Christian causes. It is true that the Christian miracle consists in a renewal of the whole time-sequence; the entrance into the Church by the door of baptism is a new admittance into paradise, accessible only to children, by the "little way" that allows us once again to climb the slope of bygone time.

But this Christian miracle does not destroy the historic nature of man, *non tollit naturam.* The losses caused by time and futility are not done away with, and it is only in living both these aspects—apparently contradictory as they are—that Christian existence, with its experience of childhood redeemed *in* growing old, is to be achieved.[8]

But man is not only the child. He is also the adolescent, with his enthusiasms, his fears and depressions, his discoveries of the depths of human nature, with the pathetic moment of the call heard and understood, the decisive hour in which the man, seemingly still too young, chooses his lot in life, his work, his state – a moment which will never return. What gain, what loss! To choose presupposes freedom, but it also presupposes confidence, hope, the unreserved gift of self.[9] It is

[6] The question here is of the *form.* It would be impossible to describe in one chapter either the content of this experience, the existent being against the background of being, or the reach of the spirit in its grasp at once of itself and of the other.

[7] Here also, we must resign ourselves to what is possible. The unfathomable mystery of temporality can only be approached here from an aspect that is relatively simple and accessible to everyone.

[8] See the very valuable book of Mouroux, *The Christian Experience* (New York: Sheed and Ward, 1954).

[9] This is one of the favorite themes of Gabriel Marcel.

human to believe, to hope, to love. And it is human also for the *mature man* to give himself wholly, to sacrifice himself to a task, to find the whole in the part that is given him. It is human for him to know the joy and danger of responsibility, and even the bitter consolation of defeats which prove to him that he has not really gone astray, that he is still a man among his fellowmen.

And in each human state there is the same looking forward and the attempt to retain, at least in memory, everything that has irretrievably fled away and to incorporate it into our onward flight. Thus the present becomes a kind of qualitative synthesis of time as a whole, modified by the continually changing relationship of the past and the future.

Time is, therefore, in no way a uniform stream; it knows mysterious moments of concentration, climaxes in which man frees himself and chooses himself. At the appointed hour of his existence he meets his own true image, his vocation and the grace destined for him. If he adheres to it, this decisive moment fills his whole life with a companioning presence which gathers it all up in a meaningful form; if he refuses, his whole temporal existence degenerates into time lost. Faith, hope, and love together make up the form of time-bound man. This is the starting-point he must use in each effort to understand his existence; we have nothing to work with beyond hope that seems so tiny, faith that is self-abandonment, love that gives itself and loses itself. Any attempt to go beyond the glory and misery of these three, *tria haec* – and every non-Christian religion would like to go beyond them – leads us astray into gnosis.

The life of whole peoples follows a similar pattern. They only can grasp what they are by projecting it into the future, aided by the mirror of memory. The measurable part of their existence, their history already lived through, in some way justifies their hope; in it they recognize certain landmarks, certain promises realized in part. It is because this fragment of being offers something like a meaning (however fleeting) that the hope that all the generations making up one people form a hidden continuity through time cannot be entirely a vain one.

This law of peoples as such is also a law of all history; the past and the future of a man or of a people cannot be cut off from the universal destiny of mankind. And this is necessarily true also of that sacred history which summarizes the dialogue between God and His chosen people.

What Gregory of Nyssa calls the *diastema* of our existence, the fundamental separateness and non-identity of our experiences, the transition from one point of view to another – why should we not find it also in the Bible?

Since God Himself has sought out the glory and the humiliation of existing in time, it is impossible to take away from revealed truth its temporal form so as to keep only a system of supra-temporal truths.

Let us recall some notable examples. "The days when Israel was a child" (Osee); what nostalgia throughout the sacred Word for the memory of that childhood—not only for the paradise before history began but for those days in which everything was young, pure and perfect between Israel and its God!

If mankind did not remember its lost origin, how could it search for it throughout all the disasters of history? If Abraham had not possessed at least that tomb in the Holy Land, how would his descendants have allowed God to persuade them to leave prosperous Egypt and bury themselves in the desert of Sinai? Certain psalms preserve so vivid a memory of the primitive grace of those times that even the events of the Covenant are not mentioned: everything is pure gift, the Law does not yet exist. Or else, when they do sing of that prodigious event, the conclusion of the Covenant made in the face of the flaming mountain, by the blood sprinkled on the people and altar and by the absolute decision of primordial faith, how clearly this Law appears as itself a grace, as a Law that is absolutely true, priceless, necessary, and *possible* for man to obey!

We must measure the distance that separates this *experience of the beginning* (which is no dream or myth) from the later theology of Deuteronomy, of Judaism, and finally, of St. Paul, to experience in this difference the inevitable aging of the idea and of the ideal. A thousand years' experience of sin has intervened; the virgin of Sion has gone astray, not only into single acts from which she could be raised up, but into a condition that is permanent and insurmountable. Is it ever possible to observe such a Law? Does it truly come from God and not rather from various mediators? Good "in itself," is it still really good "for me"? The *center of experience* is displaced, even in the times of the kings and prophets, still more during the Exile, in the age of the sapiential books and the apocalypses.

We must have the patience to leave their value at once "absolute" and "relative" to all these experiences to which sacred history bears witness. We must do so because these experiences presuppose one another in their very difference. Change from one condition to another is indispensable if each one is to be understood; but this change is itself ambiguous: on the one hand, temporal existence is understood in reference to the future, like a book whose pages are turned as we read it. And so the final synthesis, that of Christ, made explicit by Paul and John, will be more complete, more extensive, more limitless than, for example, that of the Pentateuch.

But, on the other hand, every temporal gain infallibly implies certain losses. There are texts in the Old Testament that are greater, more fully experienced in themselves than they are in the use made of them by the New Testament and in the way in which it understands them. And Christ was careful to send believers back to the greatest and most unconstraining origins.

We see, therefore, how this human law applies to sacred history and to its witness, the Biblical Word: a present experience is true and valuable only insofar as it is bound up with a certain vision and interpretation of the past and the future, with a projection of our ruling ideal, in the memory that guides us. The Bible is filled with such projections toward its own historic past. Without them, it would not possess a truth that was fully human. And the truth of the Bible loses nothing because it must undergo these inevitable divergences between modes of interpretation. It would be too facile, and even false, to say that the Jews composed their own past and pre-history to suit the experiences of much later times and that it is the task of scientific research to disengage the original and real events from this mixture of poetry and truth.

We must rather acknowledge the fact that the interpreters in the era of the kings, of the great prophets, and of the "furnace" of the Exile felt themselves entirely capable of interpreting history objectively, of proclaiming the true meaning of past events, which were more comprehensible to them than to those who had lived through them. And the more Israel learned in faith to know and to hope for a future with absolute qualities, the more clearly it was able to see, through the images of its own past, both historic and poetic, that absolute beginning from which it had set out on its course.

It is fully in conformity with the structure of human truth that a historic past (and not some myth to be de-mythologized) can orient a people towards its future through projected images (as in the account of paradise, of post-Adamic and patriarchal times), and that a primary intuition, a primary contact with the living God, such as no other people had experienced, could determine for the people of Israel their historic, messianic and eschatological history.

Biblical truth is, therefore, to be grasped only in its full context. This ancient law of spiritual and Catholic interpretation is here rediscovered from an unexpected angle. In each word the whole is echoed; each word sends us back to the whole. But the particular text may have been conveyed to us through successive and different experiences. It has been proved, for example, that certain episodes from the age of the patriarchs and previous periods have been uprooted wholly or in part from their original and living context and have been incorporated by the Yahwist or one of his successors into a wholly new context of religious experience.

Or again, a certain psalm (as Albert Gelin has shown in the case of Psalm 21) may have been composed by one of the "poor ones of Yahweh" among the followers of Jeremias. It may then have passed into liturgical use, in which the individual's hope of liberation took on an ecumenical, social significance. This significance finally became messianic when a majestic but later addition to the text came to polarize the whole text toward the future. The poor man who cries out to his God becomes that Poor Man who is the People itself, and this becomes the eschatological Poor Man, to become concrete once more in the Poor Man who died on the Cross with Psalm 21 on His lips.

All these harmonies, these relationships, these correspondences that are the result of the passing of time do not imply any diminution in the absolute truth of the Bible. On the contrary, they are assumed by the divine Word in order to make them the decisive proof of His truthfulness. For the truth of a living being is always contained in its whole reality. A man who must make a decisive choice is aware of being asked: If you act in this way, are you being faithful to your first vision and to your deepest hope? Are you thus being most fully your best self?

In the same way, the most abrupt pronunciation of the divine Word addressed to Israel always includes the relationship between the past and the future; it *creates* history while establishing the truth *in* history; it promises nothing for the future without giving proofs of its truthfulness from the accomplishments of the past. The logic of the invasion of the Word from above into human history is always a logic that, in order to show its legitimacy, makes use of the historical life of the people.[10]

This fact is evident in the harmony between the two Testaments, a harmony which, for the men of the Bible, for Jesus Himself, and for the Fathers of the Church, remained the fundamental and inexhaustible proof of the truth of the Word of God.

But this magnificent harmony is only the greatest example among innumerable other relationships, connections, encounters, recognitions and reverberations: between the religion before and after Moses, between the Law and the prophets, the institution and the event, the historic books and the sapiential books, earthly history and apocalyptic vision, the Gospel and the history of the apostles or that of the Church. The entire Old Testament (and not merely in some texts that are called messianic) is prophetically opened out toward the New, in such a way that Christ and the apostles continually referred to the Old Law to find the justification for its undreamed-of extension by God made man.

The sacred texts often, as it were purposely, allow us to discover disparities, seeming contradictions in order to call our attention to the fact that certain words or events come to us from far away, charged with much meaning,[11] with innumerable reflections, stratum upon stratum.

[10] The most sublime example, the annunciation to Mary, Queen of patriarchs and prophets, is also the clearest; the mystery of the divine decision is announced three times in a manner that is absolute, abrupt, from above (Luke 1:28, 31, 35), and is then placed in the course of the history of salvation, making comprehensible to Mary the complete and unheard-of obedience required of her (Luke 1:32-33, 36). The eschatological vision cannot be lacking (1:33), nor the revelation of the divine triune life (1:28, the Father; 1:31, the Son; 1:35, the Spirit).

[11] Here we see the reappearance, from the angle of textual criticism, of the old debate concerning the plurality of the senses of Scripture. Gerhard von Rad, in his *Commentaire sur la Genèse* (1953), has clearly shown how the Yahwist, while transposing various experiences into his new context, has nevertheless refrained from any delimitation; he leaves in doubt, he points up what is incomplete; he leaves the work of synthesis to the reader. Speaking of Gen. 22:1-19, von Rad writes: "In such an account, which has manifestly gone through many stages of internal reworkings, the content of which was, so to say, fluid up to the last, we must renounce from the outset the idea of wishing to elucidate *one* sense as *the* definitive one. It has many strata of thought, and he who believes himself to have reached the last

From a human point of view, no text of secular literature presents such a bewildering wealth of perspectives as does the Bible; one single word may have hundreds of echoes. The religious experiences of many ages are accumulated in such a word; and these unwearying meditations, in responding to the immensity of the divine Word, have finally given to its human instrument a kind of corresponding infinity. And we understand how tradition is, in a decisive aspect, anterior to Scripture:[12] Scripture confirms and completes that living history of revelation brought about in the experience that men have had with God.

Here I would add a corollary: following St. Paul and the Gospels, the Fathers of the Church considered the Old Law only as being a stage preparatory to the New, as being something essentially imperfect which future revelation was to go beyond, even apart from the rejection of the Messiah, the rejection by which Israel ceased to be the living people of God. Let us never forget, however, that Christ had to bring to perfection the age-old experience of faith of the Jewish people. The faith of His ancestors lived in Jesus, just as in their faith the Word of God had lived from the beginning and had been, as it were, incarnated in advance. But if the faith of the people of old was oriented toward the messianic future, it remained immovably rooted in its origins: in Abraham, Moses, David, and the prophets.

As Man and as God, Jesus by a supreme piety brought the religion of His people to perfection. The faith of Abraham, the exemplar of all faith; the faith of Sinai embracing the Law, sign of the promise and of the concrete commitment of Yahweh; the faith of Amos and of Isaias in the rights of the poor, the peacemakers, the persecuted; the faith of Jeremias and of Job — all this was *the faith of Christ,* leader and guide of our faith, who brings it to perfection, "the author and perfector of faith" (Heb. 12:2). His vision of the Father could not hinder Him from knowing and perfecting that fundamental human attitude of all true servants of Yahweh; otherwise, how could we, the faithful, imitate Christ by our faith?

This faith, then, did not begin with Him and does not find its unique object in Him. It is not only faith "in" Jesus, it is also faith together with Him — if we take the word in its full Biblical sense of faith in God, the God of Abraham, Isaac and Jacob, who now reveals Himself as the God and Father of the Word, His Son.

will find that there are still more beneath it. A narrator of so ripe a culture as this never has the intention of exactly delimiting the sense of such an episode and of fixing the reader therein. On the contrary, such a history is basically *open* to interpretation; whatever may be the reflections in which the reader finds himself engaged, the narrator is not opposed to them, since he is only recounting an event and not giving a lesson. To the interpreter, there is only one barrier, but this is an absolute one: the narration cannot be understood as being the a-historic representation of a religious reality common to all" (p. 208).

[12] As L. Bouyer has shown in his masterly book, *The Meaning of Sacred Scripture* (Notre Dame University Press, 1958), the subtitle of which in the French edition sums up the course of this chapter: "From the God who speaks to God made man."

The dreadful sin against the chosen people of which Christianity has been guilty for two thousand years comes in part from a misunderstanding of this unity which characterizes existential Biblical truth. Youthful Christianity was like a young man who thinks that he can turn away from his childhood and look only to the future; but the mature man looks back once more. The chosen people, in spite of everything, tried to choose God for us; they suffered for doing so – through the centuries before Christ and through how many more since Christ – for us. We are grafted on the sacred stock in a living and spiritual union more intimate than any other in the world.

The dialectic unity of love and jealousy, as St. Paul describes it (Rom. 9–11), is also the mystery of the total redemption of mankind in Abraham, the father of all who believe, in an age when there was as yet no Scripture, no tradition, no dogma, no liturgy, no law, no priesthood, no hierarchy. All this flowed (Rom. 4) from that initial self-abandonment of this man simply as man, to God simply as God. This aloneness of man in the presence of the only God was perfected on the Cross where the dialectic between Jew and pagan, between tradition and non-tradition was definitely consummated and surpassed (Eph. 2:11ff.), but in an eschatological perspective.[13]

We must always return to the final fulfillment. Arrival in the Holy Land was certainly a first achievement of the journey across the desert, but also of the Exile and of the great dispersion of the people. And so of the Son, sojourning on this earth, of the Church wandering through the desert of the centuries (Apoc. 12:14), of each believer in his hope. The whole of Scripture remains "on the way"; it is always a departure, a journey through the desert, a journey from the image to the truth, from the promise to the fulfillment, from the Word to the Word-made-flesh, but also from physical death to spiritual life, a journey from the physical presence, through the absence caused by His death and ascension, toward the eschatological presence. All this truth is made up of tension, *diastasis;* it is the truth of the *cor inquietum,* of hope and longing love.

Now it is within this human experience that the divine Word has placed Himself; this fragile web of temporal relationships is solid enough to contain the absolute Truth, which is itself a truth of eternal Relationships in eternal life.

Never has revelation fallen from heaven in order to communicate transcendent mysteries to man from without and from on high. God speaks to man from within the world, the starting-point of his own human experiences, penetrating His creature so intimately that the divine *kenosis* was already announced in the Word of the Old Law and was no more than completed in the incarnation.

Let us go on now to our second question: What kind of communication corresponds to this human experience? How does man speak? Let us first give a brief description of the essential phenomenon.

[13] In connection with all this, see the *Cahiers Sioniens,* also *The Bridge* (annually published since 1956 by Pantheon, New York); the Judeo-Christian weekly published in Berlin (noted in *Herderkorrespondenz,* June, 1957).

"To speak" signifies for man to manifest freely his intimate and personal being to someone else by means of the perceptible sign of sounds. This contains three elements. First, the self-possession of a spiritual person, present to himself, who moreover knows and understands his own *truth.* This is why true human speech is not a kind of babbling, a vain attempt to express some obscure interiority, but an exact and precise procedure. This, indeed, is what characterizes also the Word of Yahweh, in contrast to the mystical babblings or the impotent silence surrounding the summits of other religions. "It is I, Yahweh, who speak with precision, and I express Myself in true words" (Is. 45:19).

Next, to be oneself means perfect *freedom.* This is why the expression chosen by a free man is not necessitated. The language of man presupposes a choice of his means of communication that is fundamentally free. The risen Christ has, even in His physical being, become spiritual, that is to say, free. He is no longer to be known in a natural and passive way; He reveals Himself spontaneously, at the moment when He wills it. The *Verbum caro* here attains its perfection, flesh has become wholly a word at the disposition of the eternal Word.

Lastly, by truth and freedom the person is all-embracing and self-determined; that is to say, it tends to go beyond subjectivity toward a Thou (in principle toward each Thou). It exists insofar as it is intersubjective. It implies communion and interchange, and it is so in its very source.

To speak is, therefore, not an epiphenomenon of man's nature. It is an integral part of his being, and even of being as such. The recent philosophers who take the phenomenon of language as their starting-point are actually taking the most direct route to an understanding of man and of being. They tell us that the *verbum mentis,* which springs from the depths of the spirit in the love that causes it to rise and that accompanies it, does not confine the person in himself in any solipsistic way (as a superficial interpretation of St. Augustine's Trinitarian image might suggest), but rather reveals in love the mystery of being itself in the reciprocal interpenetration of consciousnesses.

The human word, if it is a true one, manifests what being is; it participates in being from its origin, illuminated from the beginning by the spirit; and by this it participates in that Word eternally pronounced in the heart of being by absolute Love. Everything was created by that Word, everything subsists in it and for it; for the nature of man, which bears within itself an inexplicable promise, has always been destined to attain its final fulfillment in the free and gracious revelation of the eternal Word.

Human language, however, is not as yet characterized by truth, freedom, and love. It must go beyond itself in two directions: toward its *origin* and toward its *goal.*

The free and spiritual language of man emerges from those deep sources with which biology and paleontology have made us acquainted, in virtue of which man is united with material creation, its summit, its spokesman before God. The spiritual man inhabits the totality of being; by his body he dwells in the whole of nature and cannot detach himself from it. His language is that of natural sounds and gestures. Thence comes that wonderful interplay in our speech between nature and spirit, those interweavings, those slow transitions from the image (imitating nature) to the symbol (already free in part) and to the sign (deliberately chosen), those transitions from the speaking body (as in dancing) to language and writing, from physiognomy to abstract logic and grammar. This richness shows us how man is limitlessly open.

Nor should we forget what present-day biology tells us about the language of the animals – the unbelievable exactitude of their communications and their signals, the prefiguring of abstraction and schematization in their mimed play, which often consists of long and complicated rituals, astonishingly close to the gesture and image language of primitive man. One whole area of the familiarity between man and nature which produced this was not lost until the present time, until the technical age. Romanticism attempted to recover, *in extremis* as it were, this dimension of human language; but it was too late. Nonetheless, man remains, whether he wishes it or not, a being in nature, and he can never completely detach himself from this world of natural signs. Symbolic logic can never be the whole of human logic and cannot replace it.

Here is the place to speak of the sacraments and the liturgy. Both are in harmony with this attachment of man to nature; both are not so much arbitrary and positive institutions set up at the divine good pleasure as adaptations made by God to His pre-established laws of creation. Guardini has brought out clearly the element in the liturgy that is related to sacred play, a function common to man as an individual and to all peoples.[14] We now know that Christ did not invent any one of the sacramental signs: He took baptism from John, bread and wine from the devout gatherings of His time;[15] confession from a situation common to all men, found in all religions, even in Buddhist convents. Anointing with oil, the imposition of hands form part of the Jewish ritual, in which also the liturgy of the Mass was preformed.

There is also a second transcendence of language, toward its goal. Speech does not achieve perfection in itself; it is ordered to life. Language wishes to act and to create. It is itself the beginning of action, it goes beyond itself in work and in self-commitment, "engagement." The moment comes when words are not enough, when the witness of the whole person is required, as in the love between man and woman, in political action, in the apostolate, in martyrdom. Truth is not human without the property of truthfulness which alone proves that the true and right word has reached being itself and has not fallen short of it.

[14] R. Guardini, *The Spirit of the Liturgy* (New York: Doubleday, Image Book edition).

[15] See Gregory Dix, *The Shape of the Liturgy* (London: Daire Press, 1945); L. Bouyer, *Liturgical Piety* (Notre Dame University Press, 1955), p. 122.

Thus in the Bible, the various aspects of truth (*veritas, veracitas, fidelitas*) are all expressed by the same word, *emeth.* God Himself is bound by His Word, no less than man. The Word of God, like that of man, is open to existence; it bears within itself the witness and the force of the presence of the living God, in contrast to the mute idols of the nations, incapable of a true word, without fidelity or reality.

The Word, having exercised His prophetic mission, entered into His definitive phase through the Eucharist and the passion. St. John calls this "to the end." What speaking, discourse, could not bring about, since it provoked only growing resistance, the immolated Word could accomplish – the Word who spent Himself drop by drop on the Cross, the Word that finally resounded in that terrible and inarticulate cry in which everything was summed up, everything that had been said, everything in the divine communication that was incommunicable.

No man would ever finish speaking (". . .all the books in the world could not contain it"); it is action alone that brings it to an end. But actions themselves would never end either; the last word is suffering and death, in which man sums up his whole being before the Father. This is the word that is his testament, the witness and seal he puts to his whole life. Human time and human speech became in His death that unity which God Himself willed in His kindness, since He chose as the final expresson of His divine unity the expression of His revelation and of His trinitarian essence.

We mentioned the sacraments and the liturgy in connection with the first way in which human language must go beyond itself: toward nature and the organic sign. We must mention them also in connection with this second way. In the liturgy and the sacraments the Word of Christ makes itself act; the truth witnessed and assured to us becomes truth efficacious and victorious in us. This second transcendence – let us never forget it – is attained only by the total gift of self; there is no Christian liturgy without the sacrifice of the Cross. We might say, indeed, that fundamentally the two are identical.

This is the way, then, that man speaks: a free spirit who knows truth, he at the same time expresses nature and he expresses himself in his existence. And it is such speech that God has chosen for His revelation. This comes back to saying that revelation presupposes a fundamental analogy of being in the order of creation, but that this analogy is precisely described (according to the Fourth Lateran Council) as being "*in tanta similitudine major dissimilitudo.*"

Free human speech, indeed, presupposes, as we have seen, a natural speech which is not a matter of free choice, since man is a corporal organic being. Between God and the world no such necessary link exists – creation, revelation, redemption are all His free choice. But there is nonetheless a true analogy: as the spiritual speech of man presupposes a natural speech, so the speech of revelation presupposes the speech of creation. It presupposes precisely this analogy of being, and therefore the natural knowledge of God, or, in religious terms, the natural and existential contact of the creature with the being from which it comes forth, *cognitio per contactum* (St. Thomas), all during his individual existence and throughout the whole historical duration of peoples and civilizations.

And this analogy is continued. As the free word of the spirit represents, in relation to natural speech (like that of animals or of a baby), a completely new degree, in the same way when God reveals Himself in human history, He acts as a sovereign who proclaims, acts, chooses, reproves, judges, and has mercy according to laws known to Him alone, laws that are in no way to be deduced from existence or from history. And yet, that such a free word of the spirit exists is already a matter of human experience, even before God reveals Himself. God takes hold of that experience in which man freely raises himself above the level of nature and attains to the Word – and it is in this way that God shows that He is the free Master of mankind.

From this let us draw three consequences which will lead us to our conclusion. First, God speaks by man. Not only what man says, but *everything that he is* becomes God's instrument. Obviously, what he is and what he could be is manifested in all its fullness only when God makes of man His alphabet, His expressive and intelligent instrument. If ever God in His supreme liberty decided to make Himself man, to adapt Himself to the modes of expression of His creature in order to reveal His divine depths, to pour out the abyss of His fullness into this other abyss of emptiness and need, to find His glory in the abasement of the Cross and the descent into Sheol – if God ever took this decision (and He did so before the creation of the world, and the creation of the world was the first step along this road), then from the very beginning His Word must have chosen human existence and experience as its mode of expression.

Man, even in revelation, therefore, *will never reach God otherwise than in man.* The curtain of secondary causes is not torn apart; on the contrary, the more God radically reveals Himself, the more He deliberately hides Himself in a human nature. The Word which at one time seemed to resound from heaven in a certain "in itself" has clothed itself in the flesh of Jesus Christ, in the sacraments of the liturgy, in the Word of the Church, in the writings of Doctors and theologians, in ritual, in imagery, in the conduct of the hierarchical activity of the Church. It is always man who is there, and more and more man.

He is called to meet God; he knows Him in living faith, in those secret touches in the depth of the soul that make His presence and His action evident. But we approach the Father in no other way than in the humanity of His Son, and we participate in Their Holy Spirit only in the real and mystical Body of Christ. To love God we must love our neighbor; in the humility of fraternal love we learn to know the eternal I and Thou.

But if man is the speech of God, still he never becomes God. In order to know God, man must at the same time realize himself and deny himself. He is what God says; he is never He who says it. In order to reveal God, he must in turn hide himself, forget himself, efface himself. He will never succeed except in sacrificing all his experiences and his positions, his abilities and his arrangements, so that God can use him, as a typesetter uses the letters laid out at his disposal.

Secondly, the particular Word of God which we call Biblical revelation, which remains the center of the divine speech, necessarily transcends itself toward a word of all mankind by its referring itself back to creation and forward to the coming of the Kingdom, the day of Yahweh, the resurrection of all history in God. Christ, at the center of history, reveals its origins and its goal; He includes what is called natural religion[16] just as much as eschatology. The religion of the patriarchs has certain roots in that of Canaan; Abraham bows before Melchisedech, that pagan ancestor of David at Salem, later exalted to become the type of Christ. In the Bible there are holy men before Abraham, brought before us by the sacred writers: Abel, Henoch, the triad of Noe, Danel and Job recalled by Ezechiel. Others remain on the margin of sacred history.

The God who was to be the God of Israel and who was to call Himself Yahweh was already – under strange and even disconcerting names, names of Canaanite divinities, of gods of mountains and storm, of that cloud of divine forces which must have originally made up the *Elohim* – the God the revelation to come. In the name and at the command of the God of Israel, the sacred writers made themselves responsible for this identification and responded to it.

And the more the messianic vision enlarged the religion of Israel and opened out to its gaze a universalist horizon, the salvation of all nations, the more also the theological reflection of the priestly code became capable of composing a correspondingly universalist account of creation, and even (an astounding thing!) of anticipating the covenant with Abraham in the covenant with Noe formally concluded *with all mankind*, with all flesh, with all living things, and this for "all generations to come"; and the sign of this definitive reconciliation between God and the world is simply a natural phenomenon – the rainbow. "When the bow appears in the clouds, I will see it and I will remember the eternal covenant that exists between God and all living beings, that is, all flesh that is upon the earth" (Gen. 9:16).

From where else, the priests of Israel asked themselves, comes that wonderful stability of the cosmic order in spite of the fall of the human race? They understood the mercy of God, who revealed Himself to Israel but who also supports and protects the whole universe and all the families of mankind with their idols and their false religions.

And, thirdly, from the fact that the Word of God wills finally to unite itself with all mankind born of God, nothing human can remain

[16] Or, more precisely, the religion derived from creation in the concrete, a religion touched by primal grace and charged with a hope secretly supernatural. But this historical modality does not call into question the existence of a truly natural religion.

foreign to it. Each human situation will be utilized: the relation between I and Thou, between man and wife, father and child, mother and son, king and people, priest and layman, prophet and temple, personal religion and ritual religion, the political community and the religious community, love, hatred, jealousy, generosity, severity and kindness, justice and mercy, faithfulness, the gift of self even to the vow whereby a man binds his liberty forever, even to the martyrdom in which he renounces his physical life.

But there is still more. The Word of God took hold of the people of Israel in their place in history, in the context of a universal development – not only in a political situation, that of the great powers of the Near East, with their dependence on the culture of the Phoenicians (whose architects built the temple of Solomon and whose poets inspired the poetic forms of many inspired psalms), but also within a framework of a different order, that of their "image of the world" (*Weltbild*), of their "outlook on life" (*Weltanschauung*), of their interpretation of life, of wisdom, of philosophy, of metaphysics, and of religion. And all this developed, particularly in the ancient world, according to certain uniform laws that ruled the whole development of human nature and of the self-consciousness of mankind.

Thus we see the various dimensions of man unfolding themselves one after the other and placing themselves at the free disposition of the Word of God. Each degree of the total development of mankind could, if God willed to make use of it, present a prerequisite condition for a new unfolding of revelation. Thanks to this bond between the historic experience of Israel and that of all mankind, the laws of political history are in a certain way subject to the laws of revealed history.[17]

The fact is undeniable: because God wished to speak in human language, the revelation of the one true God waited, so that it might be understood in faith in a manner worthy of man, for a certain syncretist monotheism to be established in Egypt and Babylon; it presupposed the

[17] Since it is the sovereignly free God who chooses what He wills to engage as an aid and material condition for His revelation, our theory could satisfy the strictest requirements of the *analogia fidei* as conceived by Karl Barth. It completes (without denying) it, by the fact that it is the same God who as Creator prepares in advance in human history the materials which He will use as Revealer. The distance separating general cultural and religious history from supernatural revelation is ruled by the law of the *analogia entis* (between creation and God)—a fact which does not call into question our first point of view.

All this has always been affirmed in the classic apologetics of the Fathers and the manuals by their introducing, for example, the treatise on the Sacrifice of Christ by general considerations on the idea of sacrifice common to all peoples, as a ritual sacrifice, a propitiatory one, an interior one, etc. The new Biblical discoveries, however, allow us to demonstrate the *concrete and historical bond* within the Bible itself between "natural religion" (with all its deformities, due to sin and severely judged by the Word of God) and "supernatural religion," a bond which allows us to go beyond the always abstract juxtaposition of the traditional treatise *de religione in genere* and the treatise *de revelatione supernaturali.* Our conception in no way leads to a kind of evolutionism run wild or to religious liberalism. It does nothing but take seriously the law of the incarnation of God in man who himself is inseparable from the "numerical universal."

system of amphictonies (alliances of twelve tribes) as already established. The idea of a God who was the leader of His people had to acquire a certain universal value, to form a framework of pre-existing thought in order later to be surpassed, when Yahweh in His assembly (*in medio deorum*) confounds every other divinity.

The theme of the anointed king as the visible image of the invisible God, the vision of the world and of the state underlying a sacred statecraft, the portrait of the wise man, of the man endowed with the gift of prophecy, of the seer of supernatural things, of the mediator, of the Messiah, the upward flight of a wisdom literature magnetized by eschatology — all these themes go far beyond the domain of Israel. In His revelation God not only "utilized" all this, He not only adapted Himself to it in an exterior way; the question here is not only one of literary genres.[18] God in some way espoused each new experience.

Without wishing to interpret secular history as being a sacred history, we must nevertheless admit what the Fathers of the Church called the preparation of the Gospel, the *logos spermatikos,* the development of which now appears to us in a new and much more positive light. But the solution is now found in reverse; it is no longer Plato who is dependent on Moses, but Moses on Plato, or rather, on the ancient wisdom of Egypt. Holy Scripture affirms this in so many words (Acts 7:22). Let us repeat it: even if the total development of mankind is reflected in the Bible, we should never have the right to deduce from it a systematic theology of secular history and civilizations. We can only conclude that this development of the total consciousness of mankind — what we are accustomed to call "progress" — should also have its own positive relationship to revelation.[19]

18 We would be underestimating the problem if we considered it only from the aspect of redaction and spoke only of literary genres, as if only this external relationship existed between the Word of God and its human expression, as if God could have expressed Himself equally well in another adapted literary genre. Anyone who thinks along these lines should also think that God could as well have become incarnate in St. Paul or St. Augustine as in Jesus Christ. Such "extrinsicism" has not grasped the fact that God does not gather His words from the mouth of men in order to take them on His own, but rather makes of the whole man the Word of God.

19 In the final analysis, there can be no question of many kinds of progress in total history that remain foreign to one another. One will admit the more willingly a convergence (but never identity) between "natural progress" and "supernatural progress" the better one has understood the implication of human reflection—meditation on the past, prayer, suffering for God and by God—in the course of sacred history, in the Old as in the New Testament, in the synagogue as in the Church.

In fact, there are not two but three modalities of progress: that of revelation (ended with the death of the last apostle), that of the development of dogma (or of the Church's reflection on revelation), and that of secular history. The fact that a certain "supernatural progress" continues throughout the duration of the New Law precludes a possible objection, i.e., the development (if there was any) of mankind during the two thousand years before Christ is so small compared to cosmic evolution that its implications in sacred history can prove nothing either about the meaning of evolution as a whole or about the relationship between the two forms of progress.

It should be noted, however, that the points of view which we have developed allow us to grasp certain internal analogies which we must refrain from making into identities. On the one hand, there is an internal analogy between the progress of revelation and that of dogma, an analogy in which the resemblance bears on two

We would risk, with Albright and others, one last statement which will doubtlessly seem to the many enthusiasts for thinking along Hebraic lines to verge on heresy, but which seems to us inevitable and which the Fathers of the Church emphasized in the first place. The new stage of Western mankind attained by the Greeks with the discovery of being, of the abstract and necessary concept of the universality of reason, seems to present one of the last "conditions" required on the part of man for the incarnation. Without it, the human foundation for the universally valid human proclamation of the Gospel would have been defective. There would have been lacking not only the appropriate means of expression, but also certain human experiences, certain structures of thought needed for grasping the meaning and import of the Christian universal.

Here again we see the synthesis of revelation, the unity effected by Christ, being in a certain sense prepared and (in the domain of preparation) anticipated in relation to Christ. The synthesis of Judaism and Hellenism preceded Him, doubtless in order that the peace which He brings about in His own Body between the two parts of mankind (Eph. 2:16) should not be made outside of and beyond history, and in order that Christian faith should find ready the appropriate elements for the understanding of the mystery.

Yet human wisdom is never dispensed from the necessity of wholly dying to itself if God requires it for the use of His revelation. The wisdom of this world must admit itself to be folly to become the wisdom of God. And even in its human structure, the Biblical Word becomes an integral part of the Word that judges and has mercy. Job, the Qoheleth, the Proverbs were doubtlessly composed on the model of the Egyptian and Accadian wisdom books. But how greatly this complaint of forsaken man and his resignation in the face of the uncertainty of

points: (1) in both cases, it is the obedience and the religious reflection of the believer that brings about in a decisive way the new interventions of the divine Spirit (which is obvious for the era of the sages of Israel and of Judaism, but also for the time of the prophets); (2) in both cases, it is, in the final analysis, this divine Spirit who freely guides history and its developments.

On the other hand, there is an analogy no less internal (but that of instrumental causality) between "natural progress" and "supernatural progress," since progress in both cases means interiorization and universalization, the power to dominate a wider field of data by a spiritual elevation. The decisive progress of the Old Testament led from an awareness of the tribe to an awareness of the kingdom, and finally, by the experience of the Exile, to an awareness of all mankind (embracing in sacred history the salvation of all peoples by the mediation of Israel). The New Testament reflects an equally universal outlook in the unfolding of the Synoptics, in Paul and in John; and the progress of dogma, in turn, can be nothing other than a continual deepening by insights always more total and inclusive.

But let us not forget, for the three domains, the existence of the great law of losses and of senescence, so forcefully experienced and expressed by a St. Augustine or a St. Gregory the Great. But these losses, so evident in secular progress, should not render us blind to a certain real ascent which it would be unjust not to be willing to admit. Ultimately, there are not two progresses because there are not two kinds of universals merely existing side by side; the ("abstract") human universal of the natural order remains subject to the ("concrete") universal of Christ, in whom all things are recapitulated.

existence changes in tonality by the fact alone of its being admitted into the body of the sacred Scriptures, without mentioning the internal transformation!

How many advances and progressions are realized in the course of sacred history, how many things are abandoned along the way! We need only think of the path followed by Elias which led him in the footsteps of Moses, but in reverse. He left the Promised Land behind to find the desert, and once again he came to the terrible mountain, the manifestation of the Holy by tempest, earthquake and fire. But time has advanced. God is no longer in all this. He is now only in the *pneuma*, the spiritual breath.

The Word can, if it wills, adapt itself to a certain degree of culture, and then it goes beyond it. Even in its adaptation it avoids any compromise. God always shows Himself as being the free and absolute Person. Man must always find God by a *conversion*, by an avowal that is repugnant to him; God is never to be found in the projection of man's own desires and his own ideals any more than in any projection of Him based on some system of asceticism or mysticism. All human experiences must serve God; He has need of none of them, and He never makes use of one without transforming it by His burning touch.

His Word is freedom; it is power. It was mighty enough to draw the people ruthlessly through the desert; it was mighty enough also to draw them, in the course of many centuries, recalcitrant, stiff-necked, adulterous as they were, from the primitive consciousness of a nomad tribe up to the threshold of the Gospel by the road of humiliations. What a miracle in the midst of the Old Testament are the songs of the Servant of Yahweh! This whole work was accomplished by the living Word alone, who like leaven worked from within.

In this refractory matter was progressively revealed, not only the greatness and majesty of the transcendent God, emerging above immanent divinities, but also, more secretly, the humility, the vulnerability of the divine tenderness, the solicitude of the divine Heart manifested in the humiliated heart of man. Blessed are the poor, for in all His riches God is eternal poverty. Blessed the humiliated, for God Himself in His ascension, *ascendit Deus*, is eternal abasement, eternal descent, *quia et descendit primum*. In the forsaken – Job, Jeremias, the captives in Babylon, the poor of Yahweh who cried to God and obtained no response – in all these nights, here is the revelation of the forsaken Heart of God.

After the great light of the religion of the Word, after the revelation of the true God, of His true existence and His true essence, here again is what man knew from the beginning and what the Areopagite reminds us of – *the absolute Mystery can only be adored.*

God manifests Himself in man to lead him to the adoration of Him whom no eye has seen. God sends even His Son, so that He may interpret God to us in human actions: we hear the Father in His human echo; in this human obedience even to death we learn who He is that commands. *In the response we receive the Word.* The Son-made-Man, at the summit of the universe, carries out before the Father the liturgy of the Church and of the cosmos. In Him, Word and liturgy coincide.

Of Him, Jesus Christ, we must say still more. In Him alone, but by Him for all, the divine Word is hypostatically united to man. In Him the temporality of human experience (of which we first spoke) and the eternal truth are united. Between the human and the divine nature of Christ there is no divergence; what God wishes to say of Himself He says in a human way, fully and exactly. *Consummatum est*: this is not limitless and without bounds; it has arrived at its goal. *Homo capax Dei.*

Human language (which we next spoke of), which includes progressively the whole nature, the whole moral existence, the whole history of mankind, now is seen to be united with the eternal Word of the Father. Here every ideal has become real; those who build on this foundation establish their ideal on what has already been realized in fact. The pleroma is attained, all the dimensions of time are fulfilled. And this by a humble human life distinguished by nothing except its ardent love of the Father and of men, the life of a Workman and Preacher who willed to fulfill Himself in poverty and ignominy. His glorification after death is attested by a few witnesses only. There is nothing here of which world history would have been aware. Only a man, the Son of Man.

In Jesus, the Unique, the Incomparable, aware of His oneness, the Word of God has nevertheless reached man. It is no longer a law, an abstraction; it is this very Man. All the objective spirit of religion, of the Law, of the rites, is identified with the subjective spirit of this Man who is a man like ourselves. Here is the religion of freedom. When this Man gave everything to God, obeyed Him even to death, He yet gave obedience to no other than Himself, to His own filial love of the Father. He has gone beyond all heteronomy as beyond all autonomy; the *heteros*, the Father, is at the same *to auton*, the same concrete nature. Whoever believes in the Son is free, for he has attained to total humanism.

The Word of God, which resounds in our liturgies, abundantly overflows the domain of the Church. It dominates secular history, offices and factories, science and politics. It includes all this, and this is only a small part of the treasures of wisdom and knowledge that it contains. The liturgy of the Church pays Him loving and conscious homage, while the world ignores its Master and crucifies Him anew. But this liturgy prostrate at His feet must at the end rise up to bring about in the secular world that which it has proclaimed and promised in the holy place.

Rev. Louis Bouyer, Cong. Orat.

CHAPTER 4

THE WORD OF GOD LIVES IN THE LITURGY

ONE CERTITUDE we can never doubt is that the Word of God always has been and always is living in the Church. This means that the Church would cease to be the Church if the authentic Word of God ceased to be proclaimed therein or if this Word ceased to find its mysterious realization in her sacramental life. From which fact flows this conclusion, which from many points of view is only another way of saying the same thing: it is impossible, without misunderstanding and tending to distort the very reality of the Catholic Church, to separate in fact the proclamation of the Word of God and sacramental life. We believe that the Church is infallible; we believe, therefore, that this vital connection has never disappeared, can never disappear.

But we know also that the Church is made up of men who as individuals *are* fallible, and of local or particular communities which to some extent also suffer from this sad weakness. We need, therefore, to face the situation as it is and see clearly that the concrete realizations which we have given in the past or which we still give at the present time to these great unchangeable principles, have been or still are more or less deficient. This examination should lead us to meditate more profoundly on the principles of which we are convinced, to try to make them more visibly and more efficaciously operative in everyday reality—in our personal spiritual life, as well as in our pastoral work.

So far as the proclamation of the Word of God and sacramental life are concerned, and more particularly, the relationships between them, what then was the state of affairs in our parishes yesterday? What is it still today?

The Latin liturgy, and particularly the Roman liturgy, has, without doubt, always remained an admirable presentation and carrying out of the Word of God, surrounding and permeating the sacramental celebration. We need say nothing about the Office—which since the end of the eighteenth century has become almost exclusively the concern of clerics—except to remind ourselves that we should immerse our personal prayer in the inspired prayer of the Psalter, nourish our personal meditation on the cycle of readings from holy Scripture, explained by the Fathers of the Church and, above all, illuminated by the great perspectives of the Christian mystery as the liturgical year causes us continually to return to them.

Let us speak only of the Mass, the heart of the liturgical life of the faithful. Its entire first part is a reading of the Epistles of St. Paul and the Gospels, prepared by and, as it were, expanded in a prayer which itself is drawn above all from the Psalter, but which at the same time is organized and guided by the living perception of the Christian mystery learned in the school of Catholic tradition.

And its second part, with the Roman canon which is so directly Biblical in inspiration and texture, introduces us into the sacramental mystery by the very ways in which it was developed in the history of the people of God: the Eucharistic preface still cast in the forms of Jewish prayer contemporary with the origins of Christianity; the recalling of the sacrifices of the Old Testament, "of Abel the just, of Abraham our patriarch, of Melchisedech Thy high priest"; the anamnesis of the great deeds of salvation, from the Supper to the Ascension; the great blessings flowing out from the Cross to all creation; the great doxology ascending from the Cross to the heavenly sanctuary in which we finally present ourselves, following our divine Precursor, there to say with Him: "Our Father, who are in heaven. . . ."

But how much of all this—even a short time ago—really went through the minds of the good people who "assisted at Mass"?

The priest certainly read the Epistle and the Gospel, but to himself, turning his back on everyone else, in a language that nobody understood, and without taking any pains to be heard by anyone. While he was doing this, the most devout of the faithful were reading pious fantasies about Christ going from Caiphas to Pilate when the altar-boy changed the book, or beautiful flights of fervor about Christ speaking through the Church—flights which, however, never suggested that it might be well, when His Word is being spoken in the Church in its own inspired phrases, actually to listen to it.

After this the priest, according to the formula of such pious books as these, entered "into the secret of the Canon." Then the faithful nourished themselves on profound thoughts about the infinity of God and the nothingness of man, or else on sentimental pictures of "gentle Jesus," until the moment when the sound of the bell caused them to bow down before the mystery.

This is not to say that in the life of the Church the Word of God was reduced to this material survival alone, a survival almost entirely rubrical for the clergy and, for the ordinary faithful, an almost impenetrable formality. Rather, to remain living, it carved out new paths for itself, but paths that were artificial, indirect, and often strangely remote from its primitive channels, which were either directly inspired or traditional. The living truth in the Church was in the same case, one might say, as is the circulation of the blood in surgical patients whose essential organs have been put into a state of hibernation to preserve them from the effects of shock, while the vital fluid is temporarily routed around through an apparatus of glass and rubber and plastic.

Indeed there was, in the Sunday high Mass, one organ at any rate through which some drops of real blood still coursed: the sermon after the Gospel. But this sermon had itself developed in such an autonomous way as to have become almost cancerous. It was no longer a part of the Mass, but an *entre-acte* between two parts of the Mass.

Anything could be spoken of as well as and besides the Gospel, and no allusion was ever made, ordinarily, to the other Scriptural texts of the liturgy. Moral exhortations, political comments, financial appeals, and sometimes, but less frequently, a sort of catechism lesson for adults had long since taken the place of the homily; while in large parishes or on great occasions, this was the time for one of those rhetorical exercises (with appropriate gestures and vocal inflections) which have always delighted the crowd and which, like some works of art, exist "for art's sake"—that is, in this case, for the pleasure that good people take, as they say, in listening to "a man who can speak well."

The Word of God, therefore, passed rather through other and newer channels which were developed little by little in modern times and were decidedly extra-liturgical. There were still, related to the liturgy at least materially, the great Lenten conferences; between Vespers and Benediction during six weeks of the year large doses of instruction, covering perhaps the whole of Christian doctrine, were administered. There were, above all, the catechism and religious instruction given in the schools. There were also retreats for men and even more for women who were able to make them. And then there were the "good Catholic books. . . ."

But in all this, the divergence from the liturgy and from its basically Biblical text was more than a purely material one. Undoubtedly it was always the revealed truth that was taught to the faithful. But it had carefully been stripped bare of everything that characterizes its presentation in the documents of revelation themselves and in its traditional exposition by the liturgy. It had been carefully taken apart and put together again as a metaphysico-moral system; then, no doubt because the sickly and unattractive aspect it now wore seemed vaguely frightening, it was dressed up with "literature" and adorned with a make-up of sentimentality so as to attract the educated without losing the masses.

We need not dwell on all this. It now seems very far away, though it would not be difficult, even now, to find traces of it surviving all about us. What, during recent years, has taken its place? I would say that we have, above all, brought the liturgical celebration closer to the proclamation of the divine Word, while we have modernized this proclamation itself. But in spite of many efforts, I do not believe that we have yet made a decisive effort, except in very rare instances, fully to reintegrate, to make one whole of the sacramental mystery and the proclamation of the Word, nor to restore to them all their richness and all their clarity.

We concerned ourselves, first of all, with giving our faithful exact and complete translations of the Biblical readings in their missals. Then, in low Masses for ordinary congregations we duplicated the Latin readings of the priest with the reading of these translations; and in some high Masses we have had them follow the chanted reading.

But it is just here that the best-intentioned practice often reveals the distance still separating us from our goals. This new reading was meant to be a real reading; but we have not as yet found out how to incorporate it fully into the celebration. It remains "marginal," and because it is marginal, it easily degenerates into fantasy.

Recently I assisted at Mass in a cathedral in which the distinguished Chapter obviously had the pious idea of applying the prescriptions of the *Directoire* of the Bishops of France for the *Pastorale* of the Mass. The deacon had just chanted, or rather hummed, the Gospel for the sole benefit of the pillar, which the subdeacon was comfortably leaning on. Then, while the latter was carrying the book to be kissed by the celebrant, I saw the minister of the Gospel desperately pulling at his vestments and rummaging around to extract from his trouser pocket a dirty little missal which he proceeded to leaf through by wetting his finger. Finally, having found what he was looking for, he stammered out, almost inaudibly, a translation that had been carefully emasculated—stripped, in particular, of all its allusions to the Old Testament.

Here before my eyes was an example, not unlike many others, of the proclamation of the Word of God in the Mass of the twentieth century. The lesser ministers, apparently, were not quite sure whether this reading was or was not part of the sacred rite; the acolytes and incense-bearer had dispersed, leaving the reader alone; seemingly they had not been able to believe that this reading in the vulgar tongue could be anything more than a pleasant make-believe, quite marginal to the real liturgy.

In fact, the reading in the mother tongue, the reading that is understood, continues so successfully to look like a secondary and facultative appendage that we have far too little sense of its seriousness. In printed missals and, still more, in reading aloud, there have been permitted under the guise of translation all sorts of transpositions, amputations, modifications, and these are sometimes doubly peculiar because they have been improvised on the spot. Priests themselves, when they proclaim the Word of God in the vernacular, often seem to forget the fact that it still is the Word of God—in French, in English, in Turkish or Japanese, just as it is in Latin. They seem to think that they have the right to make it their own word, revised and corrected according to their own tastes, their habits of thought, or quite simply, a momentary whim.

It is true, nonetheless, that along with making the Biblical readings once more understandable, a happy effort is being made to make the sermon, or rather the Sunday homily, once more an integral part of the proclamation of the divine Word in the readings. But here again, though progress has undeniably been made, it is not yet so great as to leave little to be done. Instead of allowing the readings of the Mass, in all their authentic reality, set as they are in the enlightening context of the whole traditional liturgy, themselves be the source of the homily, do we not all too often find the homily, inspired by the ideas current everywhere today, itself determining the translation of the readings and even what shall be translated?

Furthermore, the readings and homilies thus restored to their proper place—in spite of present drawbacks which we may hope will prove temporary—are being complemented by an apparent innovation which is actually the revival of a traditional custom—I mean the use of "comments."

"Comments" are brief formulas by which the celebrant himself, or preferably the minister who assists him, normally the deacon, informs the faithful when necessary of what is to be done next and interprets its meaning for them. Nothing, certainly, can be more effective in showing actively how the divine Word, the Word addressed to our faith, not only has its place in the liturgy but constitutes its very texture. Yet we can say of these "comments" what Aesop said of the tongue: it can be the best and the worst of things.

How beneficial is the prompting which is discrete, precise, exact, which maintains and renews whenever necessary the intelligent and prayerful contact of the congregation with the divine Word that is, as it were, the motive power of the whole liturgical action! And how unfortunate is the "comment" that turns into a torrent of words, drowning everything! Such "comments" (and we see too many examples of them) drive prayer away from the liturgy and finally substitute for the liturgy a kind of night-school course for retarded students *on the liturgy*. For comments are felicitous only if they really aid the liturgy and do not rather cause it to be forgotten, concealed behind a kind of sermon-flood that duplicates it.

I have just said the word that germinally contains what is perhaps the most severe criticism which the coming generation will make of our best efforts it we let them slacken and sink in midstream. For the characteristic of the present liturgical movement, a stage which, perhaps, we must go through but which we must certainly not get bogged down in, is what I shall call the *Mass in duplicate*.

My criticism of the past has been severe enough so that my colleagues today will not be scandalized if I now try to imagine what a liturgist of the twenty-first century, who perhaps is not yet born but who will surely not object to our speaking about him, might well say of us all some day. I imagine the young and rash Aristarchus saying something like this: "In the middle of the twentieth century, some worthy men, filled with good intentions, who erroneously thought of themselves as eminent liturgists, had substituted for the old Mass with three priests of the preceding centuries a Mass of their own invention with two priests. The first priest said the rubrical Mass, the Mass said so as to conform to the rules, the Mass of which almost nothing was audible, but which they tried to make a little more visible than in the past by means of those devices which were the favorite liturgical playthings of those days long ago: the altar *versus populum*, the "podium," etc.

"While this Mass was going on, and approximately in synchronization with it, another priest went on talking, talking, usually the more untiringly the less he had prepared what he was going to say. At certain moments he read, out of a missal designed for the faithful, a mish-mash of periphrastic translations which he garnished according to his own taste. To vary the figure, between these *membra disiecta* he spread out a flood of comments and exhortations on which floated in disorder all the conventional phrases then current: 'Mystical Body,' 'Catholic Action' (specialized or not), 'helping the worker,' 'presence in the world,' 'the Christian family,' 'responsibility of the laity,' etc.

"Since nobody can talk continuously, he occasionally took a breath, giving the faithful time for a fine unanimous *Et cum spiritu tuo*. Or else he had them sing a Gelineau psalm (always one of the most popular two or three). When the first priest had finished his Mass and retired with his paraphernalia, the second priest was seized with the vague notion that there had not been enough praying. And so there was an *Our Father* and a *Hail Mary* for the Chinese babies, for missionaries, for our dear departed. . . . And the show was over."

I will cut short here the words of our liturgist of the twenty-first century, which are as impertinent and also as profoundly unjust as those generally are of people who get involved in writing about the life of the liturgy with insufficient respect for the great figures of the past. Naturally, he exaggerates. But, among ourselves, future fossils of the twentieth century, is there not some truth in his criticisms? They present a caricature; but would we dare deny that they contain some elements of truth?

What, then, prevents things from going as they should in spite of all our touching good will? The trouble is, it seems to me, that we have tried to make something new out of old materials. We have changed our methods, but we have not really changed our habits of thought.

We have kept our rubrical, formalistic notion of the sacred rites. We have kept our old way of proclaiming the Word of God, a way little in accord with tradition and therefore lacking in freshness and vigor, as a result of our not having lived the Word ourselves. We have thought it sufficient to color the Word of God to suit modern tastes and then to apply it in large strokes, like cheap varnish, to a ritual simply piled up in layers and poorly camouflaged as an up-to-date spectacle. Hence the hybrid that we now possess, in which the large pieces of new cloth are in danger of finally tearing and pulling apart the old garment they have been unsuccessfully patching.

The first thing to discover is, therefore, how the Word of God, springing from its source and kept living in the very life of authentic liturgical tradition, is naturally connected with the sacramental rites, and how behind this native bond between rite and word, there is an interior connection between the most profound idea of the Word of God and the Christian sacraments.

Then we shall at long last be able to do away with this business of superimposing on a word that is simply ritualistic, reduced to the formulas required by the rubrics and hurried through as being incidental to living worship, a word that is living and intelligible but of a more or less whimsical form and with a content that is left up to the arbitrary decisions of almost anyone.

The first truth that a study of the liturgical tradition of the Church should impose on us is, in fact, that in Christianity there are not two kinds of sacred words: on the one hand, words that are meant to say something to somebody, words that are said in order to be heard and understood, but which, for all that, are not bound up with the liturgy, are not part of it; and on the other hand, words that are bound up with the rites, words that must be said (no matter how), some of them simply because the rubrics order us to say them, and others, because in addition they have a quasi-magical power of giving the rites their sacramental content.

I hasten to add that, of course, nobody in the Church has ever upheld such a concept. But I maintain that everything that is illogical, unfruitful in our preaching and in the way we carry out the liturgy is unconsciously oriented by such a view, unconsciously flowing from all sorts of routine actions, defective practices, inadequate realizations, which tend in fact towards the obviously heretical idea that I have just formulated.

In contrast, if there is anything which has become self-evident ever since the liturgy of the Mass has been studied in its origins, it is that its first part was made to be, in the clearest possible way, the most intelligible way, the most assimilable way, a proclamation of the Word of God as a living Word, seeking the attention, the adhesion, not only of our mind but of our heart. Let us only glance at the old Roman churches—St. Clement or St. Mary-in-Cosmedin. Here the subdeacon did not chant the Epistle at the foot of the altar, carefully turning his back on the people for fear that somebody might hear him; the deacon did not solemnly go off to bump his nose on the north wall of the sanctuary. Each climbed up into high tribunes where they were visible to everyone, right in the middle of the congregation so that all could see them and hear them.

And if they chanted the texts, on tones that were simple but brought out the main accents, it was not to drown these ritual readings in the rumblings to which they are usually reduced in our times; quite the opposite, it was to make sure that every syllable could be heard clearly. The psalm chants connecting the readings, by the choice of words as well as by their melodies, aroused and prolonged the meditation of the faithful on what had just been heard. Silent prayer was the natural effect; and then the brief Collect of the president of the liturgical assembly resumed in one phrase the central theme of the previous reading before going on the next.

Thus they went on, reading, meditating, praying, from the traditional readings of the synagogue, the Pentateuch and the prophets, to the reading of the apostolic teachings, and finally to the Gospel, the proclamation of Christ in His own words, for which they stood up, chanting ritual acclamations, convinced that He whose words they heard was present to speak to them, as is signified by the lights and the incense carried before the Gospel-book as before a first epiphany of the heavenly *Imperator*.

Under these conditions the homily given by the bishop did not come as an *entr'acte* or an *hors-d'oeuvre*. In the person of the successor of the apostles, of him who in the midst of the assembled Church was the very *locum tenens* of Christ Himself, all the apostolic teaching of this liturgy was made present, reunited *hic et nunc* with this local assembly gathered together on this particular day, in such a way that everything the people heard was received by them as a living Word, always present, destined for them, addressed to them by Christ Himself present among them.

This whole service of readings, indeed, progressing up to the Gospel between the meditative chants of the ancient people of God, awakened better than any explanations the sense of what the Word of God is; and after this the word of the man chosen by Him to be His minister could not appear to be or be anything other than His true and apt medium.

The Word of God in the celebrations of the ancient Church remained the saving event, the personal intervention of God in the history of men, choosing and setting apart for Himself a people, then forming them little by little and enlightening them at the same time, to lead them to what St. Paul calls the intelligence of the mystery. The "mystery," in the sense that Paul gives to this word in the First Epistle to the Corinthians and in the Epistle to the Ephesians, this is what the proclamation of the Word of God in His Church opens out on.

The "mystery"—that is to say, the proclamation of Christ and of His victorious Cross coming as the achievement and the key of human history, as also the fullness and the core of all divine words which little by little and step by step were communicated by the prophets. The "mystery"—that is to say, the saving event sketched out and prepared by the first Pasch, the first deliverance; more profoundly approached in the sorrowful and radiant experience of the exile in Babylon and the return of the captives, that first resurrection after death hailed by an Ezechiel; finally carried out in the "passage" of Jesus through death, His "exodus" to the Father, containing in Himself in advance our own victory over sin and death, our own accession to the freedom of sons in glory.

The "mystery"—that is to say, the proclamation of Jesus as always living, not only in the heavenly sanctuary in the presence of the Father to intercede for us with the all-powerful pleading of His Blood that speaks with an eloquence quite other than that of the blood of Abel the just; but here also, in the assembly of His own, to reproduce in us what was already accomplished in Him once for all.

To say this is already to go from the first part of the Mass to the second, from the proclamation of the Word of God to the sacramental celebration. But, as now seems obvious, the transition comes about of itself. In passing to the Eucharist properly so called, the proclamation of the Word of God does nothing more than expand, fulfill itself. And this is precisely why, inversely, St. Paul says: "Whenever you eat this bread and drink this cup, you proclaim the death of the Lord until He comes."

The sacrament is but the focus of the actuality, of the reality always renewed, toward which the proclamation of the Word of God in the Church tends of its own accord. On the one hand, in fact—and here is the "mystery"—the Word of God is, finally, not only what Jesus said in the Gospel, but Jesus Himself—everything that He was and is, everything that He did, and above all, His Cross. And on the other hand, Jesus in His Church, through the apostles and their successors, has willed to be present forever with His whole redeeming work, with His whole risen being, drawing us all toward Himself as if by an invincible gravitation, to make of us all one single Body, one Christ, Head and Body, to the glory of the Father.

He has, therefore, given to His apostles and to their successors, the bishops, and to their collaborators, all priests, the work of proclaiming His Word, not as simply expressing ideas or merely giving the account of past events, but as having the power, the actuality, that it has on His own lips: the Word of Christ in His messengers as in Himself, the Word of God that does what it says, that brings about what it proclaims.

And so, at His command and by His power, making once more the signs that He Himself has given, announcing the meaning, proclaiming the content that He Himself has given these signs, the representatives of Christ, by His all-powerful Word, do again what He did. Or, better, it is He Himself who through their hands and their mouths gives us again today the sacred signs of His "mystery," gives us its whole hidden reality.

In particular, in the Eucharist, taking bread and wine, the nourishment of our earthly life, at the height of the proclamation of the Gospel, the good news of salvation, and repeating the words of Christ: "This is My Body . . . this is My Blood . . . Do this in memory of Me," the messengers of Christ give us in all reality, under the sign in which He Himself wished to give it to our faith, the very content of His "mystery." The Christ who proclaimed is made present. The proclamation of His life-giving Cross becomes the proclamation of what is mysteriously accomplished among us, in order to be fulfilled in us, to perfect us all together in Him.

Thus the sacramental Word is in no way a kind of magic word, any more than the other ritual words are mere formalities which we must pronounce in order to obey the rubrics but which have nothing to do with the real proclamation of anything intelligible and vital to our understanding and our heart. The sacramental Word appears, on the contrary, as the climax of the personal revelation, of the living announcement, of the actual present proclamation that Christ, always present in His Church, has just made of His own mystery.

We might say that when the divine Word has awakened, aroused, formed, fully enlightened our faith, prepared it in advance to receive the "gift of God," to recognize in the Word that God says to it the creative Word, the Word of life, then this same Word speaks the final word, the decisive word, the word in which it gives itself, that is to say, in which it is Christ who gives Himself to us with all His gifts; this, then, is the sacramental Word, the consecrating Word.

Under these conditions we see how the Word proclaimed is not complete, loses its end and meaning without the sacrament. For, once more, it is proclaimed in the Name of Christ, by the apostles of Christ, as His Word, as the Word in which He promises us and gives us, *hic et nunc*, the "gift of God." Inversely, it appears also how the sacrament is fundamentally denatured if it is no longer the gift made to faith fully formed, fully enlightened, the gift of what is announced by the Word, the gift made by that Word itself, recognized as the Word of Christ, of Christ who is Himself the living Word of God and who remains always present, always living in His Church.

This is what is stated with supreme clarity in the very prayer in which and by which the Church consecrates the Eucharist, that prayer which is the Eucharist properly speaking, prayer in which the Word of God to man and the response of man to God are one.

The Christian Eucharistic prayer is, in fact, the perfect realization of a type of prayer which flourished in the last ages of Judaism and which was, as it were, the sign of the highest developments of the Word of God itself in His people. It is the prayer of the man who welcomes the Word of God and understands it with the intelligence of a faith wholly permeated with love. As we see in the great prayer of Esdras, the Jewish eucharist already recognized in the Word of God, in His creative Word, not only the revelation of the meaning of human history, but the great creative and redemptive force that leads that history towards its blessed goal by the decisive events in which God Himself has intervened.

The Eucharist is thus the act of gratitude *par excellence*: man's recognition that everything is finally God's mercy, and on this foundation, the upsurge of faith that gives itself to Him, that abandons itself completely to Him who has given us everything.

But already in the Old Testament, as it approached the New, the eucharistic prayer became fused with a new ritual, which might be called the ritual of messianic hope. In the Jewish communities which the discoveries of Qumran have made better known to us, we see how already the common meal of those who waited for the "consolation of Israel," as St. Luke says, had become the superior equivalent of the ancient ritual sacrifices. It became this by the eucharist, the prayer of thanksgiving that the head of the community pronounced after the bread had been broken, over the cup shared by everyone.

In the giving of thanks for these foods, in the giving of thanks for the coming together of these chosen ones whom God nourishes with His own hand, these elements were seen as the first fruits of the new Manna which God will give to His own in His kingdom, and the gathering itself was seen as the preparation for the messianic banquet in which all the saints will sit at table with the Son of Man in the company of the patriarchs and the prophets.

When Jesus was present on Holy Thursday at a reunion of this kind, He consummated the hope which actuated the Jewish eucharist by proclaiming the definitive Word of God, the Word of crucified love, and by producing thereby the definitive intervention of God in the history of His people.

And so, henceforth, under the earthly food His own recognize the Food of immortality. Celebrating the Eucharist of Jesus, the Eucharist of the Word of God-made-flesh, in which the divine Word itself, fully revealed and fulfilled, now makes but one reality with the response of man, fully open to the love of God shed forth in his heart by the Spirit of Jesus, the Church thus "proclaims" the death of the Lord, the mystery of the life-giving Cross, in the "proclamation" *par excellence,* in which she "recognizes," as well, in the breaking of bread, the definitive "gift of God" which is given to her, the gift in which it is God Himself who not only gives but is given: for us on the Cross, for us always and to us in the Mass.

And now, let us come back to earth. Or rather, let us come back from the primitive practice, a practice immediately expressive of its meaning, to our practice today.

Here is the first thing we should look to: that the true reading, the reading of the Word of God which is made so as to be heard, may once more become for us priests, and through us for our faithful, the ritual reading, a visibly sacred act, an act in which religious dignity and the truth of the reading go together. And for much greater reason let us never allow ourselves in reading the Word of God to stumble over it, to hurry through it. Let us honor it by the very way we read it; let us respect it in its text; let us transmit it without having the impudence to lay dirty hands on it.

This, obviously, requires that we have a translation of the liturgical readings of the Mass made to be read aloud publicly and solemnly, in which the fidelity to the text will be equalled by the clarity and dignity (that is to say, above all, the purity) of the language. But even when we have such a translation, we shall still need to know how not only to accept it passively, but to apply ourselves to it intelligently, so as to bring out its value simply but fully. Our habitual use of a language that nobody understands has made us unaccustomed to the effort needed for making ourselves heard and understood, the effort needed for reading while thinking of what we are reading and for helping others to think of it. This is the first thing that we priests have to relearn.

Some people will say: But to restore to the proclamation of the Word of God in the Church its reality and therefore its intelligibility, must we not have very bold liturgical reforms, particularly in the use of the vernacular? Possibly this is to be hoped for. But these reforms will not come—and even if they did, they would remain sterile—so long as we ourselves do not make ready for them. And it is not by tinkering at random with the present liturgy that we shall prepare for them. It is by respecting the liturgy in itself, though not with the respect of rubricists, which is like that of conscientious undertakers for a corpse. It is by understanding it better and trying intelligently to make the best of it. It is by giving to our faithful, in our preaching and also in all other forms of religious instruction, a doctrinal formation directly drawn from the Word of God read in the school of the Church, as she instructs us herself in the traditional liturgy rightly understood.

Above all, we ourselves need to learn to pray a prayer nourished by Scripture, inspired by the prayer which is itself inspired by God, the Psalter, guided by the liturgical orations and especially by the great Eucharistic prayer and by the whole praise of the mystery that makes the fabric of the liturgical year.

Thence we shall come to form our faithful in the same prayer, not only by theoretic teaching, but also by those vigils made of prayer and meditation on Scripture which we now see being revived according to the example of the ancient liturgy. And so we shall re-create, in our parishes and in our Christian gatherings, the spiritual atmosphere, the profound reactions of thought and of heart, in virtue of which the liturgy will be able to revive, because we shall have harmonized the rhythm of our interior life with the very rhythm of the life of the Church when she created the liturgy.

In this connection, just as it is urgent to react against the abuse of a "liturgy in duplicate," which superimposes on a Mass that is liturgically correct but buried under a hermetically sealed cover, a pseudo-liturgy of our fancy, so it would be false passively to await the solution to our problems to come about by means of an act of authority, through which the hierarchy would solve them all by heaven knows what *deus ex machina* in which we would have no part.

Recently in an English magazine, a Catholic writer with the assurance of an ultramontanist wrote that it is a waste of time to study the ancient liturgy in order to prepare for a liturgical revival. After all, said he, the supreme authority of the Church is not bound by anything and could freely give us an entirely new liturgy, answering to today's needs, without any further concern for the past. We need only, therefore, wait for this grant with confidence. A strange way, indeed, to exalt the authority of the Church, and one which strongly resembles, however little it might seem to at first sight, the apologetic approach of the modernists who said that the Church was above the Gospel, since it was her own fabrication. The logic of such a position, exalting authority for its own sake, is the same as that of the cynical Anglican bishop of the eighteenth century who said that the Anglican Church did in fact teach the Trinity, but that only an act of Parliament would be needed to make it unitarian.

Authority in the Catholic Church is very far from accepting such flatteries which, in reality, do it injury. In a document which the Holy See recently sent out to the bishops to ask their counsel on a possible reform of the liturgy, it was made quite clear, on the contrary, that there could be no question of the Church's fabricating a new liturgy, but rather of going back to a more pure realization of the traditional liturgy, a realization which would allow it to be adapted to modern needs without losing anything of its original vitality and of its unchangeable foundation.

This is exactly why any liturgical restoration carried out by authority requires of us that we rediscover that traditional spirit, which is not a spirit of passive obedience, entirely external and indifferent, but a filial spirit, a spirit of respectful and loving understanding. It is in hearing again the voice of the heavenly Father, as our Mother the Church teaches us to do, in the living treasure of her liturgical tradition—and not only to hear it, but to understand it, to respond to it in faith, to give ourselves to it in obedience—it is in these advances of a faith reborn at its source that liturgical life, that sacramental life, that Eucharistic life itself will once more become for us what it is: *the mystery of faith.*

Rev. A. M. Roquet, O.P.

CHAPTER 5

THE WHOLE MASS PROCLAIMS THE WORD OF GOD

THE LITURGY of the Word is commonly thought of as being distinguished from the Eucharistic liturgy, even as being opposed to it. Many factors favor this regrettable dichotomy. We still use the term *Foremass* to designate the first part of the Mass, which suggests that it is not part of the Mass properly so called. Or we use the term *Mass of the Catechumens*, in contrast to the *Mass of the Faithful*, although this contrast is, as we know, rather foolish since the faithful assist at the *Mass of the Catechumens.*

This contrast has historical justifications, certainly: the liturgy of the Word originated in the liturgy of the synagogue, while the Eucharistic liturgy goes back to the Last Supper. But we must not forget two facts: first, that the liturgy of the synagogue was formed during the epoch of the Exile, far from the Temple and its sacrifices, while our liturgy of the Word ends in the Sacrifice of the New Covenant; and secondly, that the celebration of the Supper included proclamation, catechesis (the washing of the feet with its explanation, the discourse at the Supper), and chanting (the *hallel*).

It is true that in ancient times the celebration of the Eucharistic liturgy was in some cases not preceded by the liturgy of the Word, as in the Mass *in coena Domini,* the Mass of Holy Thursday, in Rome; and aliturgical synaxes were celebrated which were not concluded by the Eucharist. But it is only by archeologizing that these established facts can be projected into our present Mass, in which, for centuries, the liturgy of the Word and the Eucharistic liturgy have been inseparable and have constituted one single celebration.

A perfectly legitimate kind of liturgical casuistry in resolving the problem posed by accidental lateness in getting to Mass has been unduly generalized in the minds of the faithful, to the point of their thinking that only the Eucharistic liturgy is important, for it alone "counts" for obeying the precept of assistance at Sunday Mass. This generalization of a casuistic solution has been crystallized and, as it were, institutionalized in certain places by the sound of the bell rung by the server at the moment when the celebrant unveils the chalice.

Again, the appearance and the way in which we carry out our celebration of the Mass can contribute to strengthening this distinction in the people's minds. The first part of the Mass is taken up with reading and singing: readers, the subdeacon, the deacon take the place of prominence. During the second part silence reigns; here the priest appears as the chief actor, isolated in an action which thus seems more concentrated and more important. Again, many priests who read the Foremass very quickly seem to put much more recollection, deliberation, solemnity into the consecration (and then feel free to recite the second part of the Canon with a speed suggesting that, the consecration being taken care of, the words which follow have only the importance of accessories).

The present liturgical renewal is, certainly, already reacting against this division which ends up by making of the liturgy of the Word a kind of prelude, a catechism lesson coming before the celebration, or an edifying preparation with which more fervent spirits may occupy themselves while waiting for the carrying out of a sacramental mystery which is infinitely more valuable than all this complex of words and chants. We are all convinced of the fact that the liturgy of the Word is truly a liturgy, is truly a celebration, that the Mass is a single, homogeneous action from beginning to end. We need, however, to find ways to establish this unity solidly in the minds of everyone. To this end, let us consider the Eucharist in its most specific and central characteristics.

I think that it is necessary at this point to advance a theological thesis which might, moreover, be described as very nearly *de fide.* This is that the sacramental act of the Eucharist consists wholly in the consecration. All the other sacraments are carried out in the application of their matter to the subject: there is a baptism when the catechumen is plunged in the water, confirmation when the candidate receives the anointing. The consecration of the matter is only a preliminary sacramental and one which, in the case of baptism, is not indispensable.

The Eucharist, by contrast, is entirely accomplished in the consecration of the bread and wine. The distribution of the gifts is the normal completion of the Eucharist, but it is not constitutive of it. This is what theologians mean when they say that while Communion is an integral part of the Mass (without it the Mass is mutilated, incomplete), it is not an essential part (without it the Mass would be nonetheless a true Mass).

This is because the consecration of the Eucharist does not only accomplish transubstantiation; if this were true, then the consecration would have the sole purpose of producing the Body of Christ, which then would be used to carry out a sacrifice and Communion. The consecration, which certainly accomplishes transubstantiation, accomplishes at the same time the whole Eucharistic mystery: it is thanksgiving, sacrifice which consequently includes offering; it is even communion inasmuch as it re-presents the Sacrifice of the Cross, which gathers together all the scattered children of God and gives them access to the Father and inasmuch as it produces on the altar this one Bread that unites us in one Body.

But this is the transcendent point of view of faith, a point of view to which speculative theology is legitimately attached. This point of view, profoundly true as it is, is almost beyond the reach of human intelligence, imagination and action, which need to break up such a profound mystery into successive words and deeds. The Mass consists precisely in extending in time this indivisible mystery, contained, if one may use the word, all in one point. It includes, therefore, from our human point of view, which is that of the liturgy, successive phases, in such a way that when the Mass has been completed, the Church has laid out as well as possible all the richness of the mystery. Our mistake consists in wanting to make these two levels rigorously coincide in such a way that the Mass would consist of a succession of parts in which each, as in a mechanical operation, would have its own proper effectiveness. It is this mistake which breaks up the Mass into distinct parts, crystallizing to an exaggerated extent an analysis which is doubtlessly useful from the pedagogical point of view, but which can end in minimizing the mystery, in making the Mass seem to consist only in a consecration, to which—in order to lengthen and give solemnity to the ceremony—trimmings made up of purely human gestures and prayers almost without sacred content have been added. This same mistake poses false problems like that of the epiclesis, in connection with which we find Bossuet outlining in a very interesting way the doctrine which I have just been trying to explain.

He has just been giving examples of complex sacramental celebrations in connection with which one has always the tendency to ask at what precise moment the sacrament properly so-called is carried out. And he answers:

> On these occasions, the things that are celebrated are so great, have so many different effects and so many different relationships that the Church, not being able to say everything nor to explain the whole extent of the divine mystery in one place, divides her operation, although it is most simple in itself, as it were, into various parts with words fitting to each, so that the whole makes up one single mystical speech and one single moral act.
>
> It is, therefore, to render the whole more understandable that the Church speaks in each place as if she were then carrying out the action, and without even considering too closely whether she is doing so, or if, perhaps, she is going to do so; quite content that the whole is found in the totality of the act and that at the end we have been given an explanation of the whole mystery which is the fullest, the most living and the most understandable that could be imagined.
>
> ...And to come back to the Mass, when we ask God now to change the bread into His Body, now to receive with favor the oblation that we make of it, now to have His holy angel present it on the heavenly altar, now to have pity on the living, now to grant that this oblation may give solace to the dead: do we believe that God waits to do each of these things for the moment in which we speak to Him about them? Certainly not.
>
> All this is a consequence of human language, which can only explain itself part by part; but God, who sees in our hearts with one single glance everything we have said, are saying, and wish to say, hears all and accomplishes everything at the fitting times known to Himself, without our needing to trouble ourselves as to the precise moment in which He does so; it is enough that we express everything that happens by fitting actions and words, and that the whole, even though it is carried out and proclaimed step by step, represents to us in unity all the effects and, as it were, the whole face of the divine mystery.[1]

It is the application of this principle that allows us, for example, to solve the problem of the Offertory. If we see the Mass as made up of rectilinear, successive actions, we shall be tempted to consider the Offertory as being the first act of the "drama" of the Mass, and we shall tend to consider the Offertory as a moral preparation (we offer ourselves) or a cosmic one (we offer creation) while waiting for Christ to offer Himself after the consecration. In reality, the Offertory is not so much a first act, having already in itself the value of a stage. It is already the whole Sacrifice, in its preparation. It is not only offering, it is already sacrifice and already communion. The consecration that consummates it flows back upon it and colors it in advance.

I have spoken of the Offertory only because the case of the liturgy of the Word may well be compared with it. In a linear and successive view, this liturgy could easily appear as a moral and intellectual

[1] *Explication de quelques difficultés sur les prières de la messe á un nouveau catholique,* ed. Garnier, pp. 617-619.

preparation, as a prayer-meeting before Mass. Since the heart, the center of the Mass which irradiates all the rest, is the consecration, and since this "Foremass" is an organic part of the Mass, the liturgy of the Word is profoundly connected with the Eucharistic liturgy, it is qualified by it, it is itself Eucharistic.

This may disconcert our imaginations, which represent all actions, even sacramental ones, on the model of mechanical actions, that is to say, those in which only efficient causes seem to be at work and in which the categories of before and after seem to be unbreakable. But this presence of the end in the means that make ready for it is constantly to be found in the domain of the sacramental. It is thus that all the sacraments, which are ordered to the Eucharist as to their end, draw from it all their supernatural realism.

For example, baptism only regenerates because it is ordered to the Eucharist; it is common teaching that a catechumen who would consciously refuse the Eucharist would receive only a sterile baptism. It is in this way also that every sacrament acts even before being received by a person who orders himself to it as to his end: the candidate for baptism, truly converted, is justified before receiving the water by "the very thirst that he has for the faith"; the penitent is absolved before receiving absolution by the desire that he has for it.

This homogeneity of the liturgy of the Word in respect to the Eucharist is further explained by the fact that the Eucharist taken in itself *is* Word. This is true of all the sacraments. We know the famous adage of St. Augustine: *Accedit verbum ad elementum et fit sacramentum.* But what is true of any sacrament is always still more true of the Eucharist, the sacrament *par excellence.*

Obviously, the Eucharist is effected by a word. As the Office of Corpus Christi says: *Verbum caro panem verum verbo carnem efficit.* "The Word made flesh, by His word makes of His flesh true Bread." But it would impoverish the Eucharist terribly to see in this "word" exclusively the sacramental formula, just as it would be to reduce to this formula alone the *verbum* of the Augustinian adage we just quoted, or the *verbum* that St. Paul joins with the bath of water to define baptism in the Epistle to the Ephesians (5:26).

In the first place, the very confecting of the Eucharist (not to mention the catechesis of faith which precedes it) is carried out in the context of a thanksgiving—that is to say, of a proclamation of the blessings of God—and this thanksgiving is so essential to the sacrament that it has given it its very name.

This confecting of the Eucharist is itself included in a narrative: *Qui pridie quam pateretur;* and we should take note of the fact that the tract *De defectibus Missae,* when prescribing a renewal of the consecration because of a defect of matter, rules that it should always begin with this account.

Every sacrament is a sign, a profession of faith. The consecratory act itself has the value of a manifestation, "They recognized Him in the breaking of bread" (Luke 24:35). "As often as you eat this bread and drink this cup, you proclaim the death of the Lord until He comes" (1 Cor. 11:26). This cup is that of the Blood of the New Covenant. But the Covenant includes, before the effusion of blood, the promulgation of a law, a proclamation made in words. "All these words that Yahweh has spoken, we will obey" (Ex. 24:7). And this is *mysterium fidei,* the mystery of faith; that is to say, in this consecration of the bread and of the wine is recapitulated the whole economy of salvation, the whole paschal mystery revealed to men and professed by them in this sacrament. Finally, Jesus prescribed that it be renewed as a *memoria* of everything that He is and everything that He did.

Far from being removed from words, therefore, the Eucharist requires the Word, the proclamation of the wonderful works of God, the preaching of Christ, the announcement of His passion and resurrection, the promulgation of the Covenant. The liturgy of the Word is required by the Eucharistic celebration; without the liturgy of the Word, the Eucharistic celebration is incomplete, it runs the risk of turning into a kind of magic or routine devotion. "The flesh profits nothing. My Words are spirit and life."

This connection between Eucharist and Word, the existence and, in some way, the necessity of which we have just been considering, is not only a fact which we can be content to affirm. It illuminates the very nature of the liturgy of the Word, which must possess certain characteristics of the Eucharist.

1) In the first place, the liturgy of the Word is *Eucharistic* in the proper sense of the word. That is to say, it is not only an instruction meant for the faithful, but also a *thanksgiving* addressed to God. Certainly a word ought to be intelligible, and we should concern ourselves with this intelligibility. The reader should turn toward the faithful; the proclamation should be properly pitched, distinct, audible; the translations should be clear. But intelligibility should not be the supreme law of the liturgy of the Word. This is not merely an instruction. It is the proclamation of the *mirabilia Dei* made to the honor of God. It should, therefore, be solemn, poetic. *Praedicare* is a synonym for *laudare* and *benedicere.*

We are not fulfilling this law when, for example, we read the Epistle or the Gospel in a merely prosaic fashion; when we systematically substitute reading for chant; when we silence the sacred ministers in favor of a mere reader or interpreter. I will not mention here, although this is part of my subject, the poetic element of the chants which go with the readings, since this will be treated expressly in the following chapter.

2) In the second place, the liturgy of the Word, which expresses the *mysterium fidei,* ought itself to share in this mystery. The Eucharist is not a thanksgiving that strives in a void to sing the marvellous works of God; it actualizes them. It is not merely a symbolic *memoria*

addressed to the mind; it is a real Presence, an actualization of the divine here and now. And so the Word, which is organically bound up with the Eucharist, beyond its usual value as an inspired Word bearing a divine message, possesses an actuality, a reality, a presence of the sacramental order. What is said, exists; what is proclaimed is done.

Here we encounter the mystery of the liturgical year. The Eucharist contains the whole *mysterium fidei*—that is true. But in some way it unfolds this mystery through the celebrations of the liturgical year; it is the changing part of the Mass—therefore chiefly the liturgy of the Word and the Preface—that allows the one Eucharist to be spread out through the successive feasts and seasons.

The liturgical year is not a ceremonial variation that clothes an unchanging Eucharist, like the different embroidered and bejeweled robes that are put on an old statue, which itself remains always the same block of wood, more or less roughly carved; the liturgical year is the redemptive mystery itself, signified by and contained in the Eucharist, which is celebrated variously in the Church according to the season. The *hodie* of our feasts draws its reality from the fullness of reality belonging to the Eucharistic mystery itself.

It should, of course, be noted in this connection that the degree of this fullness varies greatly between the celebration of a great mystery of salvation, of a simple Sunday *per annum,* of a "feast of ideas" (St. Joseph is not more of a Worker on May 1, nor Mary a Queen on May 31 than on any other day of the year), of a feast of a saint celebrated with the texts of the Common, of a votive Mass, etc. In many cases, the actualization of the liturgical texts is derived solely—though this is to say a great deal—from the reality of the Eucharist, our daily Bread, and from the liturgical economy of the Church, which, in providing this text for this particular day and not for another, gives it a special virtue.

Here we reach the third characteristic which the liturgy of the Word receives from its connection with the Eucharist: I mean its communal quality. The Eucharist is not a solitary meal, but a banquet; the Eucharist necessarily requires the assembly of the baptized; and the assembly of the baptized calls for the Eucharist, is ordered to it. Similarly, or rather by way of a consequence, the celebration of the Word is communal; it is a proclamation addressed to the Christian people. It is not enough, therefore, that the various individuals present should be made aware of the liturgical texts by some means or other (practically speaking, by reading them in their missal); these texts should be publicly proclaimed to the assembly, should reach their minds by way of their ears.

As we see more and more clearly, the missal, although it serves as the providential means of salvaging our inaudible celebrations and as an indispensable instrument of liturgical and Biblical preparation, is not a panacea sufficient to remedy every deficiency or opaqueness in our celebrations. And even if we were to grant the impossible—that all the faithful in an ordinary congregation possessed missals and knew how to use them—it would still remain true that the Word of God is a *word* before being a text, that it should be *heard* rather than read (which does not exclude its also being read), and that even if it were perfectly understood by each individual by himself, it should be proclaimed to the assembly as such.

The homogeneity of the liturgy of the Word and the Eucharist has led us to bring out clearly its theocentric aspect and its connection with the mystery; but it also obliges us to consider its anthropological and pedagogical aspects. If the sacraments are a witness to the *mirabilia Dei,* they are no less *propter homines.* The Eucharist is thanksgiving for the gifts of God; it is the offering to God of the Sacrifice of Christ and of the Church; but it is also the gift of God to men, food and remedy for men. It is not only the Lamb immolated for the glory of God and the salvation of the world; it is also the Lamb eaten at the family table, it is the Manna that sustains the faithful on their pilgrimage through the desert, satisfying all their desires and all their needs, *omne delectamentum in se habentem.* It is Bread to be broken and distributed.

We must, therefore, assure a solemn celebration of the Word, but we must also seek to have this Word assimilated by the Christian people, taken as a whole and taken as individuals, one by one. We must not let it be said that "the little children begged for bread and there was no one to give it to them." It is not enough, therefore—although this is indispensable—that the Word of God in the liturgy be religiously and solemnly proclaimed. It must also be heard and understood by those to whom it is addressed. Otherwise it would no longer be truly a word: it would be a mere stimulus to edification and reverence providing a general impression of beauty and mysteriousness, like that given by the majesty of the altar, the glow of the lights and ornaments, the dignity of the sacred actions.

For the Word to remain a word, that is to say, for it to reach minds and hearts, for it to create a spiritual bond between God and men, three activities are necessary: reading, catechesis, preaching.

Reading, first of all. This reading has its own requirements, even if it is done in Latin. Latin itself (does this need to be said?) is a language that has meaning. Even a reading in Latin ought to be heard, to be resonant, intelligible, at least materially. Even when we are reading in Latin, it is absurd for us to read so that nobody can hear it, to read facing a wall, to read in such a way that the text seems to be a sort of meaningless chant or dithyramb. In my childhood I was greatly impressed by a priest who read the Epistle and Gospel of the Mass in such a penetrating, intelligible way that one was certain in hearing it, even without understanding, that the words constituted, at least for the priest himself and for those privileged people who knew Latin, a message charged with meaning.

But there is no need to say that this is not enough. The Word of God should also be proclaimed in the mother tongue of the faithful. If the Word is not understood, it is not a word. And if it is understood only through the intermediary of a missal and individual effort, it is no longer the Word of God proclaimed in the official worship of the Church and so received by me. In such a case, I receive the Word of God, certainly, but by the intermediary of an instrument which has no authority, and in the solitude and uncertainty of my personal research.

In the present state of legislation this intelligible proclamation can be made only by way of duplication, that is to say, by a reading in the mother tongue coming after, or, as the case may be, superimposed on the Latin reading of the celebrant. What inconveniences result from this duplication? Its usual and immediate inconveniences seem to me quite negligible. So far as the readings are concerned, the priest is not the normal minister in any case; the reader who reads the translation from the ambo in a dialog Mass takes the part of one of the ministers in a solemn Mass. As to the chants such as the Introit and the Gradual, it is the celebrant who actually does the duplicating here when he reads them for himself in the Missal. (I will not mention the Orations, which are not the Word of God, and which pose special problems.)

But this duplication has accidental inconveniences which, in practice, are of considerable importance. For example, when the priest is alone without the aid of a reader, or again, when the Mass is solemn and includes long pericopes such as those of the passion, then successive readings in Latin and the mother tongue become very onerous, if not impossible.

But the duplication seems to me regrettable, above all, because of its generally unfortunate effect of setting up an opposition in the minds of priests, first of all, and then of the faithful, between, on the one hand, a word that must be spoken not to be understood, but simply to have been spoken for the sake of obedience, of following the rules, even for the validity of the sacrament; and, on the other hand, a word that is spoken only to be understood and which, as such, seems external to the sacred celebration. And so may we hope that the Holy See will one day satisfy the desire which it approved at the time of the Congress at Lugano: that the celebrant may be able to proclaim the Word of God directly in the language of the faithful.

If some day the Holy See allows this direct proclamation of the readings in the language of the faithful, the consequences of such a permission must be fully evaluated. The reading of the vernacular translation will cease to be an expedient, recommended and useful no doubt, but juridically facultative; it will become an obligation. This reading will no longer be a kind of parallel or appendix to the liturgical celebration; it will be part of it. It will no longer be given as a kind of aid in making the Word of God intelligible; it will be given as *being* the Word of God. The qualities of solemnity and of intelligibility, now separately entrusted to the Latin and to the vernacular readings, will henceforth both belong to the one reading in the mother tongue.

We can easily see all that this implies. To deal with such heavy responsibilities successfully, we must prepare ourselves now. It would be a mistake to consider the present situation as being so provisional that it does not matter how we deal with it while we are waiting for the happy days when the permissions we hope for will descend on us from heaven. I shall, therefore, close my parenthesis about the direct reading in the mother tongue, which is not yet possible, and return to the realities of the present considered as preparatory to progress—progress which in great part depends on our efforts, even though we do not possess the authority that alone can settle the question.

We must, then, say and continue to say that the vernacular translation of the Word of God *is* the Word of God. It may be only a translation, but so is the Vulgate itself, otherwise the Epistle and Gospel would have to be read in Hebrew and Greek, something which nobody has as yet required.

If this translation is to be presented as the Word of God, it must, above all, be a faithful one. Let us admit the fact that during recent years we have too often allowed our zeal for adapting Scripture to the understanding of our people to outweigh our care for fidelity. But what is the use of making understanding of Scripture effortless if what the people understand is something other than the Word of God, if it is a Word that has been arranged, accommodated, its harshnesses softened?

I mean, of course, the harshnesses that properly belong to it. There is no question of canonizing obscurities that come from translating without sufficient care or knowledge, or from using archaic or artificial language. And again, we must not confuse unusual expressions that are due to lack of skill in translating with expressions that are truly Biblical, technical, irreplaceable. Not to go into this subject at length, let me content myself with illustrating what I have to say with a few typical words. The words *tribulation, magnify, trespass* are outmoded, no longer meaningful, and so should not be used in translating, but the words *glory, bridegroom, thanksgiving* belong to Biblical language as such.

Here, I believe, an important remark should be made. In translating a text that is not a sacred one and that is concerned with expressing more or less rationalized and abstract thought, we may legitimately transpose and adapt. Here, doubtless, there is a certain value in raising the classic (though all too brittle) distinction between form and matter. Provided that the thought of the author is rendered exactly, the phrasing of it does not particularly matter.

But such latitude does not exist in translating Biblical texts. First, because the Bible uses concrete language in which the thought is incorporated in the images. Next, because in the Bible it is the words themselves that are inspired. Mallarmé said that one does not make a poem with ideas, but with words. This is true also for the Bible, a poetic Book and a divine Book as well; we cannot allow ourselves to translate the Bible with any kind of words. To take an example at random: we have no right in translating a Biblical text to replace a passive form with an active one, or a personal form with an impersonal one which, while it seems to say the same thing in different words, in reality does not say the same thing at all, and, moreover, muffles certain sacred resonances of the original text.

We feel all these requirements more acutely than we did a few years ago by reason of the progress of Biblical theology itself. Now we attach an importance to certain key words, to certain themes which we did not perceive, or at least did not perceive with the same clarity when we had a more superficial knowledge of holy Scripture.

Certainly, the Bible is difficult. To be understood, it demands initiation, catechesis. But we must resist the temptation to incorporate this catechesis in the translation. What may be all right in a missal meant for individual reading and initiation—for example, the introduction into the text of glosses put between brackets—is not permissible in a text designed for public liturgical reading. In vocal reading, the brackets cannot be heard; and so the gloss seems to be an interpretation, that is to say, an adulteration of the Word of God.

Such glosses, such interpretations are doubtless indispensable. But they must be left in their proper place—in catechesis—and not be introduced into the Word of God itself. Otherwise this Word will no longer have objectivity, fixity. We end up with a multitude of translations which may shake the people's faith in the Word of God, for they may imagine that it can be indefinitely remodeled, remade, transformed according to situations, hearers, or the fancy of the translator. As things are, the faithful hear a Word that changes from priest to priest and from parish to parish, and is not the same as the Word he reads in his missal. And from the pedagogical point of view also the drawbacks are great, for it is impossible to memorize so protean a Word.

It is, therefore, highly desirable that for public proclamation we arrive at a text which will be as faithful, as objective, and as uniform as possible. The Word of God will remain difficult, because, in a certain way, it really is difficult, but it is the task of catechesis external to the Word itself to bring in the needed clarification of it.

The reading of a Word which is faithful, beautiful, solemn, intelligible, should then be completed by catechesis. This, it seems to me, should be carried out in two principal ways, by "comments" and by preaching.

By "comments" I mean brief, illuminating statements given by the reader just before or after the reading. Such statements are necessary, and they differ from preaching on other scores than that of mere brevity. A comment is not a short homily; a homily is not a long comment. These two adaptations of the Word differ in their purpose.

The comment is necessarily brief, since it is inserted in the celebration itself, the rhythm of which it should not interrupt. It has a twofold purpose: first, to make clear the meaning of the Word of God in itself by some information placing it in its Biblical context; secondly, to point out the timeliness of this Word in the celebration and at the precise point in the celebration where it comes.

Preaching, on the other hand, consists in explaining and developing what has been proclaimed by the Word of God and in applying it to the present community, to its moral and social needs, to the sentiments with which it should be carrying out the celebration. I have no intention, obviously, of giving a treatise on preaching during the Mass, on what is called the homily. If I did not at least mention it, however, I should risk giving the impression that the homily is a foreign body, an importation into the liturgical celebration. We must affirm, on the contrary, that the homily itself is a liturgical act that belongs to the celebration as such.

This statement has its basis in all the preceding considerations. In fact, does not the temptation to consider the homily as being an *entr'acte,* or rather an interlude, flow from the false idea of the Mass as being made up of two semi-independent parts between which a neutral period can be set up? If we are convinced of the unity of the celebration, we shall be less inclined to call this unity into question by interpolating a heterogeneous element. And, placed precisely at the point where the liturgy of the Word is joined to the Eucharistic liturgy, the homily derives from this organic situation some of its special characteristics.

These remarks may perhaps be of some use; for if today the word "homily" has come back into fashion, it is by no means certain that all those who practice it are sufficiently certain of its true nature. The *Larousse* of the twentieth century defines the homily as "a familiar instruction on religion, and chiefly on the Gospel." "Familiar," certainly, in the sense that it should be common, pastoral, in contrast to an "occasional" sermon such as might be given at a funeral, or a panegyric. But not "familiar" in the sense that to give a homily one can speak without preparation, casually, without any plan. Given normally by the celebrant clothed in his priestly vestments, coming after the solemn proclamation of the Word of God, being itself, in a derivative but nonetheless real fashion, the Word of God, the homily must never be "familiar" in the sense of vulgar or common.

And, like the liturgy of the Word and the consecratory liturgy, the homily also should be "Eucharistic," that is to say, leading to praise, prayerful, filled with the sense of the mystery, charged with the divine.

Unquestionably, the liturgy of the Word is not a scholarly exposition; it belongs to an order more poetic than rationalistic. But this is no reason for giving a homily, meant to interpret and make personal the Word of God, that has neither head nor tail. We often hear homilies which too closely resemble notes from the missal or the "Liturgical Year." The homily cannot simply present or reproduce liturgical texts; this only duplicates them and is boring. Rather, it should order, clarify, adapt the contents of the liturgical texts so as to make them more assimilable.

On the other hand, though it should be in continuity with the liturgy of the Word, it does not have to be enslaved to it. Except for the great feasts in which the theme of the homily is imposed, there are many Sundays *per annum* on which the preacher can freely pursue some one subject and connect his homilies so as to give methodical instruction in it. If the homily is reduced to being never anything else but a commentary on the pericopes proposed by the liturgy, it can hardly avoid a great deal of sameness from one year to another and is likely to leave untouched important sections of Christian doctrine. To be homogeneous with the liturgy and the Bible, the homily is not obliged to take its *material* from them; it is enough—and this is already a great deal and is not so easy to do—that it be faithful to their *manner*, which is concrete, historical, and fitted into the economy of salvation.

When it is successful, when it binds together and crowns the liturgy of the Word, the homily introduces the people into the Eucharistic liturgy. And this imposes on it another characteristic which I might define, for lack of better terms, by the words "timeliness" and "self-commitment." A homily which is merely an exposition, even a Biblical and liturgical one, could be the same in this parish and in another, could be as appropriate today as in the times of St. Augustine or St. Vincent de Paul. But every good homily ought to be of the present time, that is, adapted to the people actually present, here and not somewhere else, today and not yesterday.

This does not call for journalistic up-to-dateness, but pastoral awareness. It is essentially connected with the fact that the pastor has the care of his flock, puts himself in their place and says to them the words which they need here and now, just as the Eucharist he celebrates is not the Eucharist in general or the Eucharist of the fourth century, but the Eucharist of today: "Give us this day our daily bread."

And again, if it is a simple exposition or a chapter from a Biblical or liturgical manual, the homily will be deficient in its function of leading to self-commitment. Just as the Eucharist is received by a man to bear fruit in his daily life and ultimately to bear fruit in eternal life, so the homily should lead to action, to conversion, to a more realistic and effective charity. To repeat, the homily is not a more or less pleasant intellectual interlude; it is a vital stage in the celebration. It should aid those who hear it to celebrate the Eucharist better, to participate better in the Sacrifice.

All this is much easier said than done. I should like, therefore, to point out some obstacles to a true proclamation of the Word of God. I will limit myself to those on the pastoral liturgical level, which is that of this report, since those other fundamental difficulties which are of the pedagogical, catechetical order and those related to the general mentality of priests and faithful today will be dealt with in later chapters.

First of all, I must repeat that good readers are extremely rare, both among lay people and among priests. I have often had the opportunity to organize liturgical celebrations, especially during Lent. I have never found a really good reader, either among lay people or curates or seminarians. I have often found that pastors are the best readers. Does this come from the difference of age, of generation, of authority? I do not know. In the celebrations of which I am speaking, I have never been able to obtain anything but feeble, unintelligent, uninspiring readings. This throws the celebration into disequilibrium: the preacher having more authority, more conviction, more naturalness in his personal word than does the reader charged with presenting the divine message, which is primary.

It is absolutely necessary, therefore, that our seminarians take some good courses in reading. Certainly there are such courses in seminaries here and there, but they are not very effective because our seminarians do not take this question seriously. I often have the impression that seminarians and young priests who believe so fervently in personal devotedness, in the direct apostolate, in Catholic action, feel that the art of reading aloud is rather frivolous, something connected with the theatre.

I tell them that we have two commanding reasons for making ourselves understood when we speak, two reasons that flow from natural law. First of all, we have a duty in justice towards those who hear us and who have the right to understand what we are saying. Next, we have a duty in professional conscience, the care we should have for doing our job well. A priest whose words are hard to understand is a workman who does not know the fundamentals of his craft.

We must also acquire the habit of giving a slower rhythm to our reading, as to all our ceremonies. Most readers go too quickly, without taking the necessary time, without paying enough regard to the punctuation, without knowing how to vary the tone or to emphasize and stress important words. The reader's haste often is caused by that of the celebrant; the reader is afraid of finding himself left behind.

Yet it is inevitable, other things being equal, that the vernacular reading should take longer than the Latin. Latin is more compact than most modern languages; moreover, the celebrant, in the case of a simultaneous reading, does not want to make himself heard. We might at least hope that the celebrant be patient enough to wait for the end of the vernacular reading before going to the middle of the altar after the Epistle, and before kissing the book after the Gospel. But would it not be still better if the celebrant formed the habit of reading the texts, even when doing so in a low voice, always slowly and appreciatively, not of getting through them as quickly as possible, and when his reading is being duplicated by that of a reader, of regulating his pace by that of the latter?

There is one particular difficulty of the liturgical order here which we should respectfully submit to the proper authorities—the poor choice and poor distribution of liturgical pericopes. Certainly, the fact that the present choice of pericopes has been approved by the Church ought to inspire us with a great respect for them and with the desire to make the best possible use of them. But this does not prevent us from hoping that certain texts might be eliminated—among the Epistles particularly—that have little bearing on the present, for example, some of St. Paul's expositions concerning charisms and ministries that are of interest only to historians, and others substituted which would be more nourishing for Christians of every age.

Considerable reformation is also needed in the way the pericopes are cut out of the complete text. Certain extracts from St. Paul begin with the conclusion of developments without which the extracts are unintelligible. Certain Gospels also would be much clearer if they began one or two verses earlier. And some Epistles and Gospels would gain by having one or two verses cut off, verses which seem to be conclusions but which, in fact, are only accidentally connected with what goes before.

For all this, we submit our hopes confidently to the highest authority; we can do nothing by ourselves.

In conclusion, I am not going to enumerate precise remedies for these various difficulties. I have mentioned some in passing; others belong to reports concerned with the liturgical apostolate, which has not been my concern here. I would like, above all, to avoid concluding with the kind of recipes that provide a refuge for laziness. I have, I trust, sufficiently shown that the proclamation of the Word of God, far from being a detail or a section of the Mass, is coextensive with the whole Mass; it is easy to understand, then, how our whole effort at liturgical renewal must be directed toward a re-evaluation of the liturgy of the Word.

In order not to leave such a general conclusion vaguely in the air, I would like to tie it down to two points: we must rediscover the sense of the community; we must rediscover the sense of the sacred.

We must rediscover the sense of the community. If too many priests proclaim the Word of God poorly in the Mass, it is because they have lost the sense of their function with regard to the congregation, the community. The priest is the celebrant—the very word itself implies an assembly, a congregation over which he is to preside. The more priests are concerned with addressing their people, the more they will understand that they are not celebrating for themselves nor for God alone, but also for their people, and the more they will feel the need to make themselves heard, to make themselves understood, to give their people the Word as nourishment, not as a ceremony.

And as for the faithful, the more they forget their individualism, the more they will let themselves be formed by the chant and actions carried out in common, the more they will understand that they are to communicate also in the hearing of the Word of God. The more they get into the habit of answering and responding to this Word by their attitudes, their acclamations, their singing of psalms, the more they will understand that this Word is not only proclaimed in their presence, but addressed to them. The more they act and communicate in the liturgy of the Word, the more they will understand its homogeneity with the Eucharistic liturgy in which they communicate in the precise sacramental meaning of the word, and the more they will perceive that this Word addressed to them should engage them in action and reaction.

And finally—but here liturgical pastoral care opens out into pastoral care in general—the more this liturgical assembly becomes the privileged expression and meeting-place of a real community of charity, of mutual devotedness and evangelization, the more this assembly will become sensitive to the Biblical Word, which is the Word of God addressed to each one of us, certainly, but to each of us inasmuch as we, each and all, form part of the people of God.

Secondly, we must regain the sense of the sacred. This rediscovery has certainly begun. But it is, perhaps, as yet too limited to what is without doubt the center and summit of the sacred: the Blessed Sacrament, the Eucharistic Sacrifice, the altar. The liturgical renewal is real and profound in many souls. But it is not yet sufficiently concrete. I mean that the convictions derived from it have not yet sufficiently permeated daily behavior. With many people—as happens in all conversions—truly liturgical ideas and intentions still coexist side by side with routine and uninspired ways of acting.

Our sense of the sacred must be manifested at every moment by the way in which we treat the Word of God, giving it a respect and affection comparable to that which we give to the consecrated Bread. This will manifest itself in many ways: by the solemn and also intelligent way in which we read the Word of God in our own language, in which (we cannot repeat it too often) it is also the Word of God; by the respect for the vernacular reading, during which the priests or the servers should not be found talking, moving about or even praying. We should not find the missal lying on the floor behind the altar; nor missals that are dirty and torn and have never been cleaned and mended; nor readings that are meant to be solemn proclamation made from miserable little pocket reprints.

Our sense of the sacred will also manifest itself by our respect for the often rude authenticity of the texts, by the discretion and dignity of our comments, by the religious, contemplative, apostolic character of our preaching, which should avoid all academic pretension and frivolity, all moralistic banality, all pietistic unctuousness.

The sense of the sacred, the sense of the assembly—we should point out again that the two go together. If solemnity and intelligence reign in the sanctuary, the assembly will be much more attentive, much less wandering. At the end of a slow re-education, perhaps the congregation will even become more punctual, because they will realize that to arrive late for Mass is to commit a twofold profanation: profanation of the assembly and profanation of the Word being proclaimed, from which one runs the risk of profanation of the Eucharistic banquet, poorly prepared for because of this lateness.

The Fathers were accustomed to say that it was as culpable to treat the Word of God with negligence as to let some particles of the consecrated Bread fall to the ground. Let us hope soon to have priests—and, as a result, lay people—who make the Word of God, after the Eucharist, together with it, and because of it, the first of their devotions.

Rev. Joseph Gelineau, S.J.

CHAPTER 6

THE CHURCH RESPONDS TO GOD WITH THE WORD OF GOD

THE BIBLE AND the liturgy have both been given us to lead us to the same goal of the new creation in Christ: unity in love. The Bible and the liturgy are, as it were, the two hands of the Spirit in carrying out the work of salvation, hands that take hold of us in our fallen state and draw us, by the "apparatus of the Cross"[1] into the heart of the mystery of the Trinity: "The glory that Thou hast given Me I have given to them that they may be one as We are one: I in them and Thou in Me" (John 17:22-23). The Bible and the liturgy find their fulfillment in the mystery of Christ: the Word of God given to men and given back by them to the Father.

How the Word that comes from God should return to Him has been described by Isaias in incomparable terms that we needs must quote here:

As the rain and the snow come down from heaven and do not return thither without having watered the earth and made it fruitful and caused growing things to spring up, without having given seed to the sower and bread to him who eats it, in the same way My Word that comes

[1] Cf. St. Ignatius of Antioch, *Ephesians*, ix.

forth from My mouth, says the Lord; it does not return to Me without effect, without having executed My will and accomplished My designs (55:10-11).

The Word of God was made flesh (John 1:14) so that flesh might become Word. God, in His Son, has revealed His Name to us so that we may confess it and so that we ourselves may receive a "new name" that no one knows but him who receives it (Apoc. 2:17). And this name is that of the divine adoption, the name that is to be given to those who become sons in the Son: "The proof that you are sons is that God has sent the Spirit of His Son into your hearts crying: Abba, that is, Father" (Gal. 4:6).

God desires that the Word He speaks to men be effective; it awaits a response. But this response is that which God Himself has willed: it is still His Word. This mystery is realized fully in the Person of Jesus. As the Prophet on whom rests the Spirit, the Christ, the Word-made-flesh, He announces to the world in human words the good news of the design of God's love. But as sovereign Priest, He offers to the Father the sacrifice of thanksgiving: in His death the homage of total obedience and in His resurrection the praise of a new and holy race of men. Thus the work of Christ is the perfect speech of God in this world, the definitive appeal of God to men and the total response of mankind to God.

Now, what was visible in the Word incarnate has passed into the mysteries of the Church. Because Christ lives in the Church, it is in her that God's call reaches each of us, and it is in her also that a response is given to the Father by each of us. The Bible and the liturgy continue in the Church the speech of God in this world restored and realized by Christ. The Church is primarily, as her name signifies, a calling, a convocation to bring together all the children of God who have been dispersed: ceaselessly proclaiming the good news, she converts men lying in the shadow of death and illuminates them by the Word of salvation. But the Church is also Eucharistic communion: she unites in the love of Christ those whom the Gospel has gathered together so that they may offer themselves through His sacrifice in thanksgiving to the Father.

The Bible and the liturgy, then, signify for us, members of the visible Church, the two terms of the divine-human dialogue: at the point of departure is the inspired Word; at the goal, the sacrament of unity. Like Christ the Prophet, the Church is always in the act of prophetic proclamation. But she is also the Bride, who, like John the Baptist, recognizes the voice of the Bridegroom (John 3:29). As the Bride, she must re-echo the word of love that is spoken to her and realize the nuptial mystery prophesied by Osee: "Therefore, behold I will allure her, and will lead her into the wilderness and I will speak to her heart . . . And she will sing there according to the days of her youth, according to the days of her coming up out of the land of Egypt. And it shall be in that day, saith the Lord, she shall call Me: My Husband!" (Osee 2:16-18).

Of this dialogue of the Bridegroom and the Bride carried out in the Church, only one aspect is to be dealt with in this chapter. Not the call, but the *response*; not the Word given to men, but the *Word given back* to God by men. Furthermore, we are only to consider this response as it is expressed in the liturgy. Doubtless the response to the Word of life is the whole life of the new man in Christ, as will be pointed out later. But every holy life must be nourished at the source of the sacraments, and the perfection of thanksgiving is the Eucharist. Nowhere does the response of the Church to the Word of God appear more clearly and powerfully than in the liturgy. To know the Church rightly, we must see her living and expressing herself in her mysteries of worship. Here we understand how she responds to the Word of God.

The most perfect expression of this response is primarily the Eucharist itself, the song of praise and thanksgiving which the Church gives to the Father in the sacrifice of Christ. We hear this response also in the hymns and supplications that fill the liturgy and that all speak "the language of God." And finally, we shall consider at greater length this response as it is to be found in the psalms, which are at once and perfectly both the Word of God and the prayer of the Church.

THE EUCHARIST: THE WORD OF CHRIST GIVEN BACK BY THE CHURCH TO THE FATHER

No sacred action shows us more clearly how the Church responds to God with His own Word than the summit of the liturgy, the Mass. The Mass appears, first of all, in its present two-part structure, the liturgy of the Word and the sacrificial Eucharist, as the expression of a dialogue between God and His Church. In the first part, the good news is proclaimed; but in the second, the Church, sacrificed with her Head and sanctified by His Word, offers her thanksgiving to God. Word coming from God, Word returning to God. In the Sacrament, proclamation becomes achievement. In Communion, the dialogue finds its fulfillment.

It is indeed in the Supper of the Lord, around the holy table, that the dialogue of the Bridegroom and the Bride attains its greatest intensity and that the voice of the Bride most perfectly echoes that of the Bridegroom. That the response of the Church in the Mass is the very Word of God is made clear to us by everything about the Mass: the very name "Eucharist" and the reality that it signifies; the course of the great Eucharistic prayer and its mystery; and finally, even the words which express this mystery.

The name "Eucharist" given to the Mass in the first Christian centuries already expresses the idea of response. Eucharist means gratitude, thanksgiving, confession, sacrifice of praise. But what can we give back to God except what He Himself has given us? What blessings can we be grateful for except those with which He has showered us? What grace can we return to Him in our thanksgiving except all that He has given us in His Son, full of grace and truth? What name is there for us to profess and proclaim but the Name that has been revealed to us in Jesus our Savior? What is our sacrifice of praise, finally, except Christ Himself, the High Priest, the Mediator between God and men, "by whom," says the Epistle to the Hebrews, "we continually offer to God a sacrifice of praise, that is the fruit of lips confessing His name" (13:15).

He Himself who has been for us the grace of God is still our action of thanksgiving, our Eucharist, our song of praise and our spiritual sacrifice. "All this," as St. Paul says, in relation to the work of resurrection in which God causes us to participate in His Son, "is for your sake, so that a more abundant grace may cause thanksgiving to abound in a greater number to the glory of God" (2 Cor. 4:15).

And also, when the Church carries out her giving of thanks in the great Eucharistic prayer at the heart of the Mass, she does nothing more than give back to God, in confession and praise, the sacred Word that she has received from God. Two words in the liturgy express this dialogue: *memores, offerimus.*

Memores: it is in memory of the graces we have received, it is in commemorating the events of our redemption that we offer the holy Victim. The Eucharist is founded on the history of salvation. First, the Preface sings the mysteries of the Savior, from His incarnation to His glorious return, thus solemnly proclaiming the good news. And then its song effaces itself before the very words of the Lord, signifying and accomplishing the mystery: "This is My Body delivered for you." And finally, it is made clear that it is in memory of the passion, the resurrection, and the ascension of the Lord that the Sacrifice is offered.

Offerimus: this is not only the Sacrifice of Jesus, it is henceforth that of the whole Church: "We and all Thy holy people." The Word of God does not return to the Father without having accomplished all that He willed. By Christ, with Him, and in Him, in the unity of the Holy Spirit, His holy people offer to the glory of the Father the *sacrificium laudis,* the sacrifice of praise. In union with the paschal canticle of the Lord, who gave thanks at the Last Supper and who intoned the *Alleluia* on the morning of His resurrection, the great voice of the Church is raised, the echo of her mystical oblation.

This exchange of a Word of God given and a Word of God returned in response is expressed still more clearly in the liturgy in the form of a dialogue properly so called. While the echo of the readings of the first part of the Mass is still resounding, the recalling of the historic events of our salvation and the foundation of our faith, the celebrant intones the Preface, the festal chant of thanksgiving. But he assures himself first that the whole assembly is one with him in heart: *Sursum corda, Gratias agamus Domino Deo nostro.* Having received the unanimous reply: *Habemus ad Dominum, Dignum et justum est,* he lifts his voice in praise. Then the whole assembly responds to the voice of the celebrant by the *Sanctus,* a song of praise that desires to include all the united voices of earth and heaven: "Heaven and earth are filled with Thy glory! Hosanna!"

Then, in response to the voice of Christ, who in the heart of the Canon seals the New Covenant in His Blood, all the chosen people give their solemn ratification, their "yes" and their signature by the *Amen* that concludes the sacred action: *Amen,* that is to say: "This is true and unshakable." And finally, the dialogue of speech is consummated in communion. Then Word and reality are fused. Sacrifice, reciprocal presence and love of the Bridegroom and the Bride are here expressed by union in one spiritual flesh which is that of the Body of Christ.

In the Eucharist, her supreme Word, the Church can say nothing other than Christ, the true and faithful Word of the Father. Her song of thanksgiving is that which God Himself has taught her: the song of self-sacrificing love.

THE LITURGY PRAYS IN THE LANGUAGE OF GOD

That the word of the Church to the Father is the echo of the Word, as we have seen in the Eucharistic action, is true not only of the mystery hidden in the liturgical rites, but is shown in the very expression of this mystery. When the Church prays, God not only prays in her, but she prays, if we may so express it, like God; she speaks the human language of God, even preferring, when possible, to use the words that God has inspired.

One privileged example from the liturgy will show us that this is true. The first part of the Mass, centered in the proclamation of the Word, at once causes a dialogue to break out: the responsorial psalm of the Gradual following on the Epistle. The movement of the sacred action, which has as its center the table of the Word, is initiated from on high; it begins by the reading of holy Scripture and the proclamation of the good news. But as soon as the first reading is finished, the community at once expresses in song its collective adherence of faith to the message it has received.

This chant could have been a composition of the Church and have been presented as a continuous hymn sung by the congregation, on the order of the *Gloria in excelsis.* It is nothing like this. Liturgical tradition shows us without question that this chant, the most ancient and the first of the chants of the liturgy of the Word, in the Mass or in the vigils, is a psalm, and a psalm sung responsorially, that is, a song in dialogue form. We shall return later to the subject of the choice of the psalms as the prayer of the Church; it is the form of this chant that should here hold our attention.

The reader of the Epistle at the ambo is succeeded by another reader, a chanter, who intones the responsorial psalm. The Church is about to respond to God with His own Word; but this inspired Word does not come first from the assembly: it is given to it as if from on high. At one time this psalm was often called a "reading," just like the Epistle and Gospel. But here the whole assembly is invited to respond to the chant-lector by a unanimous acclamation, often drawn from the psalm itself. By this cry, repeated again and again between the verses proposed for meditation, a marvelous dialogue is set up between God and His people. The dialogue of the Bridegroom and the Bride is taking place; the exchange of words is only the image of the exchange of hearts. The responsorial psalm is the "yes" given to the Word of God by the Word of God.

But now the intimate and confident exchange of the responsorial psalm turns into prayer and supplication. In spite of its impetus of faith toward the Word of salvation, the Church knows that the hour has not yet come for the new Song face to face with God; she is still a pilgrim, she is still composed of sinful members. She must plead. This is the time for the great "prayer of the faithful," always kept in use in the Oriental liturgies, which is preserved for us in the liturgy of Good Friday in the "universal litany," and of which a vestige remains in the *Kyrie* of our Roman Mass. And our Roman Orations also now gather up the needs of all to have them rise, by Christ and in the Church, to the throne of the Father.

It would seem at first sight as if the Church, in contrast to what she does in the case of the psalms, is here using her own speech and her own words. But, if we go beyond the verbal appearances to consider the interior movement of this prayer, we shall understand that it is still a response made to God by His own Word. When the Church prays, it is always in reference to what God has done for men and in the awareness that He can do the same things again. Thus Israel prayed when it represented to God His past actions in favor of His people, and when, in distress, it implored His grace for the present moment by recalling His fidelity to His covenant:

> And yet, O God, my king from the beginning,
> You have wrought saving deeds in our midst:
> By Your might You rent the sea,
> crushed the head of the dragon in the waves . . .
> You made fountains and brooks gush forth,
> You dried up never-failing rivers . . .
> Remember how the enemy insults You, O Lord . . .
> Think of the covenant . . . (*Ps.* 73:12-20).

God Himself was the first to speak and to act; will He now remain silent, or is His arm powerless? No, His Word remains as firm as the heavens; we can rely on it and remind Him of it with perfect confidence.

This is how the Church still prays, not only at the central moment of the Eucharistic action by the anamnesis and the consecratory prayer, but throughout her liturgy. When, during the Easter vigil, before celebrating the bath of baptismal rebirth, she confidently awaits God's sending His Spirit on the waters to make them fruitful, she reasons in the same way:

> O water, created by God, I bless you . . . by the God whose Word in the beginning separated you from the dry land, and whose Spirit hovered over you, by the God who caused you to spring forth from the fountain of paradise and commanded you to water the whole earth by four rivers,

who in the desert changed your bitterness and made you sweet and wholesome to drink . . .

Explicitly or implicitly, this logic of Christian prayer is to be found everywhere, from the prayers commending the departing soul to the litany prayers of the Oriental liturgies, which begin with the words: "In peace, let us pray to the Lord." The prayer of the Church is strong with the Word of God. "The effectiveness of Christian prayer," writes Divo Barsotti, "extends as far as the effectiveness of the creative Word; better, it is itself that Word, it continues creation, it carries out the redemption of the world."[2]

Indeed it carries on the prayer of Christ before the tomb of Lazarus: "Father, I give Thee thanks that Thou hast heard Me. Yet I knew that Thou hearest Me always" (John 11:41-42). The prayer of a Christian is never the cry of a man abandoned to himself; it is the ineffable groaning of the Spirit of Jesus, already laden with all the graces given by God to men. In the inspired words that reveal our vocation to us, our response to that vocation is contained. "The Bible has not truly taught us to believe as God wants us to believe unless at the same time it has taught us to pray as God wants us to pray to Him."[3] Thus the liturgy calls God by the names He has given Himself; she bestows on Him the titles which are His by right; she asks Him for favors He has already granted; she thanks Him with the very words of thanksgiving which He Himself sang while on earth.

Let us consider again her most sacred acclamations. At the heart of the Eucharistic action, the thanksgiving of the Preface chanted by the celebrant breaks out from the whole assembly. This is the *Sanctus,* the most solemn chant of the liturgy of the faithful. Here, in the greatness of the mystery, the most lofty lyricism of the Church fades away. It gives place to the hymn that Isaias heard sung by the angels in the vision which he saw prostrate in the temple of Jerusalem, and in which, as St. John would say, he contemplated the glory of Christ: "Holy, holy, holy is the Lord of hosts" (Is. 6:3). The Church adds to this chant the Biblical and messianic acclamation fulfilled in Jesus: "Blessed is He who comes in the Name of the Lord."

When she wishes to ratify the New Covenant, she does so with the word with which the Hebrew people sealed the first covenant: *Amen.* To give thanks at any time, but especially during the season of the resurrection, her preferred expression is the Hebrew cry of victory, the song of the paschal deliverance: *Allelu Yah!,* "Praise the Lord!"

Her prayer *par excellence* is also the prayer of the Lord, reported by the Gospels: "Our Father, who art in heaven, hallowed be Thy Name." She says this prayer before Communion, she repeats it at the end of the nocturns and the Hours, she uses it again in her table prayers, for this is the way that God Himself has taught us to pray, and furthermore,

[2] Divo Barsotti, *La Parole de Dieu dans le mystère chrétien,* Lex Orandi (Paris: Ed. du Cerf, 1954), 17, p. 348.

[3] L. Bouyer, in *Bible et Vie chrétienne,* n. 10, p. 22.

it is in strict continuity with His own prophetic language, the first part of the *Pater* being like a psalm of praise, and the second like a psalm of supplication.

And when the Church lets herself be carried away by her own lyric enthusiasm to create *"psalmi idiotikoi,"* or songs of her own, she only wishes to echo the divine Word to which there is nothing more to be added. The most ancient of our Christian hymns, the *Gloria in excelsis* or the *Te Deum,* speak, directly or indirectly, the language of Scripture.

THE PSALMS — WORD OF GOD AND PRAYER OF THE CHURCH

How holy Scripture impregnates all Christian prayer has been already brought out in previous chapters. Let us, then, dwell at greater length here on the phenomenon we have already mentioned more than once: the jealous preference that the Church accords in her prayer to the psalms. Certainly the Church has never been lacking in singers inspired to compose hymns and canticles in honor of Christ. Although we know very little about the liturgy of the first three centuries, any number of Christian hymns have been preserved from that era, some of which are masterpieces of poetry and of prayer. And following the lead of Ambrose and the Romans, this lyric vein has never died out in the history of the Church. However, periodically, and above all in the Latin Church, we see the will to return by preference, and even almost exclusively, to the inspired texts for use in liturgical prayer.

Various reasons have been given for this preference: the mistrust felt by the Church of new hymns, which have often served to propagate the fantasies of heretics; her prudence in the face of individual lyricism and of private and less trustworthy devotion; but, above all, the fact that the word of man, however pleasing and holy it may be, can never be compared to the Word inspired by God.

Behind this general affirmation must be seen the resolve of the Church to be faithful to the history of salvation. Since what was announced in the Old Covenant is realized in the New, is it not natural that the book of prayers of the old economy should become also the book *par excellence* of the prayer of the Church? Are not the same cries pleading for salvation, the same chants of praise and thanksgiving for deliverance as valid today as yesterday, since they are addressed to the same Savior and have the same redemption in view?

Of old, among all the Books of the Old Testament, the Book of the hymns of Israel occupied a place apart connected with its special destiny. Before expressing the prayer of the chosen people, individual and liturgical, it is presented as being the lyrical resumé of its whole religious experience, a glorious summary of the whole Word of God, given and returned. It contains, first of all, in striking epitome and in typical characteristics, the whole history of Israel, not only by recalling the great works of God in favor of His people, but also by the present and future significance of this sacred act. The Psalter is the proclamation of the creating and redeeming Word, at once in its visible efficacy, past and present, and in its eschatological bearing.

Founded on this sacred history, the psalms also translate it into confession and supplication, into praise and prayer. But otherwise than with ecclesiastical prayer that gives back a Word revealed and accomplished, in the psalmist the Spirit is at work. Here praise and prayer are still the revealing and prophetic Word. Relying on a past, expressing a present, the psalms tend toward a future—the messianic fulfillment.

For the ultimate truth of the psalms is the mystery of Christ. When Jesus came, He declared openly that the psalms spoke of Him: "These are the words which I spoke to you while I was yet with you," He said to His apostles at the time of His last apparition, "that all things must be fulfilled that are written of Me in the Law of Moses and the prophets and the psalms" (Luke 24:44).

During His public life Jesus frequently applied to Himself psalms that were well-known to His hearers. For example, recalling Psalm 22: "The Lord is my shepherd," He said: "I am the Good Shepherd" (John 10:14). And again, basing His argument with the Jews on Psalm 109: "The Lord said to my Lord: Sit at My right hand," He asked: "If David calls the Messiah his Lord, how then can He be his son?" (Matt. 22:45), indicating thereby that He Himself was the fulfillment of the prophecy as Messiah and Son of God. And finally on the Cross, it was again from the psalms that He took His last words: "My God, my God, why hast Thou forsaken Me?" (Matt. 27:46). "Father, into Thy hands I commend My spirit" (Luke 23:46).

The psalms speak of Christ. They are the very prayer of Christ. This is the unique and final reason why they are the prayer of the Church *par excellence*. The Bride can prefer nothing to the voice of the Bridegroom. So the apostles understood it as they recognized in Jesus the *Kyrios*, that is to say, the Lord whom the psalms implore or praise. Henceforth the Church will no longer name the Yahweh of the Old Covenant, but Jesus, whom "God has made both Lord and Christ" (Acts 2:36), giving Him the Name above every name.

To mention only one witness, Nicetas, bishop of Remesiana in the fourth century, expresses the unanimous tradition of the Church when he writes:

> The psalms sing the most beautiful of realities: the mysteries of Christ. His generation is expressed here, His rejection by His unbelieving people and the inheritance given over to the pagans are here mentioned; here the power of God is sung; here the passion is depicted; here the glorious resurrection revealed; nor is there lacking the ascension to the right hand of the Father. Then the coming of the Lord by fire is made manifest; the terrible judgment of the living and the dead is here declared. What more? The very mission of the Creator Spirit and the renewal of the earth is here revealed; after which in the glory of the Lord will come the eternal happiness of the just and the endless punishment of the wicked.[4]

[4] *De bono psalmodiae*, PL, 68, 371.

If this is the conviction of the Church, who chants the psalms in nearly all her sacred ceremonies, at every Mass, at every feast of the mysteries of Christ and the saints, in many sacraments of the Christian life, every day and every hour of the day in the Divine Office, if such was the thought of the Fathers of the Church and the piety of the monks, who found in the psalms the immediate and spontaneous expression of all the situations of their Christian life, why is it that the same thing has become so difficult for us? We find no difficulty in admitting that certain passages of the psalms, obviously messianic, refer to Christ, such as that line of Psalm 2 which we sing on Christmas night: "The Lord has said to Me: Thou art my Son, this day have I begotten Thee."

We admit still that the Psalter taken in its entirety is messianic, but we often stumble when we go further along this road. A way of applying certain texts to Christ, to the Church, to the Virgin or the saints, which we meet in the liturgy itself, disconcerts us and seems to us often very artificial. We find repugnant precisely the play of allegory and what is now called the accommodated sense. How can we agree, for example, that the poetic description of the course of the sun given in Psalm 18:

There He sets up a tent for the sun,
who comes out of his chamber like a bridegroom,
exulting like a champion to run his course...

can express also the virgin birth of Christ? The inspired author certainly never thought of such a thing, and the literal sense orients us in quite another direction. Briefly, all this kind of thing does not seem "real," nor apt to enlighten our faith or sustain our prayer.

Furthermore, how can one still put into the mouth of a Christian, after the Sermon on the Mount and the teaching of the Lord on the forgiveness of injuries, the terrible cries for vengeance and the frightening maledictions contained in the Psalter:

O Babylon, devastator,
happy he who pays back to you
the evils done to us;
who takes your little ones
and dashes them against the rock! (*Ps.* 136)

Is this truly the prayer of the Church? Are these the feelings of a disciple of Christ?

Let us pause for a short time to consider these entirely legitimate difficulties, for this will aid us to penetrate further into the prayer of the Psalms as it is practiced by the Church. To recognize, with the whole of tradition, the mysteries of Christ and His prayer, not only in a few more obviously messianic psalms, but in the Psalter as a whole, is to accept the force of two facts: the first belongs to the theological order and is addressed to our faith—Christ has fulfilled the psalms; the second belongs to the literary order and is addressed to our human intelligence—the language of the psalms is poetic.

First of all, Christ fulfilled the psalms because He is God and because He is Man. Being God, the Creator, the Judge, the Savior and Friend of men, it was He in whom there shone forth clearly at last all that God willed when He created, when He judged, when He saved men and made a covenant with them. Everything that was said in the psalms concerning Yahweh's intervening in favor of His people can henceforth be said of Him whose Name is "Savior," and of all that He has done for His Church.

Since the resurrection of Christ, for example, is the total and definitive victory of God, it alone can give a full and definitive sense to many of the affirmations in the psalms, as for example:

God reigns, He is clothed in majesty,
the Lord is robed in power.

With good reason, the Church has understood this Psalm 92 in a paschal sense: God the Conqueror is the Christ the King, the Lord Jesus risen in power, as said by St. Paul. In the same way, whenever the psalms call upon the Lord and speak of God, this can be understood of Christ as God. My Creator, my Judge, my Savior, my Friend is henceforth for us the Lord fully revealed to men in the Son of God, Jesus.

But Jesus is also the Son of Man. In the mystery of His incarnation He took upon Himself everything that belonged to man, his sufferings and his joys, his anguish and his hopes, his mortal state and his faith in deliverance. The psalms, then, not only speak of Christ whenever they speak of God; whenever a man is speaking in them, it is again Christ who speaks. As human history only finds its meaning in the paschal mystery of Christ, so each particular situation of every human being only finds its full truth in the light of the mysteries of the Lord. Let a poor man bewail his destitution, let a sick man make his moan, let a persecuted man express his loneliness—what other human being on earth has ever known better or felt more profoundly this poverty, this suffering, this solitude than He who took upon Himself all our sorrows and climbed the hill of Calvary in loneliness: "My God, my God, why hast Thou forsaken Me?" Or let a man chosen by God sing the grace that has been given him and the victory that has been granted him—in whom has this human blessedness been more fully verified than in the only Son, the object of all the Father's good pleasure?

Whether it is a question of the people of Israel or of one of its members, every historical situation, every human sentiment finds its ultimate truth only in the human life, death and resurrection of God-made-man. Since nothing divine and nothing human is foreign to Christ, there is nothing that the psalms say of the action of God in man that cannot be referred to the incarnate Word.

Nonetheless, this theological principle would be ineffective so far as we are concerned if the language of the psalms were not presented in such a way as to speak to us continually of Christ, as it were naturally and of its own accord. The literary genre of these prophetic writings is, in fact, what allows us to find in them a concrete expression of the mysteries of Christ. The Church preserves the psalms, not as mere monuments of the past which might serve as the basis of a historic science, nor as masterpieces of the literary culture of antiquity. She seeks in them the figure of mankind, sinful and redeemed, suffering and glorified. She finds in them the signs of what God began to bring about in His chosen people of old, what He achieved in His Son, and what He continues to accomplish in all those who believe in Christ.

Now, this lengthening of perspectives corresponds exactly to the interior movement of poetic expression. When Baudelair cries out:

"Oh, how large is the world in the bright light of a lamp,
How small, to the eyes of remembrance!,"

it makes little difference whether we know on what particular evening, in what dark room, under the light of what lamp this intuition came to him, or what memory haunted him. But the poet has given such a universal expression to his individual experience that these lines are, as it were, really our own whenever an analogous situation causes us to relive the reality they refer to. It is not only one unique moment that the poet captures in his verse, but his whole life as well, and that of all those who can make his expression their own. The symbolism of poetic language is based on analogies of situation and of experience.

It is analogies of situation also that allow the psalms to include in their lyric form everything that men can live and feel in an experience of salvation, and to include particularly the life and the feelings of Him who has gathered in Himself all human history, not only in its passing appearance but in its truth—Christ. He alone has entered into communion with the world beyond signs and language, the world into which every poet wishes to lead us by his magic.

In whom, for example, has the eulogy of Psalm 1 ever been more completely fulfilled:

How blessed the man
who does not walk the way counselled by the wicked,
but delights in the law of the Lord.
He is like a tree planted near running water,
that brings forth its fruit in due season,
whatever he does, prospers. . .

than in Him who was the one just Man whom no one could convict of sin, who always did the will of the Father and was pleasing to Him, who was planted with the tree of the Cross to bring forth the only pleasing fruit that God has ever gathered in the garden of His creation, when His due time, His hour had come, and who achieved the final victory, since death has no more dominion over Him?

It is of only relative importance to determine what persecuted man was the author of Psalm 68, or in what circumstances of his life, on what date of universal history he uttered this lament in the presence of Yahweh:

> It is for your sake that I have borne reproach,
> that shame has covered my face . . . .
> Wretched am I, and in pain,
> may your help, O God, set me free.
> I will praise God's Name with a hymn,
> give Him glory by a song of thanksgiving.

Since the Church has put these words in the mouth of Christ, rejected for the sake of the holiness of God and the salvation of His brothers but risen again for His glorification and singing the *alleluia* of His paschal victory, they find in Him the fullness of their meaning; and each Christian who is rejected because of his faith but sure of his deliverance can make these same words his own.

We could multiply examples. It is one of the miracles of the psalms that the images by which they express poetically the most fundamental sentiments of mankind and describe the social and personal situations of the religious soul are still expressive for each of us and verified in Christ Himself.

And yet, are there not certain passages in the psalms which refuse to become a truly Christian prayer and wholly our own? The maledictions and the imprecations, particularly, continually seem to spoil the marvellous cries of love and faith in the inspired texts.

Let us recall, first of all, the fact that the Bible can only be darkness and scandal for the earthly man, but that it is light for the spirit illuminated by faith in Christ. For, St. Paul reminds us, in the new economy, "our struggle is no longer with flesh and blood, but with invisible enemies" (Eph. 6:12). The dramatic struggle between the persecuted just man and the triumphant godless man, between the chosen people and the pagan nations, the struggle which is perhaps the very heart of the Psalter, is henceforth the combat of Christ against Satan and of the Church against "the world." The enemy whom I must hate and whom God will enable me to triumph over is sin and death. And this enemy is not only in other people, it is first of all in myself. This enemy is never my neighbor, it is myself.

Still more, it would be impossible to erase these imprecations from the Psalter without seriously falsifying the mystery of Christian existence. Love is never so great as when it is victorious over hatred and evil, and no one is capable of true love if he is not capable of hate, in the Biblical sense of the word, the sense in which the Lord said: "If anyone comes to Me and does not hate his father and mother, and wife and children, and brothers and sisters, yes, and even his own life, he cannot be My disciple." No compromise can be made between the kingdom of God and the world. Nothing can stand before the holiness of the living God.

This is the enduring significance of the choices of love and of hate which the psalms invite us to make: "Let sinners vanish from the earth, let the wicked be no more" (*Ps.* 103:35). This word was fulfilled when the very Son of God, taking on Himself the sins of men and their death, perished in His own flesh in the fire of the holiness of God.

Do we need to add, finally, that it is necessary and consoling for us to find in the psalms these cries of men who are still unbelieving, still in revolt, still violent? With a whole part of ourselves, we still belong to the time of preparation for the Gospel. While the psalms find in Christ the accents of perfect faith, perfect hope, and perfect love, they also preserve, in the preparation for Christ carried on in the midst of a stiff-necked people whose fidelity was short-lived, the image of everything that belongs to our meannesses and our weaknesses. Thus the psalms save us from pharisaism.

But they also keep us from remaining satisfied with our mediocrity by offering us protestations of innocence and holiness that express the loftiest justice. This justice is less that which we already possess than that to which we are called and which is always verified in the mouth of Christ and of His holy Church. No, nothing of sinful man, as well as nothing of man sanctified by the Spirit of God, is absent from the psalms.

Thus the images of the psalms, which, because of their literary poetic genre, always transcend the concrete situations which caused their birth, and which, as the inspired words of a sacred history, have an eschatological bearing, these images can always open out on the mystery of Him who assumed all the figures of this world. Bound up with the history of the salvation accomplished by God in a people chosen by Him, these images still remain the preferred ones when we wish to express our situation in faith and our relationship to the Savior. This is why the Church holds to them in her liturgy and her prayer. The Church has recognized a play of symbolic correspondences founded on the analogies of situation between Israel and Christ, between the sacraments of the Old and the New Covenants.

To take only one example, the psalmists sang of Sion as the meeting-place of the tribes of the chosen people and even of all peoples. Since it is the Church of Christ which realizes this mystery of convocation and unity, what was said of Sion can be said of the Church, the new Jerusalem, in a way which is even more true than it was of the old:

> Jerusalem built like a city
> into one perfect whole!
> Up here come the tribes,
> the tribes of the Lord (*Ps.* 121).

And since Sion and the Church reveal to us a mystery of motherhood, what is said of one and of the other can also be said of Mary, figure of the Church, Mother of grace:

> Sion—each man may call her: Mother,
> for in her one and all were born (*Ps.* 86).

In the mystery of liturgical worship, the same Lord is living and acting who was living and acting in the flesh some two thousand years ago in Palestine, and who had already been living and acting through prophetic signs in the history of the people of Israel. This is why the psalms, which prophetically express the mysteries of Christ realized in the deeds and the words of His earthly life and continued in the sacraments of the Church, are always present, always of today. If the same figures are applied to the successive events of our visible world, their reality is unique: Christ.

This reality transcends human history. Whenever a psalm verse is addressed to us, God is speaking to us; the mystery of the Son of God is proclaimed to us. Whenever we take the psalms to make them our prayer, it is Jesus, the Son of Man, who in them prays to His Father, or it is the Church who prays to her Lord and *Kyrios*. Such are these words of man and this Word of God, for the Church and for believers. Since the Bride has no other life than that of the Bridegroom of whom she is the very flesh and bone, she has henceforth no other language than His. His Word is hers. In Him it is the human Word of God.

The Bible and the liturgy, as we said at the beginning, have been given to men only to lead us to one goal, the purpose of the work of redemption—unity in love. If, going beyond the sign of holy Scripture and of the sacraments of the Church, we seek the source of their efficacy, we see the Holy Spirit at work, the Spirit of unity and love, sanctifying the world by the twofold mystery of a Word given and a Word given back.

The Word of the Father came down to us in Jesus the Prophet, and men who heard this Word with their own ears of flesh have transmitted His message to us; then the Word returned to the Father to present to Him the sacrifice of mankind obedient to His voice. It was the Spirit who caused Him to come down and take flesh in the womb of the Virgin Mary; it was the Spirit who revealed Him in glory, taken up into heaven. But the Spirit has gone before Him since the beginning of the world, and, with Jesus departed, He dwells with the Church until the end of the world to accomplish His work.

The Spirit has no face, but we hear His voice. It is He who spoke by the prophets; it is He who prays in the Church. He inspired holy Scripture, the Word of life; present in the water and the oil, consecrating the bread and wine, He makes the sacraments signs of life; He is the voice of the Eucharist.

And henceforth He who in the bosom of the Blessed Trinity is the song of love which is eternally exchanged between the Father and the Son is also in us as the dialogue between the Bridegroom and the Bride. The Spirit of Jesus is the voice of the Bride. Together the Spirit and the Bride say: "Come, Lord Jesus!" (Apoc. 22:17). Together, the Bidegroom and the Bride say in the Spirit, *"Abba,"* Father.

Rev. Francois Coudreau, S.S.

CHAPTER 7

THE BIBLE AND THE LITURGY IN CATECHESIS

TO TRANSMIT TO our fellow men the twofold wealth of the Church—the Bread of the Word and the Bread of the Sacrament, the Bible and the liturgy, the message of Christ and the life of Christ—is not this, in its twofold aspect, the unique and basic objective of pastoral work? The pastor's task is, indeed, to lay hold of these two realities, to lay hold of them where they are to be found, to bear them with the greatest care without altering or perverting them in any way, so that they may reach those who are to be taught, both children and adults. What a formidable mission, completely bound up with the very mystery of the incarnation, deeply stamped with its transcendence and its humility!

In transmitting *the Word for the sake of the Life,* catechesis unites man with God through a world of signs. It must enable him to read these signs, it must open out their meaning, it must propose to him their content.

In order to gain a better understanding of our mission, we shall use a threefold approach—*a starting point*: the destitution of a catechesis that has lost the sense of the living Word of God; *a stage*: the benefit, but the insufficiency, of a catechesis integrating the Biblical renewal; *a perspective*: the priceless, irreplaceable "accomplishment" of a catechesis "situated" in the liturgy of the Church.

This statement of the plan of this chapter indicates of itself the significance and the limits of this study. There is no question of dealing with the problem of catechesis in all its dimensions, or of showing the importance of the pastoral context which conditions its effectiveness, still less of recalling the necessity for a living presentation of Christianity and its requirement of Christian self-commitment in concrete living. Here we are dealing with one particular aspect of the catechetical ministry, the aspect defined by the theme of this book: to show the doctrinal authenticity and the spiritual wealth of a catechesis close to its Biblical and liturgical sources. We ask our readers to keep this "formality" of our discussion in mind in order to give to our analysis its true meaning, and their true bearing to the orientations we shall point out.

THE DESTITUTION OF A CATECHESIS THAT HAS LOST THE SENSE OF THE LIVING WORD OF GOD

A twofold fact obliges the catechist who is conscious of his mission to question himself about the value of his pastoral activity. Almost all children who have been baptized receive some catechesis; between the ages of twelve and fifteen years, some 80% are unfaithful to their baptismal promises renewed on the day of their "solemn Communion"; a recent inquiry revealed the same percentage of infidelity among baptized adults. This is the first fact. The second is the profound lack of interest in religious instruction, particularly among adolescents; even in Catholic schools the religion class does not hold the students' attention.

There are, of course, many causes for this relative lack of perseverance and of interest: the break-up of families; the immorality of street-corners and places where young people spend their leisure time; the dechristianization of our society and of its institutions; secularism, etc. Without denying the role of these causes extrinsic to our teaching, must we not question ourselves about our teaching itself: its content, its spirit, its method? The catechesists of every country, of every society, of every age today are asking themselves the same question: is there not too often in our present-day catechesis (not, certainly, in the teaching of Christian doctrine itself, but in the pedagogy that presides over its transmission) a formal defect which compromises its effectiveness?

To answer this question means to undertake an investigation; this is the origin of the present catechetical renewal. The first years' work along these lines brought about an improvement in the method and the techniques of religious instruction. The catechetical renewal began on the pedagogical level; this was the first wave. The second gained greater depth; without abandoning the study of the devices of transmission, it applied itself to the study of the presentation of the subject transmitted.

From this viewpoint we cannot help saying that for many decades catechesis has frequently been defective in its form, and this fact often prevents it from being a real initiation into the faith. If we must give it a name, we might call this defect the division of catechesis into three parts.

Christian doctrine is actually presented to children under three aspects, and often in three books, or in three parts of one book: the catechism manual, sacred history (the Bible, the Gospel, the history of the Church), the liturgy. Whether we consider these three elements in themselves, or whether we consider the connections that should exist between them, we must admit that such a method of catechesis, if it is not necessarily a total loss, yet normally leads to an impasse.

The program of religious instruction includes first of all the catechism manual. Obviously we are not criticizing the value of such a manual of religious instruction, nor casting any doubt—even the slightest—on the need for using it. Such a systematically organized presentation of doctrine, explained, memorized, recited, is indispensable to the orthodoxy of the faith and is required by the mode of apprehension of all objects of knowledge by a human being. The manual and its didactic study has, then, its due place in catechesis.

But the catechetical method cannot and should not be reduced to the explanation of a manual. Such a method suffers from two evils: abstraction and dispersion.

The simple explanation of formulas leaves the student on the level of the abstract, of mere concepts; it gives ideas addressed to the intelligence; it puts them in order; it is the indispensable backbone and skeleton of the faith. But an effort of contemplation is needed to grasp through these forms, true signs and carriers of revealed truth as they are, the dogmatic realities themselves, the mystery. What the eye has not seen, what the ear has not heard, what language has never expressed, this is the Christian mystery and this is the authentic nourishment of faith.

In the manual, moreover, revealed truth is presented piecemeal, as a mere sequence of facts laid out one after the other. The student cannot grasp by this means the unity of Christian teaching, all centered on the Person of Christ, in whom God reveals Himself, in whom alone we can find the final textbook of our faith. The manual, therefore, does not reveal the Person of Christ, living and present, the fullness of the living and present Word of God.

Programs of religious instruction also include the study of sacred history. The Bible, the Old Testament, the New Testament, the history of the Church—these are the books of Christians; they ought to know them as we know our family papers and family treasures. Here is usually the motive for this study; this perspective is true enough, but insufficient. Thus conceived, the study of sacred history does not become for our students a true entrance into the faith.

The face and the presence of God in the Bible are revealed to us by His whole activity and perceived in events considered as signs of what God is to His people, also in the interconnection of these events, the reciprocal link and causality of which reveal His design. Now, too frequently our sacred histories are mere collections of anecdotes and accounts, and so do not reveal this face and this presence. The events follow one another without being connected with one another, without the essential being brought out in relationship to the accidental.

The jawbone of the ass, the hair of Absalom, the trumpets of Jericho are put on the same level as the departure of Abraham, the deliverance from Egypt, the giving of the Law on Sinai. Presented without connection and without evaluation, the events of the Bible, if they are history, are no longer the history of salvation, the living expression of the living God.

And further, our books of sacred history often present a mutilated Bible; certain riches, and not the least important, are often missing. Ordinarily, the prophets, the books of Wisdom, the psalms, the canticles are all left in obscurity. All this spiritual wealth which makes up the soul of the people of God escapes the students; yet what would be more nourishing for their faith?

Programs of religious instruction include, finally, the study of the liturgy. But, alas! Just as doctrine is studied from without, both as to its formulation and its conceptual expression, just as the Bible is studied from without in Bible history books, so also the liturgy is studied from without, in the details of the rubrics, without any true perception of the inner realities expressed by the signs.

The students, for the most part, learn to place the various feasts correctly in the calendar of the liturgical year, but they do not discover the mystery of Christ lived here and now by Christians; they learn to find their way through the Mass and its successive parts, but they do not comprehend the Eucharistic and paschal action of the Mass; they learn a repertory of liturgical rites, objects, and words, but they do not know how to go from the sign to the thing signified.

Thus the liturgy remains external to their Christian life: they know the road, so to speak, because they have read the map, but they have not learned to admire the glorious view; they have not learned to nourish themselves on all the spiritual riches of the liturgy, spiritual riches which, although hidden, are nonetheless the true food of their faith.

This is the first difficulty with our three-part teaching. But there is a second to be noticed also: the absence of dynamic connections between these three elements—manual, Bible, liturgy. From this point of view, our trichotomy is still more disastrous.

Are not the Bible and the liturgy the two living sources of the doctrine formulated in the manual? Are they not the privileged dwelling-place of the presence of the living Word of God, giving to catechesis its concrete character and its personal unity? It is through the Biblical and liturgical signs that the *Credo* is to be studied. But, in the majority of cases, catechism and sacred history are studied as if they were two separated sciences, foreign to one another, with two subject-matters to be examined on, and often two different teachers. What happens when a river is cut off from its source?

Furthermore, what gives meaning to the liturgy if not the Bible? What are the sacraments but the deeds of Christ, announced and prepared in the Old Testament, accomplished in the New, represented in the liturgy of the Church as the efficacious sign of the realities by which we are saved?

And even when Bible and liturgy are not treated in separate classes, they are usually presented as appendices, or illustrations, or applications or extensions of the chapter of the catechism under consideration, without organic connections, without shedding light on one another, from a moralizing and superficial point of view, which does away with any presence and any action of the living Word of God in Jesus Christ.

Should we, then, be so greatly astonished at the relative ineffectiveness of our religious instruction and the lack of interest in religious teaching shown by our students? We must realize clearly this sad fact: a too exclusive systematization, a narrow spirit of keeping things separate, a departmentalization of mind have ended little by little in degrading the Word of God.

My readers could certainly reproach me, in this first part of my exposition, for its quality of slight caricature and of negativism, since it shows only the shadows in the picture. I am quite aware of this fact. Certainly, in practice, many pastors have already made the needed reorderings and syntheses. But should we not, in a book such as this, denounce with some vigor the evil with which we are afflicted, the sickness from which we are suffering? Only a true diagnosis makes it possible for the sick man to be cured.

At the end of this analysis, however, we must answer two objections, objections which are heard too frequently to allow us to pass them by in silence.

Is it not an exaggeration, people say, to find a relation of cause and effect between this trichotomy and the leakage from the Church that we have mentioned? There are many reasons for this leakage and some of them, perhaps the most important, are completely outside the domain of catechesis as such. This is quite true; we have evidence of it. We know well, alas, that the best instruction often results in failure because of the absence of factors, familial, academic or pastoral, that determine its effectiveness. But this realization does not reassure us in the least; it leaves our problem untouched, the problem that is occupying us here: how to give back to catechesis its true dimension as the living Word of God.

But, people also say, the catechesis that you criticize is traditional in the Church and has proved its worth. It has brought forth generations of believers. Was not this the kind of catechesis that we ourselves received, and when we look at ourselves, with all due modesty, might we not say that it has proved its merit? Here we need to dissipate a misunderstanding. In the first place, it is not quite exact to say that this tripartite catechesis is traditional. It is even relatively recent; in any case, it is later than the sixteenth century. The catecheses of the Fathers have quite a different tone; they show, by contrast, how the history of salvation and the *Credo* are united and how religious instruction is bound up with liturgical initiation.

Furthermore, to remedy the imperfections and the lacunae in this catechesis which we ourselves received, supplementary factors used to be at work, and it was to these factors that this catechesis, when it was successful, owed and still owes its success. We are all familiar with the two principal ones: a Christian family atmosphere and Christian institutions.

The Christian family is and always will be the great educational force; this is the "good ground" of perseverance in the faith; the tree that is rooted therein will normally resist all temptations. But at the present time this family life is under attack. Truly Christian homes, of truly militant quality, may be growing in number, but yet we know by experience the feeble mediocrity of the Christian life in the families of most of our students. And if the family atmosphere is less Christian today, as the Holy Father recently reminded us, is this not, at least in part, due to the fact that the poor quality of our religious instruction is beginning to make its effects felt?

As to Christian institutions, they too were and still are a supplementary factor. We know their value and their necessity; both have been recently reaffirmed. But experience shows here also that they will not be able to ensure that people will persevere in faith who are no longer nourished by the living Word of God.

No, let us look neither for justifications nor consolations. Let us look the evil in the face, the more boldly since the remedy is at hand. The Lord is faithful, He the Shepherd of His flock. The pastures are ready—the Bible and the liturgy—to give His people the food they need.

THE VALUE, BUT INADEQUACY, OF A BIBLICAL CATECHESIS

One of the major orientations of the catechetical renewal has certainly been the return to the Bible, in its profound reality, in Christian catechesis. Efforts along this line are being multiplied today, and recent works have made a decisive contribution to this field.

All the same, we should get rid of an outlook which has been and still is that of many catechists and which can keep them deluded.

This is the method called "the Gospel as the catechism." The method consists either in following the evangelical narrative step by step and thus replacing the catechism manual by the Gospels, or in illustrating the various aspects of dogma or morals with quotations or examples taken from the Gospels.

Although the context of the Gospels is that of Christian initiation, although the concrete and inductive method of the Gospels is that of religious teaching, it is still true that a systematic and organized presentation of revealed truth centered in the Creed is required for the orthodoxy of the faith.

And to reduce the role of the Bible to that of illustrating doctrine, is not this a real betrayal? It is not for us to say what faith is and then to show it realized in Abraham, but rather to look at Abraham to say what is faith. The Bible is not to be reduced to a collection of arguments to justify doctrine and of examples to illustrate it; it is the privileged witness of the Word which is expressed by doctrine. The abuse here is the more regrettable in that the applications are frequently extrinsic ones which grasp only a secondary or accidental or anecdotal aspect of the Biblical phrase or example.

The values given to catechesis by the Bible are of an entirely different order. The Bible is not a teaching outline, a collection of illustrations, a reservoir of stories, a ground of applications. What, then, is it?

It is a *presence* which expresses itself through events, deeds, acts. It is the special dwelling-place of revelation; it is the Word of God. It is God drawing near to man, approaching him in order to speak to him, to reveal Himself to him. What we cannot dispense with in catechesis is the Biblical method, which is respectful of the very mystery of God that it is to transmit and of the human being who is to be united to this mystery.

Let us try to grasp some of the characteristics of this method in order to define Biblical catechesis.

1) It is a catechesis made up of *deeds and events;* it is, therefore, a return to the concrete. The teaching given in the Bible is not given in an abstract form. When the Lord speaks, He does so in a concrete way, starting with what is sensed with an immediate experience that is quite simple and connected with life. Whether it is the message of the books of Wisdom, the language of the prophets, the teaching of Christ, or the language of the parables, the whole of the Bible is marked by this same concrete character and this same care to remain close to concrete reality.

But the Lord does not speak in words only; the Word of God is all the *mirabilia Dei,* the interventions of God in the world which culminate in the event that is Jesus Christ Himself. The Biblical events are the progressive revelation, through these interventions by God, of His face, of His presence, of His message; in a word, the Biblical events are the "epiphanies" of the Word of God. In the Bible, everything that God wants to say to us about Himself or about ourselves He tells us by means of actions.

The teacher will notice the value and effectiveness of such a method. It is the inductive method, the one which arouses interest, which sustains attention, which inspires to a course of action. But the teacher of the faith will also notice the special quality of Biblical concreteness. It is not that of a picture or a story; it is that of fact, of experience, of the real. Here is a valuable directive for the teacher of religion who is anxious to get away from "representations" and to approach "realities." The image leads to the idea (leaving us still in the realm of abstraction), but the fact leads to the reality of which it is the sign.

This is why it seems very true to say that the Bible is not made first of all to be "represented" but to be "proclaimed." The representation, or the "concrete as visualized," is in danger of keeping the student on the plane of the image, while the proclamation or the "concrete as spoken" allows him to go from the Biblical fact which is the sign to the reality of the Word of God which is signified.

2) But let us now define the second characteristic of Biblical catechesis: it is a catechesis of *signs and symbols*. While the Biblical facts are concrete and therefore close to men, they are also signs that reveal an invisible reality. The sign subsists on two planes, that of the visible and that of the invisible, in such a way that in looking at what is visible we discover the invisible reality.

Each Biblical event, in fact, is the bearer of a revelation of the Lord, of a Word of God: the call of Abraham, Moses, the covenant, the exile.... In the New Testament, the mystery of the Trinity, of the incarnation, of the redemption, is expressed in deeds; the unfolding and interconnection of the events themselves are also the bearers of revelation. Thus, the stepping-stone to lead us to the mystery, or the casket that encloses it, or the shell that protects it like a fruit, is not primarily or only the concept addressed to the *ratio*, the conceptual intelligence, but primarily the event which challenges and obligates the whole man.

The Biblical events as signs are thus akin to the knowing powers of man – be he child or adult – for whom the concrete rather than the abstract is the natural starting point. These signs are also nearer to the process of the act of faith in simple people, in its human root – adult faith does not suppress this "spirit of childhood"; and they are, finally, nearer to the mystery itself into which we are introduced by the reading of the signs. The pedagogy of the faith is at the basis of religious symbolism.

3) While the Bible causes us to enter into a world of actions and of signs, it also causes us to enter into a world of *persons and personal relationships;* here is the third characteristic of Biblical catechesis in virtue of which it also causes the religious world to appear to the students in its true light.

The mystery of God is, in fact, a personal mystery. God is not an academic course; He is a living Being, Someone and not something. His message is not a system of ideas, but the revelation of His mystery. God is a "community" of living Persons in which each Person is a subsistent relation to the two Others. And the Bible causes each of the divine Persons to be revealed to us in the specificity of His proper dynamism, as also the divine Being in the unity of His action.

To meet the Bible is also to meet a world of persons in relationship to God. From Adam and Abraham to the apostles and the saints, the definition of the religious life is the same: to stand in a personal relationship with God. Nothing is more valuable for the Christian catechesis which wishes to be both revelation and initiation than this Biblical viewpoint, which allows the students to discover religious reality in its most fundamental essence.

4) The fourth characteristic of Biblical catechesis is that it introduces us into *a world of acts.*

The Bible puts us into contact with persons who are in act. Here we find a world in movement, in dramatic activity. God calls, He awaits our response; He offers His security, but He must have our trust; He pardons, but we must repent. Throughout the Bible we find the spiritual combat, temptation and struggle, the active and militant life.

Nothing is closer to the mystery of the faith than conversion, self-commitment, decision, choice. Nothing is closer to the mystery of life in the Church, in which the Christian finds peace and life only in apostolic work for the kingdom of God. And nothing, finally, is closer to the profound needs of children, of adolescents, of young people, of those at the age of action, of choice, of commitment.

5) The Bible, again, is a *whole spirituality* which permeates our catechesis insofar as this draws from it its content and its method. Truth and challenge, interiority and peace, loyalty and hope — is not this the spirit that we find on each page, in deeds, in maxims, in prayers? Who could deny, henceforth, the incomparable value of familiarity with the Bible in forming the souls of our pupils? "Tell me who your companions are and I will tell you who you are."

We could analyze at length the characteristics of the spirituality of the Bible, the common denominator of all true spiritualities since it is that of the People of God, but this has been excellently covered in recent books. It is enough to recall here how children love the personages of the Bible, how their interior life awakens at contact with them, to be convinced of the value of such a method.

6) And, finally, the Bible is the *history of a people.* Biblical catechesis facilitates the students' entrance into the community of believers; here is the last characteristic that we wish to note. From the creation of the People to its triumphs or its failures, the same sense of solidarity always shines out in the great events of its history; thus to live the Bible in catechesis is already to live with the Church and to find ourselves united with those who share the same faith. It is no small good to

give very early to our students the sense of the Christian community and of the inter-responsibility that unites Christians with one another, and by and through them, with all men also called to salvation.

A great work of education, certainly, still needs to be done to have our catechists discover these riches, to convince them of the value of this Biblical pedagogy for their teaching and to initiate them into the method that it inspires.

But we should note also the limits of such a catechesis. We have mentioned already, and we repeat here, that a Creed is absolutely necessary. The dogmatic and moral formula is indispensable to catechesis. Doubtless, in the light of the directives of the Church, psychology and pedagogy will make more precise our knowledge of the best age at which the formulas should be presented and the best order of presentation. In any case, conceptualization is a function of the intellect which has its place in the knowledge of faith, and the study and the formulation of revealed truth is an integral part of catechetical pedagogy and is indispensable to the orthodoxy of the faith. It is the Church who, in the formulation of revealed truth, gives the Bible its final significance; she is the rule of faith.

The Bible proclaimed and the *Credo* explained are, then, both irreplaceable; and primitive catechesis is defined by the interaction of, on the one hand, a study of the sources, the events, the history of salvation, and, on the other, a study of doctrine formulated and explained, of truths systematically organized: *Haec oportuit facere et illa non omittere.* To affirm the need for the first is not to deny that for the second. But to do without the first is frequently to make impossible the learner's entering into a true faith.

The second limitation is summed up in one word: however present may be the Word of God announced and proclaimed in the Bible, the acts in which it is expressed are acts of the past. From the pedagogical point of view, this is an obvious difficulty: the child as such faces the future and is not interested in the past. But there is another difficulty. To speak only of Biblical events is to isolate the sign from the thing signified, the proclamation from the reality. The first chapters of this book have made abundantly clear the unity between the Bible and the liturgy, the second making present what the first announces and begins to realize in figure in the men of the Old Testament.

And so it is that the events and saving deeds of the Old Testament are only fully perceived, discovered and understood in the reality of the saving deeds of the Church.

To say this is to point out the inescapable need for the liturgy in catechesis. A catechesis has no right to become Biblical if it does not become liturgical at the same time. Concerning this profound unity between the Bible and liturgy in catechesis, then, we now need only to analyze the why and the how.

THE INDISPENSABILITY OF A CATECHESIS GIVEN IN THE CONTEXT OF THE LITURGY OF THE CHURCH

The liturgy confers on Biblical catechesis a threefold benefit: (1) it gives the Bible its authentic interpretation. Very early our students, both children and adults, need to gain the conviction that it is only in the Church that one can read the Bible with certainty. Biblical circles which leave room for a certain "prophetism" of individual interpretation have led to grave disorders from the point of view of the faith. It is the liturgical realities, in fact, which give to the Biblical realities their true meaning. This mutual clarification is basic in catechesis. As Father Daniélou has clearly shown, this is the way in which the sign is not separated from the reality signified, the proclamation from its realization.

2) In the second place, the liturgy gives to the Bible its quality of present reality. The history of salvation is not a thing of the past; it is going on today. It is not enough to state this to our students; they must experience it. It is, without doubt, the whole Christian life which gives the Bible its present reality, engrafting the life of the baptized into that of the people of God on their pilgrim way, engaging them to be witnesses to God in today's world, to make the choices dictated by their faith. But we might say that the liturgy of the Church constitutes, as it were, the living vital structure of this history. The liturgy gives, so to say, in an accentuated rhythm their present actuality to those major events that marked the life of the men of the Bible and of the people of God. The Bible shows us a drama; the liturgy causes us to live it. By it, from the liturgy of baptism to the liturgy of the dead, we ourselves live here and now, in reality, the history of salvation.

3) And, finally, the liturgy indicates in a special way the *passage from revelation to initiation* which should take place during a course of instruction. To transmit the Word is not enough; we must cause our students to enter actively and personally into the mystery. We must set our students "in act" in the Christian life.

Prayer, charity, the apostolate in all its forms are certainly true responses to the Word of God and true Christian commitments. The fact remains that a liturgical catechesis, starting from the rites of the Church, clearly shows the necessity for this passage from "saying" to "doing." It realizes to perfection what we might call, on the methodological plane, the vital connection between instruction and education, revelation and initiation.

The catechism manual reveals and explains; the Bible invites and calls; the liturgy introduces us, takes us by the hand; it exposes us, it causes us to understand by having us act. To use a very material analogy to bring out a spiritual reality: in learning to swim, it is useful to have the various motions explained; it is better to have them also demonstrated; but it is absolutely indispensable to try to perform them oneself in the water. So, too, for an apprenticeship in Christian life and action, carried out by a liturgico-ritual catechesis.

This strictly catechetical utilization of the liturgy is not intended in any way to conceal or to diminish the proper function of the sacraments as administered and received, their power of transforming a man from within so that he can welcome the teaching he has received and live by it. The rites of the Church, valuable as they are in showing the wealth of the *Credo,* are not to be reduced merely to outstanding illustrations of doctrine. They are this, but they are much more: the intervention of God in the life of man. They enlighten him from within, transform him, in some way place him at the height of the journey that God wishes him to travel, by engaging him in the liturgical rite.

The fact remains that, in addition to the sacramental action itself, the catechetical action, if I may call it that – a true discovery of the *Credo* through the rites of the liturgy – gives to each student a better chance to approach more nearly to Christian being and action – in a word, to Christian existence.

THE ROLE OF THE LITURGY IN CATECHESIS

But it is now time to go from the domain of principles to that of applications of the role of the liturgy in catechesis, limiting ourselves to four: (1) the celebration of the liturgy as the method of using the Bible in catechesis; (2) the liturgical year as the context and the global object of catechesis; (3) the sacramental liturgy as the principle object of catechesis; (4) the Eucharistic liturgy as the special expression of catechesis.

Space does not allow us to go into all the developments of these topics which would be useful to catechists; we shall content ourselves with a few summary indications to give the necessary filling-out and defining of our line of thought.

The Celebration

The Bible can be used in catechesis in various ways: (a) it can be "represented"; this is the whole field of images, of Biblical films and albums, sometimes very valuable, but difficult to use well; there are many abuses here; (b) it can be "explained"; the catechist presents the Biblical passage and explains it in order to have the doctrine shine out from it; (c) it can be "meditated"; this is the personal work of reflection which must be carried out by each student; (d) it can be "celebrated"; this is the liturgical way of using the Bible in Christian instruction.

From the pedagogical point of view, we must, in our teaching, respect the hierarchy of values that puts the Word above the representation, meditation above explanation, celebration above meditation. This indicates the importance we must attach, it would seem, to the liturgical way of using the Bible in catechesis.

The liturgical celebration of the Bible is a profound proclamation of the Word in the community in a ceremony similar to that of the liturgy of the Word in the Mass, with an insistence on the catechetical elements to be brought out, in order to nourish faith, inspire prayer, lead to self-commitment.

The purpose of such a celebration is, very simply, to cause the mystery of the faith contained in the event to be relived in its actuality. Students are always tempted to be satisfied with learning facts and knowing doctrine; educators must always be concerned with having their students go from the event to the mystery, from doctrine to life.

Let us take an example: a child might be quite familiar with the parable of the pharisee and the publican and be capable of telling it. He might even, which would be better, be able to find the lesson contained therein. But the concern of the educator primarily is to lead the child to *contemplate* in faith this mystery of the poverty and the true condition of every sinful man in the presence of God; next, to go from the contemplation of the doctrine explained and assimilated to the contemplation of the mystery meditated on and appreciated (*recta sapere*); then to *enter into* this disposition and interior attitude, to relive for himself here and now (*hodie*) the parable; and, finally, to give a personal response to the Word of the Lord, and thus to go from contemplation to a course of action, at once the conversion of heart and the self-commitment to Christian living presupposed in every act of faith.

Let us take another example: the child can have a very exact knowledge of the effects of baptism, which have been explained to him by means of the parable of the vine, our Lord's conversation with Nicodemus, or the appropriate texts of St. Paul. But the concern of the educator is that all this "doctrine" should become "present reality" to the child, that he should actually advert to his own baptism and that this discovery should illuminate his whole life. The "celebration" of these texts will give them their value as the Word of God, living and acting, enlightening the spirit, transforming the heart, and putting the child in the state of living the life given him at baptism.

Here is an unequalled source of catechetical wealth, and experience shows its irreplaceable value. Doubtless, let us repeat it once again, Biblical "celebration" in catechesis in no way removes the need for the necessary didacticism, the value and the urgent necessity for which we have frequently recalled. Such celebration has only one place in the pedagogical context of catechesis; yet this place must be respected. And, furthermore, such celebrations are entirely traditional in the Church, deriving from the Biblical and liturgical tradition inherited from the worship and the teaching of the Synagogue. One can find many examples of it in the Old Testament, e.g., Deuteronomy, and also Nehemias 8; the sacred text is presented and explained in a celebration that leads to self-commitment.

We have defined the purpose of such "celebrations" in catechesis. Their technique is twofold: evocation by word and action, and the creation of the liturgical atmosphere.

The central technique on which everything else converges is the proclamation of the Word, which should be done with solemnity, by a lector – wearing an alb if possible – from the missal, with incensing, procession, dialogue, etc. To the evocation of the event by the Word may be added evocation by actions. The child is, as we all know, visual-minded; the Church knows man's needs, she who in every sacrament unites action to words. But this evocation in action needs to be sober.

In contrast to a mime or a dramatic presentation, and still more to the theatre in which various parts are played, celebration has neither actors playing parts nor spectators looking on. Belonging as this does to the genre of the liturgy, it has only celebrants with various functions to carry out. Words and actions are the supports, human vehicles that are accidental and transitory, of the mystery of the Word, which itself is central and permanent.

The liturgical atmosphere gives the celebration its fundamental character, that of an action, an action that people carry out together. What is then expressed is, indeed, not only the Word of God; but, through the liturgical act of the assembled participants, their chant and prayer, their silence and their actions, it is also the response to this Word.

To analyze some of the elements of such celebration is to show its advantages. That the class which has listened to, studied, understood and recited Christian doctrine should become a community assembled in an act of faith expressed in the Church — is not this the sign of a catechesis that has attained its properly theological dimension?

Here we have not only the advantage of shared enthusiasm in the access to faith due to the religious atmosphere. But, as we know, the Christian community is the *locus* par excellence of the action of grace even before any particular sacramental action is begun. The presence of Christ in the mystery of His Word as proclaimed is "realized" in the mystery of His Word heard by the members of the assembled community. It is Christ present in their midst who, by His power to transform from within, brings souls into harmony with the teaching that is received and disposes them to give an active response in Christian living.

It remains to say that to carry out such a liturgical celebration of the Bible requires competence; a celebration cannot be improvised. This technique, like all others, follows certain quite simple laws, but to list them would go beyond the scope of this chapter. The essential thing for our purpose here is to show the place of such celebrations in the effort we are making to give its proper liturgical "realization" to Biblical catechesis. Many efforts have been made along these lines. Let us mention only the booklet *Montons á Jérusalem* of the C.P.L., which gives a schema of such celebrations, and No. 157 of the review *Verité et Vie,* which makes the application to catechesis.

The Liturgical Year

The liturgical year also makes religious instruction effective by giving it, not only its context, but also, "in some way," its object; this is the second point of application of the role of the liturgy in catechesis.

The liturgical year is, first of all, *the concrete presentation of the Credo,* in recalling the great events of our salvation; nothing is more obvious.

It recalls to us the coming of Christ: this is the season of Advent, of Christmas, and Epiphany. Thus the mystery of the incarnation is presented to our faith as being the echo of the first manifestation of Christ in creation, and as the announcement of His glorious return at the parousia. It recalls to us the life of Christ, His teaching, His miracles, His struggle, His passion, His death, His resurrection and His ascension: this is the season of Septuagesima, Lent, Passiontide and Easter. Here are presented to our faith the divinity of Christ, morals, sin, redemption, salvation, glory. And, finally, it recalls to us the presence of Christ in the Church by grace and the sacraments: this is the season of Pentecost, of Christ the King, of All Saints, of the dedication of the great basilicas.

Here the mystery of the Church, the Mystical Body of Christ and our life in the spirit are presented to our faith. But the liturgy is not only a reminder; it expresses a living reality of which it is the efficacious sign. It is a *Credo* "in act." This mystery of Christ, lived in former times in these various events by Christ Himself, the Head of the Mystical Body, is lived here and now by Christ in the members of His Mystical Body. Thus the liturgy reveals to those receiving instruction—and this is the important point—both what Christians believe *and* what they live. It teaches them that the Christian mystery is not some thing, but Some One. It convinces them that in Christianity what we believe in is what we must live by.

Who, then, can deny the twofold value of the liturgical year as being both the plan and the global object of catechesis, the concrete presentation of the *Credo,* and the *Credo* in act? Happy the students who have the liturgy as the context of their instruction, as the guide of their initiation!

The Sacramental Liturgy

In penetrating into the more specific domain of the rites of the Church, and particularly of the sacramental rites, we discover an even greater wealth and effectiveness for catechesis.

The sacraments, bringing together dogma, morals and spirituality, are the most complete and unified expression of Christian doctrine. Presented in their institution, their effects, their movement, and, above all, as the actions of Christ giving us salvation, they cause the object of our faith to appear, not in a logical and abstract exposition, but in a concrete and present form.

The pedagogy of the sacraments is inductive: it is by means of the sacred signs that the learner is led to the realities of the faith. This is what is called the catechesis of the rites. By means of the persons, actions, words and objects that are shown to us by the signs and symbols of the liturgy, nearly every aspect of the Christian mystery is expressed, to become the object of knowledge and the nourishment of the life of faith.

This pedagogy respects at once the transcendence of God and the psychology of the child. By an intelligent study of the signs we go from the visible to the invisible, from faith that is knowledge to faith that is adherence. What a vast difference there is between a catechesis that explains the effects of baptism abstractly on a blackboard, and one that slowly reveals the riches of baptism by means of the rites of the sacrament and the Easter Vigil! This revealing is not only richer and more coordinated with the whole of the Christian mystery, but far more respectful of the divine and transcendent character of that mystery.

This pedagogy is inductive and also active, not only because it leads the child to an attitude of mind, but because it causes him to enter actively into the actuality of the saving mystery. The sacramental signs are efficacious: they express what they contain, they accomplish what they signify. They do not merely recall the saving deeds of Christ; they re-present them, that is to say, they render them present, they make them events of the here and now. In the sacraments it is, indeed, always Christ Himself who carries out in the members of His Mystical Body what He accomplished on earth as Head of the Mystical Body. The sacraments are the abiding and actual presence of the saving deeds of Jesus Christ.

The study that children make of the sacramental rites leads them not only to knowledge, but to a course of action. They are formed by salvation from within; they let themselves be taken up by the deeds of Christ; they enter into the mystery. If the catechetical manual, which is a didactic exposition of Christian truths, is indispensable to the *orthodoxy* of the faith, the sacramental liturgy, which is the revelation of Christ and of His action while He is accomplishing His work of salvation, is indispensable to the *life* of the faith.

The Eucharistic Liturgy

Finally, at the very heart of the life of the Church, the center of the whole liturgy, the sacrament towards which all the others converge, there is the Eucharist. We need to treat only briefly of this as the supreme expression of catechesis.

The Eucharistic liturgy brings to the student, first of all, the wealth of its many signs. It presents a universe of objects and of persons, of actions and words whose symbolism is priceless. Alas, all this liturgical wealth is frequently ignored, left to seem heterogeneous and archaic. It is accepted because it must be, without understanding. Yet here is a language that is very concrete and therefore very close to the students, very rich since it is the revelation of the mystery of salvation. Is it not a serious mistake and a great pity to neglect such riches? For anyone who has made a serious effort to study these signs knows well that thereby he has brought new life to his teaching. And he has also enlivened the manner, the style of his teaching—not the content, because doctrine does not change, but the presentation.

The Eucharist is the summary and the center of the whole Christian mystery. It constitutes the "framework" of catechesis, in the sense of regrouping all the elements of revealed truth in a synthesis that accords with the true hierarchy of the different truths that compose it. The motif of this unique value of a Eucharistic catechesis has often been described. Let us state it briefly.

The fundamental act that sums up, that underlies, that animates the whole life of Christ is His *transitus*. He came into this world only to return, to "pass" from this world to the Father, Himself and all His brethren, both Head and members of the Mystical Body. One obstacle alone stood in His path to prevent Him from gathering all men together to bring them to God—this is sin. This is why the "passage" of Christ had to be painful: "It was necessary that Christ should suffer in order to enter into His glory." This was carried out in the three events that sum up the great paschal act of Jesus: His death, resurrection, ascension.

But this "passage," carried out by Christ as the Head of His Mystical Body, must also be carried out in His members, that is, the Church. Christ has, therefore, left to His Church His "passage" as a permanent reality, so that all men can "go from this world to the Father"; and this is the Eucharist, the "passage" of the whole Christ: the death, the resurrection and the ascension of the Head and of the members. The rites of the Eucharistic celebration are the simple expression of this doctrine; better still, they are the dramatic expression of this movement. The Eucharist is, certainly, a presence and a communion; but it is, above all, an action and a movement: the act, the movement of the paschal Sacrifice.

The great value of a catechesis that is, in each of its lessons, truly Eucharistic, based on or extending one of the aspects of this mystery, is that it causes the students, during the whole course of their initiation, to discover this act and this movement, and to introduce them into it. Is this not the central mystery of the *Credo*? Is this not the fundamental course of action of the Christian life? Thus the *Credo* is found to be revealed through the living wealth and variety of the signs of the Eucharistic celebration and to be revealed in its actuality. In this celebration it finds its summary and its realization. A precise study of the themes, the prayers, and the actions of the Mass shows it to be the most unified and the richest synthesis of the Christian mystery.

A comparison may help us to understand this quality of the Eucharist, at once simple and complex, which justifies the pedagogy we are proposing. If I want to become familiar with the great mountain Mont Blanc, there are two possibilities. One is that I might climb it myself. But I realize that people who have made this climb found that at the top of Mont Blanc they could see everything except Mont Blanc itself; they dominated it, but did not become familiar with it. Or I might make, one after the other, the ascent of the various peaks around Mont Blanc, from Brévent to Mont Joly and to the Aiguille du Tour. Then I would have a series of partial views of Mont Blanc which, when they were put together, would give a knowledge at once analytic and synthetic, unified and global, of the glory, the greatness, the beauty of the great mountain itself.

So it is, analogically, with the mystery of the Eucharist, the summary and center of all Christian doctrine. The contemplation of the different mysteries of our religion is like so many revelations of the Eucharistic mystery. When, therefore, our classes in religion are given in close connection with the mystery of the Eucharist, they are like so many glances at its liturgy, lights on its celebration, approaches to its mystery. While our instruction should be centered on the Person of Christ, it should be on the *whole* Christ in His Mystical Body, realizing here and now for us His paschal action in the Eucharist.

And so, week by week, month by month, year by year, to the rhythm of the lessons of the catechism as to that of the liturgical feasts, the student, like the catechumen, will at the same time and with the same movement penetrate to the interior of the Christian mystery, known and summed up in the doctrine of the Eucharist, while he is being initiated into the Christian life whose fundamental act is the Eucharistic celebration. Taking part in the Mass, then, no longer seems merely a law of the Church imposed from without, but the central reality of Christian life.

This point of view, furthermore, invites us to develop, to "scan," as it were, the doctrinal formation and the religious education of children in relation to the rhythm of their Eucharistic life.

The *Directoire pour la Pastorale des sacraments,* while it hopes "that the profession of Christian faith might be broken up into various commitments made over a period of time and in a progressive way, so that children and adolescents would be given only those formulas to repeat which do not go beyond their true convictions," asks further that each of these self-commitments be bound up with the Eucharist. "The profession of faith is a renewal of the baptismal vows and should, therefore, retain the character of a paschal celebration, of a completion of Christian initiation which essentially includes the Eucharist."

These statements are in line with our concern for a catechesis which will be at once teaching of doctrine and Eucharistic and liturgical initiation.

Children from six to eight years old, arriving at what is commonly called the age of reason, should be given a religious training wholly oriented toward the full celebration of the Eucharist to be achieved at first Communion, the Eucharist surrounded by the two sacraments given at the same age, penance and confirmation.

A catechesis that makes use of this sacramental richness—will it not certainly possess, together with a unique character of integration, the two essential characteristics of revelation and of initiation?

The period between nine and twelve years of age, that of mature childhood, is the time for the study of the *Credo*. We have already shown how the Eucharistic liturgy is valuable as the concrete presentation of the *Credo* and the pedagogy of the *Credo* in action.

The catechesis received from the age of twelve on, during the periods of pre-adolescence and adolescence, should be the disclosure of the Christian meaning of the profane realities that force themselves on the attention of young people when they are first confronted with the great problems of life, and should lead to a commitment to serious and active Christian living. Here, again, it is in the course of a Eucharistic celebration that the adolescent should renew his baptismal promises, in the consciousness of what the three sacraments he has already received actually mean to him, the sacraments which he must live by. But, here also, this Christian teaching should be understood as a requirement of his Eucharistic life.

Thus, the Eucharistic liturgy should appear clearly as being the structure, the resource, the soul of all catechesis. The most valuable guide of the educator, it allows him to carry out his teaching in the atmosphere of the catechumenate. The children in our catechism classes have already been baptized, but they have to discover the riches of their baptism and to live by them. When they have been baptized, confirmed, and "Eucharized," they still have to become day by day more fully what they already are. Is this not the same progress as that of the catechumenate?

There is nothing novel in this point of view. *Nihil innovetur nisi quod traditum est.* All our proposals here are, in fact, in the line of the great catechetical and catechumenal tradition of the Church. (It is, undoubtedly, in order to bring together all the efforts of the present time to return to the catechumenal tradition of the Church that the word "catechism," now too narrowly associated with the explanation and memorization of a manual, has been replaced by the word "catechesis," which better expresses in Christian terminology a religious formation organically united with the Biblical and liturgical sources of doctrine.)

CONCLUSION

And now, to conclude with an answer to the objection always aroused by any study designed not only to convince but also to lead to action. *How to do it?*

It is obvious that it is difficult to carry out this program under the conditions actually obtaining in religious instruction today. The manuals that we have to use, like the techniques, are hardly oriented to such perspectives; the mentality of parents, like that of their children, is foreign to such a unified conception of Christian formation.

Yet we must not give way to discouragement. And so I shall conclude by making three positive recommendations:

1) Let us say, first of all, that the primary need is for us to change our own mentality. Having become aware of the deficiencies of a catechesis that does not sufficiently assure a true evangelization and a true entrance into the Church, we need first of all to take time to reflect and meditate. Let us not say too quickly that we agree and are convinced of all this but that it is impossible to do anything about it. Let us rather seek always to perceive more clearly the objective to be attained, and we shall then find the means to attain it. An effort to reflect is at the basis of all progress.

2) In the second place, we are suffering in our apostolate from a kind of divorce between education and pastoral care. Each of these two activities of the Church often seems to become a "Lone Ranger." Educators should arouse their pastoral spirit in order the better to integrate their educational action in a pastoral effort that forms one whole; pastors should not be content with administrating and directing, but should also become educators. One cannot be a catechist without being a pedagogue of liturgical initiation. One cannot be a celebrant of the Eucharist without appreciating the educative riches of this celebration. This effort to understand, to coordinate, to incorporate is one of the conclusions of this book.

3) And finally, the witness of a living parish community, the people of God on their pilgrimage to God, assembled about the Eucharist, is the condition of the success of our enterprise. It is in the parish community that the synthesis is realized, the synthesis of doctrine, Bible, liturgy which our catechesis is to demonstrate. For those under instruction, it is in the living parish community that doctrine becomes life; the Bible, the history of salvation; the liturgy, the deeds of Christ.

Let us not forget that in a world in which the secular *Credo* imposes its own ukases, the conscience of children is often profaned even before they hear the Word of God. Under these circumstances, only the force of a Christian witness that is both mature and powerful can remove this hard shell of paganism, can free souls from this domination and render them permeable to the message and the grace of God.

Meditative reflection and change of mentality, the coordinating of education with pastoral care, an adult Christian community—this is the environment necessary for the catechetical effort, the great lines of which we have attempted to describe here, taking into consideration also the stages necessary to bring this about in various concrete situations. May both Catholic children and catechumens under instruction for baptism soon benefit from our efforts. The signs of this renewal are now all around us. More than ever before, there is reason for hope.

Rev. Charles Moeller

CHAPTER 8

IS IT POSSIBLE, IN THE 20TH CENTURY, TO BE A "MAN OF THE BIBLE"?

THE QUESTION IS, perhaps, badly put. It is God who judges us, not we ourselves. His Word saves us, not man's. The problem is, therefore, not to find out *if* one can be a "man of the Bible," but *how* one can be. The only force capable of conforming us to the "man of the Bible" is the power of God. Only God can make us men *of God;* the real question is, therefore, what are the *human* preparations to be made in the Biblical and liturgical apostolate.

THE PROBLEM

The union between the Bible and the liturgy is intimate and indissoluble. It is not the secondary elements of the Bible that have been taken up into the liturgy, but its living heart, the history of salvation. It is not the peripheral aspects of the liturgy that are found in the Bible, but its very life-current, that proclamation of the Word which created the people of God as they heard it and were nourished by it. The "man of the Bible" is also the "man of the liturgy," as can be seen from three examples.[1]

[1] Other examples may be found in my book *Mentalité moderne et évangélisation,* coll. *Cabiers de Lumen Vitae,* n. VII, (Brussels, 1955), which attempts to analyze

Three Aspects of "The Man of the Bible"

Baptism implies the return of the baptized to paradise. The garlands of leaves and flowers adorning the baptistry of the Orthodox at Ravenna, the four rivers flowing from the mount on which stands the Lamb depicted in many Roman mosaics, symbolize the mountain of paradise.[2] Although the dialectic of baptismal faith orients us toward the eschatological coming of the Lord – for Christianity is no nostalgic "return" of "the exiled princess"[3] – nevertheless the bond with the paradise of the first Adam can never be broken.

The re-creation is certainly to be "still more wonderful" (*mirabilius reformasti*) than the first state of man (*mirabiliter condidisti*); the transfiguration accomplished by the redemption surpasses everything that man has heard, everything that he has seen or imagined, "everything that the heart of man could conceive," yet his roots in the Adamic past still remain, for the stuff of sacred history is all of one piece, and God does not destroy what He has created. To put it in another way, the dialectic that we shall frequently note in the course of our discussion, maintained between the Old and the New Testaments, never means that the Old Law is abolished; Jesus has not come to destroy, but to fulfill. The ritual of baptism, the blessing of the water, of the oil of catechumens, of holy chrism speak continually of the Adamic paradise.

Next, there can be no question of doing away with the exorcisms that fill the ritual and the blessings of the holy Triduum[4] as being embarassingly out of date. All liturgical functions proceed in the same way: the impure, satanic spirit is driven away to make place for the Holy Spirit, the Sanctifier; still better, it is the power of the Spirit that drives the demon away. Certain apologists would like to edit the texts and rites so as to relieve them of these "indications of a bygone past." But one cannot leave in obscurity this presence of demons which is taken for granted by the liturgy, any more than one can in the Gospel narrative.

contemporary states of mind in relation to Christ, Mary, the Church, but which brings out at the same time the Biblical and liturgical aspects of catechesis.

[2] Doubtless the golden cross surrounded with stars in the center of the cupola of certain baptistries indicates that paradise regained is not "behind us," but that it is merged with the regenerated universe, the new heaven and the new earth. In the same way, the octagonal shape of the majority of these buildings reminds us that the day of the resurrection, with which the baptized are mystically united, is "the eighth," that which has no evening, for it is fullness; but this "eighth day" is also the "first," the re-establishment in glory of the first creation. Cf. *Le jour de Seigneur,* ed. Robert Laffont, (Paris, 1948).

[3] I am here paraphrasing a text of J. Daniélou, *Espoirs humains et espérance chrétienne,* in *Atti del quarto convegno per la pace e la civiltà cristiana,* (Florence, 1956), p. 70. Here also (p. 64) can be found some considerations by the same author on the Greek term *nostos* (return), which is also at the root of the word *nostalgia.*

[4] See L. Bouyer, *The Paschal Mystery* (Chicago: H. Regnery, 1950) and by the same author, "The Two Economies of the Divine Government: Satan and Christ" in *God and Creation,* Vol. II of *The Theology Library* (Chicago: Fides, 1955).

The Spirit "drives" Jesus into the desert; Christ, the new Adam, refusing to obey the devil, wins a first victory over him, an antithesis of the defeat of the first man; the expulsions of demons narrated by the Gospel are wrought by the power of the Spirit. The sin against the Spirit is precisely to attribute to the prince of demons what is the work of the power of the Most High. If Jesus drove out demons, this was precisely the proof that "the kingdom has come among you." The hour of the passion is also that of "the prince of this world," for in the desert the devil left Christ "until the appointed time," that of Gethsemani and Calvary, as John and Luke both show; the resurrection is, therefore, victory over Satan.

To try to diminish the importance of this struggle in the life of the Lord would be to destroy its whole economy, to remove its very backbone. The same is true for Christian baptism: the victory over sin and death that we must win is *equally* a victory over the demon. The last request of the *Pater* certainly also means "deliver us from the Evil One."[5]

Finally, while we must turn our backs on any naive progressivism since the essential event of history has already taken place in the resurrection, we must give as precise a content as possible to this truth: "If Christ be not risen from the dead, then is our faith vain." The essentially paschal character of the whole liturgy has been emphasized in recent years, especially that of the Christian Sunday; we must "cry out with joy to the Lord." This is the major rediscovery of the first part of the twentieth century, given in germ in the decrees of St. Pius X and developed in those of Pius XII: it is time that all Christians be invited to the feast: *tempus erat dapibus, sodales*...! But it is still necessary that the guests know something about the feast in which they participate.

Doubtless, we can never have an adequate comprehension of this mystery; but we can and should strive to gain that rudimentary understanding which St. Paul refers to in speaking of *gnosis* and *epignosis*.[6]

[5] L. Bouyer, "Le problème du mal dans le christianisme antique," in *Dieu Vivant*, n. 6, (Paris, 1946), pp. 17-20.

[6] Bultmann tries to rediscover Christianity by putting in parentheses the historical reality of the resurrection and its content, which is said to be unintelligible to the man of the twentieth century; by doing this he destroys Christianity itself and substitutes for it a dialectic of moral decision which more nearly resembles a religious philosophy than a message of the living God. "Holy Week" is holy only because it culminates in the resurrection of the Savior.

On Bultmann, read L. Malevez, "Le message chrétien et le mythe," coll. *Museum Lessianum*, n. 51, (Paris, 1954); R. Mable, "Bultmann et l'interprétation du nouveau Testament," coll. *Théologie*, n. 33, (Paris, 1955); H. Duméry, *Philosophie de la religion*, t. II, (Paris, 1957), pp. 73-96 (on the resurrection), pp. 239-249 (on "demythization"); L. Malevez, "Exégèse biblique et philosophie," in *Nouvelle revue théologique*, 78 (1956), pp. 896-1042 (comparison between Barth and Bultmann). Bultmann's own work, "L'interprétation du nouveau Testament," coll. *Les religions*, n. 11, (Paris, 1955) contains the fundamental text, "Nouveau Testament et mythologie," pp. 139-183.

These Three Aspects Are As Many Obstacles

The reader of Sartre and Malraux, of Hegel and Merleau-Ponty; the "pagan" overcome with the sadness of purely sensual love described in the novels of Francoise Sagan; young people intoxicated with a belief in nature or with the idea of giving their whole being to help underdeveloped peoples; and finally, those who allow themselves to be fascinated by the mystique of Marxist efficiency — all these, who represent various aspects of modern man, if they wish to become "men of the Bible," must accept these three aspects of Biblical and liturgical man.

If they wish to be converted to the faith, they must accept their descent from Adam; they must realize that their deepest being, according to the divine likeness engraved therein by the Creator, cannot "develop" or "expand" except at the end of a struggle with Satan; finally, they must turn to the risen Christ who *is*, in His glorious humanity, *the Man*, not "classic" or "medieval" or "modern" man, but simply Man, that is to say, the keystone of the Bible and the liturgy.

Now these three aspects arouse in men of any age, and so also in modern men, a fundamental opposition, or, at least, an uneasiness which paralyzes religious commitment.

For how many Christians, even those whose education has been on the university level, is not the problem of human origins summed up in "the story of the apple"? The difficulty seems still more deep-rooted when we confront the vision given by the Bible and the liturgy — man as first "constituted" in a state of justice and holiness, later to fall (*in deterius commutatum*, says the Council of Trent) — with that of science, which, rightly or wrongly, discerns in human history an ascending line, at least in what is of the essence of man: from a state close to that of animals, man has raised himself to that of *homo faber* and then to that of *homo sapiens*.

This last state — if we must believe certain extrapolations, the scientific character of which is much under discussion — is growing progressively more profound in the universe, leading mankind to a state of concentration, of unity and of spiritual communion, the call to which was implicit from the beginning in the "human phenomenon." On the one hand, we have a fall, a "descent," followed by a re-ascending; on the other, an ascent which, so far as the fundamental line of evolution is concerned, is progressive and homogeneous, in such a way that if we can still see how Christ is the "Omega" of creation, it is hard to see how He can any longer be the "Alpha."[7]

[7] The attempt of Teilhard de Chardin, *Le phénomène humain*, (Paris, 1955), is well known. It was completed by *L'apparition de l'homme*, (Paris, 1956) and *La vision du passé*, (Paris, 1957). A good introduction to his thought is furnished by C. Tresmontant, *Pierre Teilhard de Chardin His Thought*, (Baltimore: Helicon Press, 1959); in an unfavorable sense, see A. Frank Duquesne, "De Schweitzer a Teilhard de Chardin," in *Construire*, 10 (1955), pp. 487-497.

One of the best commentaries on *Le phénomène humain* is that of D. Dubarle in *La Vie intellectuelle*, (March, 1956), pp. 6-25. The problems raised by this hypoth-

Similar difficulties arise concerning the devil.[8] Modern man is fascinated by all forms of the irrational; the devil, who passes for a master in such matters, greatly preoccupies him, if one can judge by the frequent use of such terms as "demonic," "demoniac," "satanic." At the same time, he is skeptical about the existence of the devil, for he would willingly agree with Valéry's Faust that men no longer need a devil in order to be damned, since they are the most wicked animals in creation and the most evil.

In a more general way, modern man attributes to psychic or physiological causes phenomena that the "ages of faith" attributed to the influence of the prince of darkness. In the Middle Ages it was thought, for example, that impure dreams and their physical consequences were due to "incubuses" or "succubuses," or again to "kobolds" who weighed down the breast of the sleeper to smother him in a spasm in which sensual pleasure and the agony of death would mingle. But today we know that these phenomena are quite normal; too frequent occurrence of them might call for some examination, but it would be that of the doctor, not of the confessor or exorcist. Yet the Church still has us sing in the Office of Compline: "*Hostem nostrum comprime, ne polluantur corpora* – Repress the power of the enemy, so that our bodies be not soiled."

Must we eliminate this strophe, certainly connected with these monastic terrors by which the twelfth century, as described by Emile Male, was haunted, but which we still find incredibly widespread in the milieu of the monks of Athos? Or should we recite this text and put in a kind of parentheses the words that displease us, or "transpose" them or "adapt" them, as we are fond of saying? Or again, how can we take seriously the belief, affirmed in many passages of the Bible and in some important liturgical texts, concerning the presence of devils in water? Is it possible seriously to believe this, for example, in connection with the bathing and swimming so widespread today, all of which are not, I imagine, "satanic pleasures"?

And, finally, a last example which sums up the preceding by generalizing them: the book devoted by the *Etudes Carmélitaines* to *Satan* is a witness, probably involuntary, to this dualism between the "Satan of psychology" which is discussed in a remarkable series of medical, literary, and artistic studies, and the "Satan of theology" who

esis (which is a bold extrapolation) are, from the theological point of view, the following: In this perspective, is there a place for the initial "break"? Where can be placed the final, eschatological "break"? Is not the liberty of the person practically subsumed and absorbed by this kind of "physics of the spirit," which is the essence of the system? Furthermore, as L. Malevez remarks in "La méthode du P. Teilhard de Chardin et la phénoménologie," in *Nouvelle Revue théologique,* 79, (1957), pp. 579-599, there is a marked antithesis between the vision of the phenomenologists (freedom, the risk inherent in the human adventure) and the evolutionistic optimism of Fr. Teilhard; in this last article, on p. 579, a more complete bibliography will be found.

[8] Cf. my article "Réflexion en marge du 'Satan' des Études carmélitaines," in *Collectanea mechliniensia,* 19 (1949), pp. 191-203, used as the introduction to the English edition of *Satan* (New York: Sheed & Ward, 1952).

can easily be pushed back among the imaginative myths created by a "primitive mentality." Doubtless, the psychological facts must be analyzed; the problem must be posed, but I fear that this book does not contribute to clarifying it.[9] Yet, how can a modern man participate wholeheartedly in the baptismal ceremonies or how can he live the Easter Vigil with his whole being, if there remains in him any uneasiness, any hesitation concerning the reality of this devil who, as the whole liturgy declares, has been vanquished by the resurrection of Christ?

I have myself verified the fact of this uneasiness. During the academic year 1956-57, I devoted a course to the resurrection, not as a fundamental point of apologetics for our faith in the divinity of Jesus, but as a "mystery of salvation." And I soon observed that my audience, composed for the most part of student assistants in medical laboratories, were not following me at all. The problem raised by the ignoring of the mystery of the resurrection both in religious instruction and in Christian living apparently did not strike them. (And here I am anticipating my third and last example.) And my developments of the work of redemption as a victory over death and the devil seemed to them to depict some mythological combat, absolutely unreal; all this, which still forms the heart of the paschal mystery, remained completely closed to them.

Now it is not permissible to surround the deeds of the Savior with a more or less prudent skepticism, limiting ourselves to only those passages of the Gospel that are immediately accessible – or at least are believed to be – to twentieth-century man. If the Synoptics distinguish Christ's works of healing from His exorcisms, it is because they attribute to Him a singularly acute power of "discernment of spirits"; to say that sickness alone really exists would be to state that Jesus was deceived on a point, the importance of which we have already mentioned. And to say that the Church should also shade discreetly, or even hide in her storehouse and never bring out again, the texts of her exorcisms, would be to attribute to the Spouse of Christ a possibility of error in a matter in which her power is one which the Savior Himself communicated to her.

Everything is all of one piece: the life of Jesus, His messianic mission, His resurrection, Christian baptism, the paschal liturgy, all presuppose a struggle with the Evil One and a complete victory over him.

Concerning the resurrection itself, with its corollaries, the ascension and the outpouring of the Spirit, the reaction of a pious Christian lady,

[9] *Satan,* in *Études carmélitaines,* (Paris-Brussels, 1948). This work is extraordinarily interesting; it should have finally presented a synthesis which would at least sketch out this meeting between psychology and theology; but from every other point of view one can only rejoice in this courageous effort that the *Études carmélitaines* have been carrying on for several years to inaugurate the necessary dialogue between modern science, especially of the psychological order, and theology, especially of the mystical order. (The English edition omits some of the essays included in the French, and includes some other essays; the introduction by Fr. Moeller helps to remedy the defect noted above. *Trans. note*).

recounted to me by her pastor, will save me any lengthy commentary. When this good lady on her deathbed heard her pastor say: "And consider, my child, that you are going to rise with Christ," she answered quickly: "Don't bother me with all that, Father." Then, after a moment's silence, she added: "Obviously Christ had to rise from the dead; He merited it after His suffering and death on the Cross; but as for me, what need have I to rise again? What is important to me is that my soul should be saved and be as soon as possible with the good God; the resurrection of my body would add nothing to this."[10]

Approaching a Solution

Our problem is that of every age. The threefold procedure which I am about to sketch – to *believe and proclaim* the Word that saves, but also to *distinguish* the various kinds of obstacles that keep us apart from it, and to *explain* it profoundly so as to reach man in his most fundamental vocation – has been gone through in each historic era. What was done by the Fathers of the Church – and they have a privileged position here, which is the reason why they are read in the Breviary – has been continued by theologians; the fortunes and misfortunes of theology should not make us forget its essential mission. We should not, therefore, think of the present age as being any more removed from the Bible than any other, nor, on the contrary, as being particularly close to it; in any time, good or bad, the obstacles and the stepping-stones are more or less equal.

To regain our belief in the effectiveness of the Bible and the liturgy and so truly to proclaim the Word that saves.

We need, first of all, to believe in the effectiveness of the Word of God precisely because it is the Word *of God;* the words of Karl Barth, "The preaching of the Word of God is itself the Word *of God,*" "*praedicatio verbi Dei est ipsum Verbum Dei,*" are in point here.[11] But I am acquainted with priests, and they are not among the least eminent, who certainly know that the Bible is the Word of God and that the liturgy is one of the privileged proclamations of the Church; when necessary, they say as much in their answers to questions or when their instruction outline leads them to speak of the Bible once a year in their Sunday preaching; but I fear that these same apostolic men do not sufficiently believe in the Bible on the practical level.

They prefer humorously but skeptically to "your old Bible" to those of their colleagues who extol it as useful in the presentation of the Christian message – as, for example, in presenting this message to visitors at some great exposition. When the question comes up of how best to

[10] Cf. the excellent book by F. -X. Durrwell, *La résurrection de Jésus mystère de salut,* 2nd ed., (Le Puy-Paris, 1954); cf. also P. de Haes, "La résurrection de Jésus dans l'apologétique des cinquante dernières années," coll. *Analecta Gregoriana,* vol. 59, (Rome, 1953), and the excellent study by K. Rahner, "Auferstehung des Fleisches" in *Schriften zur Theologie,* t. II, (Einsiedeln, 1955), pp. 221-227.

[11] Cf. my article "Prédication de la Parole et oecuménisme," in *Irenikon,* 25, (1951), pp. 313-344.

give a concrete image of human anguish, such men would prefer to exhibit the more than life-size photograph of a young woman at the wheel of a luxurious Jaguar, dreamy-eyed, smoking a cigarette, one hand on the half-opened door – in a word, a kind of *"Bonjour Tristesse."*

Although the Book of Proverbs might inspire various images along the same lines, I would prefer a good reproduction of a fresco or a picture representing the expulsion of Adam and Eve from paradise, or perhaps, since Christian hope goes beyond anguish, an image of Abraham leaving Ur of the Chaldees; for I am afraid that the young lady with the cigarette would not strike the man in the street very much more than would the covers of some sporting magazine or *True Romances*.

And there are priests who do not believe any more firmly, at least on the practical level and even when "adapted to the people," as they say—those poor "good people" whom we would so often saddle with the burden of our laziness and our routine ways of thinking – in the instructive force of the liturgy when it is celebrated as it should be.

It was once suggested that to help people understand that the resurrection is not merely a past event, an apologetic argument, but the present reality of the glorious Christ in whom and also by whom we believe and are saved from death, a photographic montage be made representing the risen Christ, with a paschal candle in the same vertical line but a little higher, and the whole framed with small pictures representing various aspects of the Easter Vigil and the Mass. This project was turned down, because, it was stated before any serious experiments had been made, that the symbolism of the paschal candle was out of date, at least so far as its effectiveness for the man of today was concerned, whether farmer or city worker. And it was said that in any case such a photographic montage would be a meaningless puzzle.

The objectors had forgotten two things: first, the man in the street is much more skillful at deciphering such "composed" photographs than nine-tenths of the clergy, who, since they seldom frequent bars, small restaurants, night clubs and the like, are not in a position to unravel the complexities of such "non-sulpician" art; and secondly, that the symbol of the paschal candle may be out of date, but if so, then the Easter Vigil is out of date also, since it is all carried out around the candle as the center of the action, in the middle of the choir.

But no, it was considered preferable to run no risk of forcing the millions of visitors to the exhibition to ask one another questions about the pictures or to search for the meaning – better to inspire them with something "modern" along the lines of exhibits put on by manufacturers of ceramics; better for the visitors to find themselves in the familiar atmosphere of a kind of Christian bargain-basement than in the unfamiliar landscape of Biblical imagery.

Such mistrust too easily passes for down-to-earth realism or worldly wisdom; it is more widespread than one would think possible; it is a younger brother to that craze, now fortunately extinct, for replacing certain Biblical symbols with objects taken from the world of machinery:

tractors instead of sheaves of wheat; a radio tube instead of the flame of a candle. Why not, then, instead of a composed photograph showing, around the hand of God reaching toward the hand of man as painted by Michelangelo, the splendor of the world from nebulae to the flowers of the field, from mountains to the faces of newborn children — why not, instead of such a picture, simply present a real "life-size" aquarium?

The reader will put into my examples, where necessary, the required grain of salt. And there are exceptions: for example, a brochure published by the J.O.C. of Brussels for their world conference in Rome. In the center of a page meant to show in concrete form the hopes of men and also their sufferings and trials is a reproduction of Michelangelo's Jeremias. The editors of this brochure certainly wanted to be "popular," at least I presume they did, for if the "good people" were not the readers that these pages had in view, then one would have to look for them in the moon. Yet these editors did not think that an image taken from the "old Bible" would, because of its lack of modernity, escape the understanding of the thousands of young workingmen to whom this brochure was addressed.

If I have pushed this point a little too far and not brought out very clearly as yet the nuances of which I spoke, it is because everything else comes down to this same question. Pastors who have celebrated the liturgy with care and fidelity, preparing for it with the same care, the same faith, and the same love that they would put into the production of a play, know its supreme effectiveness. Here the drama is sacred; it is real; it contains what it represents and communicates it. The "backstage" of this "religious theatre" is no damp, chilly, slippery little alley from which we are, as it were, separated and protected by the tawdry finery of the actors, the lights, the tatters and boards of the theatre as summoned up by Kafka; it is the power of the living God raising us from our spiritual death.

Those who have prepared their voices by learning how to read well — we must neither declaim nor weaken the Word of God, but proclaim it — those who have trained their voices to sing the supple and living chant, those who have accustomed their bodies to carry out the hieratic gestures which are just as much a language as are words, which are themselves "words" to understand, texts to decipher, to spell out, to read; those who have with their whole being made ready for and lived an Easter Vigil know how truly the liturgy is the Word of God, efficacious, "converting" hearts, piercing like a sword even to the division of soul and spirit.

To Distinguish Among the Obstacles

Next, it is important to distinguish from one another the three kinds of obstacles that present themselves; many mistakes would be avoided if care were taken to exert our efforts in the right direction here.

The first obstacle is that of the "*man according to the flesh,*" "who can understand nothing of the things of the Spirit." If, for instance, a man thinks of himself as "without father or mother," if he wishes to find his greatness in launching defiance at a universe that he declares absurd, as Malraux believes; if human truth consists in the arbitrary choice of a liberty that is radically autonomous, left to its own choice alone, with no transcendent reference to a divine absolute, as Sartre believes,[12] this is a new form of the will to make oneself God without God, to "will infinitely without willing the Infinite," as Blondel says.

To this attitude there is no answer except, "Not to us, O Lord, not to us, but to Thy Name give glory."[13] In the same way, if one denies the sacredness of the universe in which we live and which we are transforming,[14] if the primacy accorded to technique is radical to the point of excluding all forms of symbolism, the way is closed to the world of the Bible.[15] To the extent, therefore, to which men of the twentieth century pretend to identify themselves purely and simply with its technical achievements and with its radically autonomous and anarchic idea of liberty, they close the way to becoming "men of the Bible." To accept being transformed into such a man is to be converted; it is to cause the "old man" to die.

Here the Word judges us; it causes the vein of our "unutterable personal absurdity" to show itself in order to fill us with the power of God, that God whose service is a royal rule, *cui servire regnare est,* according to the phrase of the liturgy.

But there are also obstacles arising from the *difference between two modes of thought and expression,* both of which seem legitimate, but

[12] Cf. "La foi en Jésus-Christ," in my essay *Littérature du XX siècle et christianisme,* t. II, (Paris-Tournai, 1957), 5th ed., the study on Sartre; in t. III "Espoir des hommes," 3rd ed., (Paris-Tournai, 1958), the study on Malraux.

[13] This attitude does not imply passivity in the bad sense; nor does it presuppose that the existence of God reduces human history to a "commentary" or a "thanksgiving" of a submissive and infantile sort, as A. Camus seems to think in *The Fall* (New York: Knopf, 1957). H. Duméry, in *Philosophie de la religion,* Vol. I, (Paris, 1957), pp. 50-91, tries to show that the liberty of man remains intact (conscience, as described by phenomenology, is "act-law," this last term being made up by the author), for God is beyond determinations and essences; He is "trans-ordinal" (on this view, which attempts a synthesis between Biblical materials and a very Dionysian theodicy, see, by the same author, *Le problème de Dieu en philosophie de religion,* (Paris-Brussels, 1957), especially chapters III and IV; this last work is practically the first part of *La Philosophie de la religion*).

Duméry's work perhaps pushes too far the use of purely philosophical reflection on the categories of Biblical thought; one frequently has the impression that he neglects the privileged character of revealed images, implying, in certain cases, the transcending of the human spirit by the mystery of the living God; in other words, the reaction against the insistence on emphasizing the "Semitic" aspect of revelation often goes to extremes along the lines of a "Hellenization" which is equally dangerous; but this does not prevent this book from raising very clearly some of the problems sketched in this essay; it is for this reason that I give some references.

[14] The fact that man can "transform" the universe, and, in this sense, dominate it, implies in no way that it thereby loses its sacred character; it is only the hypertrophy of technology that causes this aspect of reality to be lost to view; cf. H. Duméry, *op. cit.,* pp. 114-130.

[15] The religious sense is founded on the certitude of the presence of a "second" reality in what we see, hear, breathe or touch, giving them a mysterious significance. This sense of the sacred has nothing to do with the affirmation that there exists somehow in a kind of "metaphysical heaven," an "intelligible duplicate," an invisible duplicate of this world; it is a question of the same reality, unique, known by science or philosophy, but *also* illuminated by a significance wholly projected on the real and rediscovered

which seem hard to reconcile – if one even should or could do so; carried to its conclusion, this "difference" can become real opposition.

Here we face the problem of the "categories" of Semitic thought, which are distinguished today in a way that is probably exaggerated from those of "Hellenistic" thought.[16] This age-old dialogue is conveniently defined by the words Athens and Jerusalem, chosen by Léon Chestov as the title of a famous essay. Let us say from now on that we must no longer separate and oppose, but rather *distinguish in order to unite;* this is, if I am not mistaken, one of the meanings of those celebrated words of Pius XI: "We have to remake ourselves spiritually as Semites." These terms indicate the following twofold course of action, while they allow us to express various shades of meaning in the words, "man of the Bible."

First, to the extent to which the New Testament is rooted in the Old,[17] it is necessary to disengage the "originalities" of *Hebraic thought.*[18] Thus the psychology and, consequently, the anthropology of the Old Testament ignore all dualism: the word "flesh" (*basar*) does not mean the

in it. These terms, familiar to modern phenomenology, simply mean to say that the sense of the sacred is nothing other than a new dimension that illuminates the visible world and orients human vision toward the transcendent God.

Who does not see that the liturgy is nothing other than the "sacrament" of the divine Word in gestures, colors, sounds? The idea that Malraux has made up of Christian art is an example of narrowness due to agnosticism: he sees art as sacred; but, since there is no God, no "land of promise" to journey to, the sacredness of art is identified for him with the defiance launched at an absurd world; hope also is defiance, accusation of the world. It is true, certainly, that it is man who unveils the sacred character of the universe, since he is greater than the world, but while it is he who projects this sacred aspect on the world, he discovers it at the same time; on all this, see H. Duméry, *op. cit.*

[16] Here are some titles: O. Quick, *The Gospel of Divine Action,* (London, 1933); A. Festugière, *L'idéal religieux des Grecs et l'évangile,* (Paris, 1932); K. Prumm, *Christentum als Neuheitserlebnis,* (Freiburg, 1939); C. Tresmontant, *Essai sur la pensée hébraïque,* (Paris, 1953) and *Études de métaphysique biblique,* (Paris, 1955); E. Rust, *Nature and Man in Biblical Thought,* (London: Lutterworth Press, 1953); T. Boman, *Das hebraïsche Denken im Vergleich mit dem griechischen,* (Goettingen, 1954); J. Hessen, *Griechische oder biblische Theologie,* (Leipzig, 1956); G. Azou, *La parole de Dieu,* (Paris, 1956); P. Christian, "Humanisme occidental et pensée judéo-chrétienne," in *La Revue nouvelle,* 24, (1956); J. Giblet, "Orientations de la pensée biblique," in *La Revue nouvelle,* 24 (1956); H. Duméry, *Philosophie de la religion,* v. II, p. 92, n. 4 (this long note contains some important comments).

Having rather exaggeratedly "hellenized" with the generation of Reitsenstein, today we are "judaizing" perhaps a little too much; the Old Testament itself "hellenizes" in certain parts; Palestine at the time of Jesus was permeated with Alexandrine influences. The problem indicated here should be dealt with in two ways: first to bring out in theology and in catechesis the originality of Hebraic thought; then to study more closely the problem of the connections between the two types of thought. Let us not forget that the first scholar to bring out the contrasts between these two types of thought was R. Bultmann in *Das Urchristentum im Rahmen der antiken Religionen,* (Zurich, 1949), and earlier in *Die Geschichte der synoptischen Tradition,* (Goettingen, 1921).

[17] See L. Bouyer, *The Meaning of Sacred Scripture,* (Notre Dame Univ. Press, 1958) and *Liturgical Piety,* (Notre Dame Univ. Press, 1954); Anglican theologians, whose work Fr. Bouyer knows well, have often brought out this continuity.

[18] The question is that of distinguishing the *categories of thought* implied by the Biblical texts from *revelation* properly so called, which makes use of these categories but always goes beyond them; this does not mean that this revelation can be *separated* from the Semitic vehicle of which it makes use.

body (for which there is no word in Hebrew), but the whole created being ("body and soul," if we are thinking of man as envisaged by our Hellenistic way of thinking) in his basic weakness, both ontological and moral, before the living God; the word "spirit," then, does not mean primarily something which is discarnate, but life in its aspect of power, which exists supremely in the living God, the Lord of "spirits" and of all "flesh."[19]

Furthermore, the vision of the Bible gives value to historic time. While Hellenistic thought (as also that of many religious systems of philosophy outside of the Judeo-Christian tradition) seeks to save man from the cycle of the eternal recommencement of time, Biblical man knows that history has a meaning, is oriented toward the realization of the kingdom, for this history is *holy.* God has "entered" it, never to leave it, for by it is realized the design of salvation. From this point of view, creation is the first stage in the history of the covenant, just as, inversely, the new covenant of which Jeremias speaks is also a re-creation.[20]

This very fact indicates another essential aspect of Biblical Semitism, typology: the events of the history of salvation are types of a divine action which, in a manner always similar but also progressively more profound, saves His people from situations which, humanly, are equivalent to death, but which the power of the Lord transforms into instruments of liberation.[21] This is why the deluge, the exodus, the passage of the Red Sea, the crossing of the Jordan, the exile in Babylon, as types of the action of God upon His people, have been taken in a definitive way into the Christian liturgy.

And, finally, certain peculiarities of Hebraic style – parallelism, the parable genre, accounts which seem to make the role of secondary causes evaporate into thin air, a language that is concrete and dynamic (every Hebrew verb expresses a movement, an act; the "word," *dabar,* is a reality, a creative force), as also, and perhaps above all, the literary genres of which we are going to speak at greater length – are enough to indicate the originality of this vision.

The ancients, Celsus, for example, called this originality barbaric; a spirit formed by Greek culture could not admit that God had "entered"

[19] Cf. P. van Imschoot, Théologie de l'ancien Testament, coll. *Bibl. de théologie,* III series, v. 4, *L'homme,* (Paris, 1956); and E. Jacob, *Theology of the Old Testament,* (New York: Harpers, 1958). As I shall show further on, the term "spiritual life" too often connotes the idea of a "discarnate" life, while it really means a life that is, above all, interiority, certainly, but incarnated (projected, structured, as phenomenology would say) in a condition of life become, in the spirit, participative in the power of God.

[20] E. Jacob, *op. cit.;* this point of view must be harmonized with that of the complement *time-eternity* which also underlies the Biblical scheme of things: creation and the covenant lead man to the eternal; they manifest the eternal in the temporal. (H. Duméry in *Philosophie de la Religion,* v. I, pp. 131-138, carries the philosophic transposition too far.)

[21] J. Daniélou in *The Lord of History,* (Chicago: Regnery, 1958) shows clearly how allegorism (of a dimension mainly vertical) and typology are quite different things. See also C. Charlier, *The Christian Approach to the Bible,* (Westminster, Md.: Newman, 1959).

into history and that the "flesh" could rise again.[22] Here we see a dividing line, a parting of the waters in universal religious thought.

On one side there are the religious systems centered on the repetition of (always identical) phenomena, of which "myths" are the "pseudo-history"; they preach release or the return to primitive indetermination; all the heretical gnoses, whether dualistic or monistic, finally, do away with time and ignore any "sacred history."[23] On the other, there is the Judeo-Christian tradition, according to which the world created by God is the place in which a hope is being realized; the "*cosmos*" exists for the "*chronos*," for the time of God;[24] the incarnation of the Word in human flesh represents the climax of this historic pedagogy. The greatest originality of Hebraic thought culminates in the "scandal" of the incarnation.[25]

Yet the "Platonism of the Fathers" and the Aristotelianism of St. Thomas Aquinas show that there are secret paths facilitating the dialogue

[22] In this connection, we must certainly be on guard against a naive realism which would purely and simply project into the divine reality the spatio-temporal images implied in the Biblical themes which I have just mentioned; through "temporal" history, it is, finally, the union with the eternal God that is realized. But man is an incarnate being in a world, a place, a time, a history; he expresses himself on all the levels of his consciousness: psychology, imagination, ritual and social institution, and, finally, history (to say nothing of the "conceptual" level to which all theologies strive to raise themselves).

Moreover, the vision of the eternal divine does not imply the rejection of these concrete "projections"; there can be no question of leaving them aside once the eternal vision is attained; they cannot be considered as mere scaffolding to be destroyed when the house is built. Man is primarily an "incarnate consciousness" — the vocabulary of phenomenology here comes rather near to the Biblical vision. His religious life can never be released from these roots in the concrete material world willed by God, so that he can raise himself into a purely a-temporal heaven of metaphysics; it is always in time and through time that He is reached whom the Bible calls the Eternal, the Lord of hosts.

Furthermore, the Biblical images are privileged by reason of divine revelation; they are not, as it were, illustrations of purely human origin, the value of which would be more or less interchangeable from the moment that their end was attained; they are eternal *types* of God's action, symbols whose choice was aided by inspiration. In a word, the vision of the Old Testament — and therefore, that of the New to the extent to which it is rooted in the Old — is to be safeguarded because it is guaranteed by the special protection of the revealing God granted to the sacred writers.

Of course, as the third series of obstacles shows, we must not put on the same level all the literary procedures of the Bible. But, according to their basic viewpoint, according to their permanent centre of gravity, easily recognizable, the originality of Semitic thought is to be respected. Here should be read the celebrated text of Celsus, with a pertinent commentary, in de Labriolle, *La réaction païenne,* (Paris, 1942), pp. 117-126.

[23] On the content of the gnostic manuscripts recently discovered at Nag-Hammadi, see J. Doresse, "Les gnostiques d'Égypte," in *La table ronde,* n. 107, (Nov. 1956), which gives a good *orientation;* one can see here clearly the antithesis between the Judeo-Christian tradition and that of the gnoses on these points (in the "gnosis" of certain texts of Qumran, the dualism comes from Iran; cf. J. Daniélou, *The Dead Sea Scrolls and Primitive Christianity,* (Baltimore: Helicon Press, 1958).

[24] H. Azou, *La parole de Dieu,* (Paris, 1956), pp. 161-162.

[25] And therefore in the "scandal" of the resurrection; cf. in L. Cerfaux, *Christ in the Theology of St. Paul,* (New York: Herder & Herder, 1959) the wonderful pages on the Greek opposition to the message of the resurrection. When "Hellenistic" thought pretends to be exclusive of any other mentality and, consequently, of religion, when it is hardened to the point of not being willing to recognize its natural incapacity not only to discover but to understand the incorporation of the plan of salvation in human history, then it unites with the pride of the "carnal" man and thus becomes an obstacle

between Athens and Jerusalem. If we must distinguish, then, we must also "unite."[26] We may remind ourselves continually that the Hebrew way of thinking knew "nothing about purely material realities, that it did not separate the visible from the invisible world, that the man of the Bible is a person united with other persons in an active commitment and that his God is Someone to be listened to";[27] but we must also discover the possible harmonies with the philosophy and the humanism that still make up a good part of the classic education of the West.[28]

Secondly, we must remake ourselves as Semites, but we must do so *spiritually*. The words "man of the Bible" do not only mean the humanity that God educated progressively in the course of the old economy; they signify also, and above all, the man who has appeared in Jesus, born from on high, "of water and the Spirit," according to the *new* Law.

In Jesus, the economy of salvation has passed from the flesh to the spirit; it has put off everything in it which attached it too closely to a particular physical ancestry, that of Abraham, brought about by physical

of the first kind we have mentioned, that which the Biblico-liturgical Word has to break up by its power of converting.

I should add that all purely human thought (including the Semitic vision insofar as it is a *thought* of man) which pretends to stretch on the Procustean bed of its *natural* categories the unimaginable fact of the incarnation of God in history, condemns itself by that very fact; Semitic thought, cut off from the light of revelation, becomes ingrown as a purely earthly messianism, which becomes, finally, idolatrous — the various "millenarianisms" of history are a degradation of theological thought on the level of a "carnal" Judaism, prisoner of space and time; "Greek" thought, pretending to be self-sufficient, lacks the discovery of the central event in the history of the world, God amongst us. The majority of heresies have not had very different causes.

[26] H. U. von Balthasar, in Chapter 3 of this book, states that the maturation of Greek thought along the lines of the discovery of the notion of being was providentially willed by God as a necessary stage in the understanding of the mystery of the incarnation.

[27] H. Azou, *op. cit.*, pp. 161-163.

[28] The ancient civilizations in which we instruct school-children are reduced more or less to two, the Greek and the Roman, to the neglect of the third, here the most important, the study of which was united with these others until the sixteenth century — the Hebrew. Young people must be familiarized with Biblical history at least as much as with the *Iliad* and the *Odyssey* — about which, in any case, if things continue in the present direction, they will no longer know anything in two or three decades. By "Biblical history" I mean, not a collection of isolated anecdotes the miraculous character of which can hardly be distinguished from that of fairy stories, but the history of that divine pedagogy, traced out more and more clearly in a *real* history, running parallel to, but also interwoven with, that of the Near Eastern Greek and the Latin West.

Children must enter fully into this sacred realm. If the teaching of the plastic arts, architecture, sculpture, painting is brought in, by way of surplus, to illustrate this dialogue of the two Testaments, for example by the study of early Christian painting and sculpture in which, continually, the figures of the Old Law are contrasted with those of the New, harmony in distinction, and also unity, can more easily be brought about between Athens and Jerusalem; we shall see fewer little "part-pagans" divided between the humility of the crucifixion, taught in sermons, and various kinds of Christian humanism, from that of the "muscular Catholic" to that of the person fascinated by the dream of a "Christian communism."

While I cannot develop or modify this idea here, yet mav I say that I believe that such an enlargement of academic formation is necessary, is *most urgent.* My essay "Bible et humanisme," in *La Bible et le prêtre,* coll. *Études de pastorale,* n. 5, (Louvain, 1951) gives a series of concrete examples drawn from the climate of the Greco-Latin humanities.

generation and by circumcision, not of the heart but of the body, to use St. Paul's words. It has transcended everything that would risk its being imprisoned in any particular culture, however privileged, in any country, even the "land of promise"; the economy of salvation has in Christ become universal, "catholic"; for "there are no longer either Jews or Gentiles, Greeks or barbarians, but all are one," and this is the "freedom with which Christ has set us free." In Him, all cultures are called to be evangelized; all, in a sense mysteriously willed by God, can aid men the better to understand something of the mystery of salvation.

One most remarkable indication of this fact, I think, is the sovereign liberty with which the writers of the New Testament used one or another form of culture. Christianity is, from this point of view, a crossroads of cultures; this aspect of being a meeting-place, a kind of estuary where sharply contrasting cultural visions flow into one another, already realizes something of that uniting which, as we have said, is as important as distinguishing between Athens and Jerusalem.[29] We should, therefore, emphasize not one or another type of thought, Semitic or Greek – or Persian, Babylonian, Egyptian – but God's sovereign freedom in using them; the final word here is the risen Christ who "makes all things new."[30]

A twofold dialectic, then, begins to be indicated: of integration and of transcendence. Of *integration* first, because we can never reject the Old Testament; the history of Israel is our own because the still imperfect phase which it represents is not located in the bygone past, but, on the contrary, is one level – inferior, no doubt, but indispensable here on earth – of our own spiritual edifice.[31] At every moment mankind must be going from the flesh to the spirit, from the race born of the flesh (in the Biblical sense) to the new birth; thus initiation into Biblical thinking remains indispensable. Marcionism is always a heresy. So long as we are pilgrims to the kingdom, we are the Israel of God – Israel according to the spirit, certainly, but still Israel.

And then, transcendence, or, better, *transfiguration*.[32] We must ceaselessly continue to enter into the liberty of the children of God; we must, with St. Paul, make the painful transition from a vision too narrowly Judaic to the discovery of justification in faith and in the Spirit, renewing us "day by day to the image of our Creator." Thus we rejoin the first Adam; we find in the Old Law what goes beyond it and rejoins its universal design, man, the image of God, before and beyond the

[29] St. Paul, for example, in explaining baptism contrasts it with circumcision when he is speaking to Jews, compares it to illumination when he is speaking to Greeks, and identifies it with the rite of immersion in the Jordan, symbol of the death and resurrection of the Lord, when he is speaking to neophytes. In other words, according to the New Law, the major originality of the inspired Word is precisely to be "new," designed from the outset to go beyond everything that we call "categories of thought."

[30] The synthesis of the two types of thought is not syncretization (like Huxley's); in his case the residue that comes out of the mixer is impersonal and adogmatic; Biblical symbolism is, on the contrary, always historical and personal.

[31] Alain, *Histoire des me pensées*, 5th ed., (Paris, 1936), p. 294.

[32] The term "transcendence" should be understood in the sense of the paschal "passing-over," not in the sense of something beyond all formulations.

promise made to Abraham. The man of the Bible, then, is in tension between an Old Testament pole and a transcendent one, that of the Pasch; this man, according to the promise of the Old Law, according to its realization in the Lord, the Master of the new economy, is our judge.

In addition to the obstacle of the "man according to the flesh" and that set up by different modes of thought, there is a *third series* of *seeming and unnecessary obstacles* which negligence and routine, and ignorance as well, have heaped up in our path.

We cannot ignore the essential fact of *how the books of the Bible were composed.* For example, when the existence of at least two documents (J and P) put together in the Pentateuch is explained, many false problems vanish; the only elements common to the two (or three) documents are, in fact, positively pointed out by the sacred writer. Or again, the framework of the six days of creation served the purpose of inculcating among the Jews (and indirectly among Christians) respect for the weekly day of rest; but the essential truths stated here in Genesis concern the creation of the whole universe, "matter and spirit," space and time (the *ta panta* of St. Paul) by the all-powerful Word of God. In the same way, what is stated in Exodus is the reality of the great prodigies connected with the going-out from Egypt under Moses, and not the exact number of "ten" plagues, no more and no less.

Certainly we cannot eliminate the literary framework of each of these documents, the symbolism of the garden of paradise, of the four rivers, and many others, since they are at the origin of a whole theological and iconographical tradition; but we must arrive at the *meaning* of these images and these accounts.

And then, we must remember to take into account the various *literary genres* used in the Bible. Judith, Tobias, Esther certainly seem to belong to the class of "inspired romances"; the apocalyptic writings obey very precise literary laws, and we need to understand clearly the bearing of images, such as those of the heavens rolled up like a book or of the stars falling down to earth; St. Augustine gives us an example of this. In the same way, we have no right to put the trumpets of Jericho, Josue causing the sun to stand still, the shadow going back on the sundial, etc., on the same level as the course of the history of salvation, the great prophetic vision of the deliverance from the Babylonian captivity as a second Exodus, the image and the foreshadowing of the paschal "passage" of Jesus in our midst.

Without speaking of "de-mythization," (for Bultmann seems to forget that the message of Christ always comes to us enveloped in human representations – inspired, doubtless, but this fact does not change their nature –) we must classify the sacred texts according to their literary genres, we must "take the shell off," to use a happy phrase of Msgr. Chevrot's, in order to find the transcendent meaning.[33] Although, for

[33] May I take this occasion to thank Monsignor Chevrot for the valuable remarks he kindly made to me on this theme.

example, the geocentric representation of the universe is that of the Bible (as well as the most spontaneous for the imagination of men of all ages), it is in no way guaranteed by revelation or bound up with the essential truths of revelation: "heaven," "the ascension," Satan "thrown down into the depths" and present in the "waters of the great abyss," etc. – all this and much besides must be explained by taking into account the heliocentric vision of antiquity.[34]

And, finally, we must keep before our eyes the fact of the progress of revelation from the Old Testament to the New: the practice of *herem;* a conception of the sacred which is sometimes very formalistic as, for example, in the episode of Ozias touching the Ark; polygamy; the very "human" desire to be avenged on the enemies of God (who are also our enemies) – all this and many other phenomena are an imperfect phase in the history of the people of God. To forget that the purpose of revelation is precisely to teach us how God uses "the things that are not, the weak, the unworthy, the despised," how He makes use of our weaknesses to mould this lumpish human material, to cause it to "rise" by the leavening of the Word, to lead it progressively to form the new man: to forget all this would be to miss the dynamism of the Bible seen as a whole.

We must get rid of those little books of Bible stories which go from Esau and Jacob to Joseph sold by his brothers, from there to David and Goliath by way of Samson and his jawbone of an ass, to end with Jonas swallowed by the whale. Nine-tenths of the "ineptitudes" with which Krouchtchev, for instance, taxes the Bible and which have caused millions of working-people to lose their faith, so easy is it to spread propaganda on this point, are found in this third category of obstacles.

The theologians have already said all this in the silence of their studies and even in congresses and conferences; but nine-tenths of those who take part in our Latin liturgy are still no further along than the Bible of Ecker (even revised) and are deeply troubled by the fog that surrounds them. The people want from their priests, far more than the organization of "dramatic" and "musical" concerts or the setting-up of various activities, enlightenment on these questions. The continuous reading of the Bible in parish services would provide a convenient opportunity for affording such enlightenment; the homily could be given along the lines of such explanations.

Certainly, the story of that hermit in the Egyptian desert who believed that God was a sort of an august old man with an enormous beard and white hair, and who was very much upset when he was told that God was "incorporeal," shows that we must go about this work with prudence and indulgence; but there are too many impertinent young people who have "pulled the beard" of God, thinking that it will remain in their hands, for us to put off any longer giving these explanations.[35]

[34] On this subject, cf. D. Dubarle, "The Theology of the Cosmos," in Vol. II, *God and Creation,* of The Theology Library, (Chicago: Fides, 1955).

[35] Is any reminder needed that a great effort of pastoral work and catechesis is

To Explain Profoundly

If we really believe in the effectiveness of the Word, if we distinguish between the three kinds of obstacles that may prevent us from understanding it, then we can attempt that kind of profound explanation which resembles the Biblical and liturgical catechesis familiar to the Fathers, or the commentary made by a candidate for a "bachelor's degree in the Bible" in the thirteenth century. All this is included in that "extremely profitable kind of understanding which one may have of the revealed mysteries when, zealously, prudently and piously, one shows the connections between them as well as their connection with the last end of man."

In undertaking this kind of explanation, our first aim should be *not to adapt, but to convert.* We would do well to banish the equivocal term "adaptation."[36] We are now happily free of bowdlerized editions of Shakespeare or of Don Quixote "adapted for young readers"; let us also, then, get rid of Bibles "adapted for easy reading"; let us not prevent the queen of Sheba from hearing the wisdom of Solomon! Furthermore, let us stop trying to adapt modern man to his Biblical "colleague"; certain poorly inspired theologians have in this regard abused the sciences of antisepsis and surgery; by cutting away here and there some unpleasing growth, veiling some too visible nakedness, they have succeeded too often in creating a completely "modern man" whose higher nature is completely existentialist and whose body and emotions are "authentically free."

The Bible knows only one way of salvation: to be converted, transformed into the new man. This is something more than, it is *something entirely different from "becoming what one is,"*[37] for the man of flesh has no right to consider himself in any way the man according to God. Such a man must be re-created by the Spirit Himself in the Word and the sacraments. The image which should be placed at the center of liturgical pedagogy is not the man resulting from some "humanistic" equilibrium to be achieved by careful adjustments — and, naturally, completely academic ones — such a man then to be declared "fit for service," the service of God, because he would be at once ignorant of God's call and not repugnant to it.[38] The *only* image is

needed to answer this urgent need? More and more the results of these researches must be made concrete on the level of school and other texts.

[36] The theme of the *Conversations de Saint-Sébastien,* in 1957, was concerned precisely with the language of the Church confronted with the modern world. It goes without saying that my remark about "adaptation" does not refer in any way to the necessity for revivifying a certain sentimental and abstract phraseology which is still at large, and for going beyond a certain "chancery style" so foreign to the soundest instincts of modern man; here we must most certainly "adapt" and even "replace."

[37] According to the word of Pindar, used by Goethe, which serves as the starting point of a whole type of humanism.

[38] We can understand how Charles du Bos, in his *Journal,* Vol. 1, (Paris, 1946), p. 347, said to Gide that "equilibrium" was the word, the state which he did not wish at any price; the Greek element was absent from his "composition," he added, and he saw in Gide's too refined concern for equilibrium the major temptation for

that which the risen Christ presents to us, as Guardini has said so profoundly.[39]

The baptized man is the man that God wills we should be, that He creates in us. The East has especially emphasized this point: the Lord transfigured in the light of Thabor is the image of man *par excellence,* which explains the importance of the feast of the Transfiguration in their liturgical year, and the aspect peculiar to Byzantine art.[40] This "man of the Bible" is a hundred times richer, greater, more capable of development than the man envisioned by any of the ephemeral "humanists" succeeding one another in the course of history. We shall never finish the inventory of the unfathomable riches of the Bible; humanisms of the present and of the future will be dead, and very dead, while the sacred Word will continue to reveal to us new aspects of man. It cannot be otherwise, since it presents him to us "according to God," who is Life.[41]

While profound explanation is not "adaptation,"[42] still it should facilitate the conversion of the whole human spirit. All the domains of our being must be evangelized; those black clouds which have nothing to do with the cloud that covered the tent of witness must all be dissipated. We must not confuse what is mysterious by reason of its essential being, because it is beyond the reach of discursive reason, with what is mysterious because it has not yet been sufficiently developed or elucidated.[43]

him to turn back to the purely profane and to refuse the divine: the *Stimmung* of romanticism seemed to him closer to Christianity.

[39] R. Guardini, *The Lord,* (Chicago: Regnery, 1954). We must completely reconsider man starting with this glorious humanity of the transfigured Savior. We must not try to put in the shade what seems to us to go beyond the "human"; we must make of this a starting-point, for the question is one of a "conversion," that is to say, of that *metanoia* of our heart, of our intelligence and our spirit which will open them out to the transcendent revelation of the Man "from on high."

Thus the impeccability of Christ in no way diminishes His humanity, it *augments* it; when we say in the liturgical invocations that Jesus is "true God and true man," the last words do not mean primarily a "composite of body and soul," but the image of God according to which we were created. Human "nature" is also a divine "vocation"; it *is* in conformity with what it should be as "nature" when it responds to the divine call, when it identifies what it wills to be with fidelity to its vocation of sanctity in the love of men and the love of God. The image of God is fulfilled in us when it is irradiated with this love, when, in the glory of a life delivered from sin, it is henceforth only presence to men, in charity.

In other words, if man is the more "man" as divine grace in him conforms him more perfectly to His Creator, we can understand how the new Adam, glorious, is "the Man." Doubtless, the impeccability of Jesus flowed from the hypostatic union; but here we are in the presence precisely of the archetype, of the sovereign model of all humanity; each man must tend toward it as toward a limit which is certainly inaccessible—for Jesus is the Son of the Father, while we are sons by adoption—but which orients his whole life according to God; *there is no other true type of man.*

[40] In my essay *Espoir des hommes,* (Tournai-Paris, 1958), pp. 125-129, I tried to discover the causes of the complete misunderstanding of Malraux on this point.

[41] Is it necessary to repeat that there is here no trace of passivity which would alienate man?

[42] Cf. *supra,* p. 136; it is in connection with what is *essential* in the Biblical message that we cannot speak of "adaptation."

[43] This explanation is that of G. Marcel, in *Positions et approches concrètes du mystère ontologique,* (Paris-Brussels, 1933).

For this reason, the need still exists for Biblical apologetics; there is, perhaps, a tendency to forget this today. This kind of apologetics does not consist merely in distinguishing carefully between different kinds of obstacles – this is its negative aspect, that of clearing away– it consists also in bringing out, from within, the harmonies between the man of the Bible and certain valid aspects of man in the twentieth century.[44]

Our second aim in undertaking to explain the Bible profoundly should be *to bring out the kind of "human nature" implicit in the Bible.*

1) One theme runs all through the Bible, that of *God seeking man before man seeks Him.* From the "Where art thou, Adam?" of Genesis to the parable of the lost sheep in the Gospel, the loving patience of God is revealed. The Old Covenant is the history of the strategems of the Father's love, seeking ways to bring the prodigal son back home, to gather together in the divine fold a stiff-necked and rebellious people. The final strategem is given in the parable: "They will respect my son." But they did not respect Him; Peter himself denied Him with an oath, and, on the eve of the ascension, none of the apostles had yet understood; even, as a response of the liturgy repeats, "on the day of Pentecost, they were gathered together in fear of the Jews."

It was necessary, then, that the Spirit, as on the first days of creation, should come to seek these fearful and obtuse disciples, no longer in shadow and mystery, but in storm and wind, in the surge of power from on high, in the shattering and uprooting of the very foundations of their interior dwelling, in the outbursting of its incorruptible force.

The same law goes through the history of the Church. St. Paul was struck down on the road to Damascus, caught by the heavenly Pursuer of whom Francis Thompson speaks; Augustine was, as it were, "taken aback" by the *Tolle, lege, tolle, lege* sung by a child and at last forced to see himself as sinner and as pursued by the pardon of God; Francis of Assisi, loving life and chivalric romance, met Lady Poverty coming to meet him and espoused her with his whole soul.

We are here at the heart of our daily experience.[45] What matters is not to be worthy of being loved, but to be loved as we are, at the very heart of our unworthiness; Mauriac has illustrated this clearly in a work such as *Vipers' Tangle.* It is easy to love a person who conforms to the ideal image that we make of him, but very difficult not to condemn one who does not with a "nothing but" judgment ("You are nothing but a money-grubber," "nothing but a liar"), the kind that kills as surely as a sword. Yet we must love not only in spite of infidelities, but in some way because of them,[46] in a forgiveness that truly effaces[47] the fault and re-creates us.

[44] J. Guitton, *Jesus,* (Paris, 1957), and also in the whole of his work, *La pensée moderne et le catholicisme,* maintains this permanence of apologetics in present-day Christian currents of thought.

[45] While we should not carry too far the celebrated distinction made by A. Nygren, between Eros and Agape, still it brings out the *prior ipse dilexit nos.*

2) The humanity of our divine Savior, He whom the Oriental liturgy calls "good and the Friend of men," is revealed in another aspect of the pedagogy of the Old Law. Israel had first hoped for a temporal kingdom, sign of God's blessing; but each time that the promise was about to be realized the hand of God seemed to be gently withdrawn beyond human reach. Hardly had the royal house of David been established when, beneath the riches and wisdom of Solomon, an unsuspected hollowness was revealed; never did the restoration after the Babylonian Exile equal in visible splendor that known by the holy City under David; messianic hope then had to project itself in a vision more and more apocalyptic.

This law of the *delaying of the kingdom,* which obliged the chosen people to pass beyond earthly, flesh-bound hope to true theological hope,[48] is found operative also in the history of the Church. On the one hand, she must strive to hasten the coming of the kingdom by manifesting the justice and the charity of Christ,[49] for the kingdom is to come *in* this world, but it is not *of* this world; as soon as we begin to believe that it is definitely established, see, it recedes, as if God took pleasure in destroying His own work.[50]

The Christian soul goes through the same suffering, that of "prayers unheard." Those who have lost a son, a husband or wife; those sinners who have prayed that their soul and their flesh might be delivered from those adulterous loves which have revealed to them the fire of physical passion, and who have had the feeling that they remained alone in front of a wall of silence – all these understand the words of the Bible: "How long, O Lord, will You be silent? See, our body is stretched flat on the earth; see, our throats are parched; arise, why are You sleeping, Lord? Do not forsake us." But God is silent: *Jesus autem tacebat;* God sleeps, *Jesus autem dormiebat.*

It is only by accepting the will of God in prayer that peace will return to the soul and even a smile to the face, for those who have faith have gone through the experience of the desert, or better still, that of the new exodus from Babylon, through the death of human hopes apparently blessed by God.[51]

[46] C. du Bos, "L'amour selon Coventry Patmore," in *Approximations,* Vol. VII, (Paris, 1957), pp. 347-397, illustrates this theme admirably. See also *What is Literature,* by the same author, (New York: Sheed & Ward, 1940).

[47] The scene in Tolstoy's *War and Peace* in which Natasha asks pardon of Prince André shows clearly the need for a mercy that will wipe away sin and recreate the sinner.

[48] This is the dialectic that I have tried to make perceptible, with the aid of literature, in Vols. III and IV of *Littérature du XX siècle et christianisme.*

[49] It is important to recall that in the twentieth century the duty is imposed of giving this "charity" institutional forms, since the needs are so great and since political structures so clearly appear as the only ones capable of satisfying them on a grand scale (as also, alas, of imperiling them).

[50] The play of Hochwalder, *Das heilige Experiment,* admirably illustrates these "delays" of the kingdom.

[51] One would never come to an end in quoting the commentaries of the Fathers who see in the events of the Exodus or the Exile the history of the human soul; the best-known example is probably that of Origen in his *Homilies on the Book of Numbers.*

What I have just indicated of the history of an individual soul is also true of all societies. Each political and social development goes through the same phase of earthly hope,[52] hope of seeing justice and peace established; it is a strict moral duty to foster and promote them. Yet the word of Valéry, written in 1919, has lost nothing of its truth: "Our civilizations also now know that they are mortal"; we might even paraphrase this by saying "Our *Christian* civilizations also now know that they are mortal."

What is left of Christian Egypt and its glorious and holy Alexandria? What memory remains of Antioch, that city in which for the first time the disciples of Jesus were called Christians? What remains of Caesarea, the city in which the first baptism of a pagan took place, that from whence St. Paul set out to go to Rome, that in which Eusebius and Origen studied, in what was one of the most beautiful libraries of antiquity? There is nothing left. Alexandria is nothing more than a port; at Antioch the guides do not even tell "legends"; as for Caesarea, there are only a few ruined houses; and the blue sea, for nearly two thousand years, has beat against those scattered columns once set up as the foundation of a jetty by Herod, the megalomaniac kinglet.

Here is not only an accidental epiphenomenon but a mysterious *law* of death hidden in the heart of life; every person and every society must, then, take this law into account. Whether it is a holy city or a religious society makes no difference, on the level of the *visible* success of justice and peace; sooner or later defending the city of God as incarnated in *temporal* institutions leads to a crusade or a holy war; but, since the transition from the Old to the New Law, a crusade can no longer be the last word in the pedagogy of the kingdom.[53] We must strive unceasingly to foster any manifestation of the kingdom in this world, but we must never forget that it is not of this world, and so be ready to give ourselves wholly over to God.[54]

Jesus' word to Peter is true for all of us: "When thou wast young, thou didst gird thyself and walk where thou wouldst. But when thou art old . . . another will gird thee and lead thee where thou wouldst not." The delaying of the kingdom, without ever justifying any abstentionism on the earthly plane, teaches us hope, for it teaches us to die in order to rise again.

[52] This is equally true of the *respublica christiana* of the Middle Ages in the West; here was a realization of the "kingdom," and one strongly influenced by the Old Testament climate. However great it may have been, it was not the less marked by the precarious quality of this earth.

[53] Hochwalder's work, mentioned above, shows very clearly this inescapable transition to the crusade, with all the ambiguities that it implies.

[54] This does not mean that the Church should abandon without a struggle the temporal structures of the institutions of a mixed nature into which she has succeeded in breathing a Christian spirit; the question is of our having the will, the profound disposition of which St. Paul speaks when he says that "We must use this world as if we were not using it."

3) The image of *Jerusalem* allows us to grasp the interlinking of the two dialectics we have mentioned. Jerusalem is the humblest of cities compared to the ancient capitals of Egypt, of Assyria, or of great Rome; but it was consecrated by the divine promises; at the same time, the Lord punished it for its infidelities. Jesus, the Man-God, wept over Jerusalem, for He loved it as only a Jew could love his City of David, and He also was a son of David. He loved its walls and its beautifully fitted stones, as a man can love the work of his hands; He loved it as only God could love this temple, which, towering above the brook Cedron and the valley of Josaphat, seemed to be proclaiming the hope of the resurrection of the dead; He loved to contemplate it and to walk in it, as God "found His delight in walking in the Garden in the cool of the evening."

It was from the heart of this love, at the climax of that long imprecation which also seems like a kind of sob turning into a tempest, that a few days before His death, on His way back to that kindly Bethany in which He found His friends, He spoke those words which tear our hearts each time the liturgy brings them back to our lips: "Jerusalem, Jerusalem, thou that dost kill the prophets and stone those that are sent to thee! How often would I have gathered thy children together, as a mother-hen gathers her chicks under her wings, and thou wouldst not! Lo, your house will be left to you desolate."

The city today, torn apart by the absurd "frontier," divided among Christian Churches on the very place where Jesus died that all might be one, remains the mysterious symbol of her whom God loves even in her sins and of her who carries out unceasingly the passage from the hopes of earth to true hope in God, theological hope. This image is Biblical and liturgical, for Jerusalem is the figure of the Church, and if "the Church makes the Eucharist, the Eucharist also makes the Church";[55] it reminds us that it was in His city-temple that Jesus died and rose again, and that it was there that He saved His people. Jerusalem, at the heart of the Bible and the liturgy, incarnates some of our most ineradicable hopes.[56]

Our third aim in undertaking a profound explanation of the Bible should be *to bring to light all the potential stepping-stones* between the mentality of modern man and the Bible. The search needed here is not some variety of concordism; the harmonies that we are going to suggest have neither more nor less value than those which St. Augustine discovered between Neo-platonism and the Bible.

They are no *more* valuable, because the man of the Bible is always beyond the concepts we consider most adequate; neither are they *less* valuable, for if the platonic harmonies were legitimate, then the consonances which we can discover between certain, quite unplatonic, aspects of the modern world and the man of the Bible are legitimate

[55] H. de Lubac, *The Splendor of the Church,* (New York: Sheed & Ward, 1956), Chap. IV.

[56] T. Maertens, "Jérusalem, cité de Dieu," coll. *Lumière et vie,* n. 3, (Bruges, 1954).

and valuable also.[57] Bringing such stepping-stones to light is a task that is always precarious and always necessary; the five points that I am going to sketch out are only chosen to give a general idea.[58]

1) There is, first, the *concrete and existential mode* of contemporary thought. Phenomenology "might be in a sense the union of Jewish realism with Greek idealism";[59] it ignores the dualism of body and soul, since man is an incarnate consciousness, in a concrete situation, projecting himself, expressing himself at various levels – the psychological, the imaginative, the institutional, and, above all, the historical. In other words, the whole man appears in act (*"la gestualité"*) or, more simply, in those individual and collective actions that go beyond the antinomies of abstract analysis; the liturgy, for this reason, is a concrete, existential mode of action of the entire man.[60]

From now on, instead of being concerned with "essences or abstract natures" in human nature, for example, the philosopher takes as his starting-point the concrete situation of the person, in the "human condition," to use the term popularized in 1933 by the novel of Malraux. This "condition" may be ineluctable – man is a being made for death (*zum Tode,* Heidegger says) – but it can also concern one or another way of being, in good health or not, rich or poor, intelligent or mediocre.

Man is, then, always envisaged according to a dimension that is called "historical"; his consciousness must necessarily be engaged in acts; these, in turn, have their echoes in the behavior of other people, for man is not only, nor even chiefly, what he thinks or what he hides, but what he does; and he is responsible for his acts; he is free, and so responsible also for the course of events. The primacy of *praxis* in Marxism, its insistence on the dialectic of history which at once transcends man and is his own work, are in the same line (even though the Marxist saying: "We must consent to necessity, in this is liberty" is worlds away from the liberty of indetermination of Sartrian existentialism).

We may allow ourselves to find here a consonance with the man of the Bible. He is the ruler of creation, since he is to "increase and multiply and fill the earth and rule over it"; he is the image of God precisely by reason of this rule exercised over the universe. The vision of the Bible, equally concrete and dynamic, ignores the dualism of soul and body (at least in most of its texts) but insists on the responsibility of man with regard to this world (the sin of Adam has had cosmic effects). Furthermore, it puts at the heart of the message the history of salvation, and it assigns to man a final blessed-

[57] They are, moreover, in profound accord with the Aristotelian-Thomistic synthesis.

[58] See my article "Modern Man and the Bible," in *Lumen Vitae,* X, (1955), pp. 63-76, in which I describe these same stepping-stones in a somewhat different way.

[59] H. Duméry, *op. cit,* v. II, p. 94, note.

[60] The merit of modern phenomenology lies in this restitution of the total and concrete dimension of man; but St. Thomas had already made it the center of his vision.

ness which is not to be uniquely that of his intelligence, but is to engage his entire being, since at the end of time we shall reign with Christ over a new earth.[61]

We must certainly not replace the purely material messianism of Marxism with some revised version of a millenarianism too hastily baptized; and certainly also, the differences here are more important than the resemblances between existential thought and the Hebraic vision,[62] but these differences do not need to be stressed here.[63]

2) A second stepping-stone, akin to the first, is the insistence of modern thought on the *values of solidarity and intersubjectivity.* Solidarity is primarily the sense of the collaboration of all engaged in the same task, political or social. The spirit of the team is one form of this, but it is found more deeply still in the sensation of having set out on the same adventure, with the same human destiny. The famous example of the island of the condemned in Pascal is a foreshadowing of this in that seventeenth century which was preparing in France for the glory of Versailles. The "unanimism" of Jules Romains, Georges Duhamel and Charles Vildrac examines more thoroughly the mutual link between consciousnesses, for example at the "death of someone," according to the title of one of the most beautiful novels of the author of *Men of Good Will.*

But, above all, according to the view of a Gabriel Marcel, man is transformed in his very being by one or another encounter: Orpheus is not truly Orpheus until he has found (or refound) Eurydice, for we *are* the bond that we have with another being, truly welcomed in authentic exchange, just as truly as we have caused this bond to be tied. Here is one of the aspects of what the author of *Homo Viator* calls "the mystery," that is to say, a problem that goes beyond its own data and cannot be resolved from the outside.[64] Between solidarity and the communication of consciousnesses we can discern a whole gamut of human relations following the line of a growing interiority.

And solidarity expands equally on the horizontal plane. The intercommunication of world cultures becomes a condition of their development: we are on the eve of a new era in the sciences of comparative religion and civilization. While this obviously implies the danger of syncretist relativism, the potential wealth of this world-wide humanism (according to the phrase of Malraux) is certain. Equally, the social dimension spreads, like a film of oil, over all problems, not only on the national level but on the planetary. And, finally, the immense

[61] To the extent to which Marxism is "a Christian truth gone mad," the problem of the Bible and Marxism could well be studied.

[62] C. Tresmontant, in *Études de métaphysique biblique* does not perhaps distinguish clearly enough between Biblical thought and certain modern systems which have, apparently, been inspired by it.

[63] Our purpose here is rather to bring these stepping-stones to light.

[64] G. Marcel, *Homo Viator,* (Paris, 1944), pp. 15-38. (Eng. trans.—Chicago: Regnery, 1951.)

interest awakened by the underdeveloped countries creates the sense of responsibility for our whole planet.[65]

Here again, taking due account of differences, a harmony may be discerned with the theme of the people of God. Beginning with the call of the personal God to which man may respond by obedience (or refusal), the community, the *qahal*, the *ecclesia* is built up. It is God who owns the land of promise and it is to Israel as a people that He confided its development, which excluded the *ius utendi et abutendi* of Roman law. Just as Biblical man only fulfills himself in obedience to the Word, so the people of God arrive at their fulfillment only by hearing and obeying; the reading of the Law is, in fact, always communal; the acclamations and prayers that accompany it are communal also.

Finally, not only does the planetary dimension of human solidarity find an echo in the increasingly universalist preaching of the prophets, for example in the famous chapter 60 of Isaias; not only is the message of salvation universal because it implies the material and spiritual cosmos (to use Hellenistic terms), *ta panta,* says St. Paul, but also because it envisages all times and all places, all the cultures of the past and present and because, very precisely, as I have said, Christianity appears here as a meeting-place of world cultures. Biblical man should rule the world in its entirety; he can only do so in and by the people of God, who, grown as numerous as the sand of the seashore or the stars of heaven, should fill the earth. "In your name," God said to Abraham, "all the tribes, all the nations of the earth, shall be blessed."

One achievement dear to our contemporaries is that of reintegrating woman into the building-up of society and the realization of world-wide humanism. Now, it is to the human couple that the Bible promised rule over the world; taking up, in fact, the theme of man as the "image of God," that is to say, the ruler of the universe, the sacred writer deepens its meaning by saying that God "created them male and female," saying to them: "Increase, multiply, fill the earth and rule over it." In the same way, in the second account of creation, the woman is "bone of the bone" of Adam, and "flesh of the flesh," for she expresses what is most intimate in him. But she is also "a help-meet like unto himself"; this image of him is also his aid, precisely the aid which he must have in the carrying out of his task as king of creation.

The love of man for woman is, then, bound up with the dialogue of each with him or herself, and also with motherhood, with that rejoicing that breaks out in the Bible each time a woman becomes aware that a young life is awakening within her. This maternity, this family, is not ingrown; it does not deserve the "Families, I hate you," of Gide, for it opens out upon the infinity of the world that is to be filled and ruled. The Biblical family, far from the being the enclosing nest in which germinate the complexes, prejudices and pseudo-principles which the

[65] The book of Tibor Mende, *Regards sur l'histoire de demain* (Paris, 1954) is an interesting index of this.

child inherits, is, on the contrary, the cradle of the great human adventure, that of the peaceful conquests of technique, and the cradle also of baptism, according to the word of Bernanos that was developed, as if in advance, in the *Five Great Odes* of Claudel.[66]

3) These last lines lead us to a third stepping-stone, that of *human love*. It is meeting that achieves the communication of consciousness; the body here takes on a new significance well brought out by contemporary phenomenology. The body is, indeed, our means of acting on the world; we know the word of Bergson concerning technique as being "a human body immeasurably enlarged." But, among the various kinds of action on the world, there is one which attracts attention in a very special way because it signifies to each person the presence of another or others; the body is, then, also the means whereby human consciousnesses manifest themselves, communicate themselves. Doubtless, by the same title, the body is as much an obstacle as an instrument, but the phenomenology of perception is endeavoring to describe the "reading" of this complex language which the body *is*.

One would, therefore, tend to leave aside the distinction between carnal and spiritual love; the attempt is rather to unveil the meaning – the *Sinn*, as the Germans say – inherent in the gesture of the whole being, for example in the mutual giving of the marriage act. In an almost unhealthy mistrust of all "Platonism" or of what is called by this name, present-day psychology strives to describe the phenomenology of the body as sign, as language, as the means of presence to someone else. So in art, the language of the senses, the word of the whole person, as, for example, in dancing; so in friendship, in which the least flick of an eyelash becomes communion; so in wedded love, finally, in which the humblest, most secret and most intimate gestures strive to "express," in a definitive self-commitment, what the consciousness of each person is.

In other words – and this approach is important – modern phenomenology unceasingly carries out that return to the concrete individual being which St. Thomas made a necessity for all critical thought. The attempts of phenomenology are bold ones, certainly, but they are fundamentally healthy and enriching: thus the progress of love between husband and wife witnesses to a growth of "spiritual," altruistic sentiments, but these are registered in simpler and simpler gestures, which are more and more sensory and concrete.[67]

The vision of Biblical man also emphasizes in its own way the unity of the person in his being and his action. The most concrete, the most colorful language, that of the Canticle of Canticles for example, expresses the love of God for Israel His bride with a realism that scandalizes only the puny natures that have been stunted by three centuries of pious

[66] In this connection see the book on "Woman," by F. Buytendijk, an excellent answer to Simone de Beauvoir's *The Second Sex.* (French translation by R. Micha and A. de Waelhens, Paris-Brussels, 1954.)

[67] Let us repeat that in the Christian vocabulary "spiritual" does not mean "discarnate," but "filled with power, incorruptible."

hypocrisy. The Bible is neither puritanical nor "jansenistic,"[68] as is shown by the famous chapter 16 of Ezechiel, one of the most beautiful but also one of the crudest. The same word means "to wed a wife," that is to say, to possess her carnally, and "to know"; we see to what point the "body" is, in the vision of the Bible, "language" and communication; it will be fully this in its glorious state, at the resurrection.

The dialectic of the Bible, without ever disuniting man from his corporeal and sensory way of acting, leads him by a divine pedagogy which delivers him from the chains of his "carnal" condition to orient him towards pure language, perfect communication, reciprocal transparence, analogous to that of the Persons of the Blessed Trinity among themselves.[69] Biblical man is responsible for the destiny of this world; he is thus responsible in solidarity, as a people, and also as a married couple; finally, he is to develop himself progressively, under the breath of the Spirit, into a kind of language, a word that he is becoming and that finally he will *be,* in a love open to the infinity of God and of the world.[70]

4) *Depth psychology,* our fourth stepping-stone, dear to the man of the twentieth century, reveals, beyond our reflexes and beyond our explicit consciousness, the role of the unconscious and the subconscious; without denying the danger of the irrational,[71] the contact with that mysterious world "below" can nourish what J. Monchanin calls the "supra-consciousness" which puts us in relation to God.[72] The most vital core of man does not consist in the solitary and hardened affirmation of his individual autonomy, but in availability, welcome, receptivity. Here

[68] The quotation marks indicate that I do not mean to describe historic Jansenism, but a kind of deformation along moralizing lines.

[69] However, it is important here to emphasize one difference: it is not "the face of the world" as it appears to us which is the final speech of God, for "the figure of this world is passing away"; it is to be progressively transfigured; thus our bodies will be conformed to Christ's glorious Body. But, here again, it is precisely the idea of the body as the sign of presence which can help us to understand something of what glorious bodies will be like: does not the glorified Christ, as I shall mention later on, realize in His being as man transfigured the most perfect presence possible, first to His apostles, then to the Church and so to each of us, by His Eucharistic Body? Will not heaven and earth be renewed to the extent to which our bodies, having passed through death and the resurrection (which is not some kind of reanimation but a new life) become only a means of knowledge, play, dance, music, language that is artistic as well as loving, among one another?

Instead of which, as things are now, our words are quite as much a risk of betraying ourselves, or even a means of hiding ourselves, of protecting ourselves from others, of defending ourselves against a kind of dissolution which seems to threaten us, as they are our total opening out to charity, to the life of others in us. Can we not see something of this perfect "speech" that our glorified bodies will become in those dancing and musical flames which vibrate in Dante's Paradise: the most unbelievable presence in the most humble "earthly" realities is here united with the music of the spheres, with that interior embrace in which the crystal clarity of water is united with the power of light and the furnace of charity. Cf. A. Masseron, *Pour comprendre le Divine Comédie,* (Paris, 1939).

[70] Yet there will always persist that insuperable limit which distinguishes creature from Creator; and, also, the bond with sensible life will always subsist, at least to the extent to which it will have contributed to the formation of the true personality.

[71] See my contribution, "Le retour à l'irrationel et à l'immatériel," in *L'homme nouveau,* coll. *Études de pastorale,* n. 1, (Louvain, 1947).

[72] J. Monchanin, *De l'esthétique a la mystique,* (Tournai-Paris: Casterman, 1954).

is an original experience, in which the affirmation of self goes along with the discovery of a reality that transcends us at the very moment in which the consciousness projects itself into it.[73]

The psychology of art helps us to grasp this articulation in which liberty and love, affirmation of self and welcome are all joined together. The Claudelian distinction between *animus,* the discursive intellect, and *anima,* the faculty that is moved when the poetic "current" runs through it, causes us to perceive this union of acting and being acted upon. Such "passivity" is a privileged form of action; we take in, then, as if it were our own life, what the poet summons up; we have a real knowledge of it, by a mysterious contact with life itself.

Thus, for example, the solitude of Christine of Pisan is ordinarily one more fact lost in the ocean of the past; but when we read the poem *Seulette suis, sans ami demourée,* she comes near us, she fills our heart to such a point that the tears she sheds seem to be our own, her loneliness seems to be ours; we find ourselves "inhabited" by someone who is at once a being other than ourselves, the mysterious Christine of Pisan who lived in the fourteenth century, and ourselves.[74]

This faculty is found again on a supreme level, that of mysticism. What certain Biblical passages call "spirit" and distinguish from the soul and body, what St. Thomas calls *intellectus* and distinguishes from *ratio,* what spiritual writers call the "fine point of the soul," the "holy of holies," the summit of the spirit, and which they distinguish from the surface faculties of man – this is the possibility of welcoming the visitation of the divine Spirit. The personality of the saints and mystics shows that man is at the height of his being when he accepts the gift "of loving men *with* the very love with which God loves them." These words of Bergson remain true; psychoanalysis itself confirms this since the majority of neuroses are brought on by the fear of taking root in the "not I," that is to say, the fear of renouncing our anxious attachment to ourselves.

Furthermore, we must not identify what French classicism calls the "character" (think of La Bruyère, for example) with the whole man;[75] the view of romanticism already orients us more directly toward the fundamental availability that we have mentioned.[76] The "humanistic" ideal here would be to unite the precise characteristics of classic psychology with the lyric flexibility of romanticism; thus we approach,

[73] I am here purposely using the vocabulary of phenomenology.

[74] It is not necessary to quote H. Bremond, *Prayer and Poetry,* and many other studies on the poetic mystery; it is more important to attract the attention of modern man to this "prayer which does not pray but which causes prayer" which can be a most useful introduction to the discovery of activities of the mystical order.

[75] Cf. my contribution, "Liberté et verité dans la critique littéraire," in *Liberté et verité,* (Louvain, 1955).

[76] Romanticism, on the European level, represents a positive value, the role of which was of capital importance in the return to the religious sense; this must obviously not be confused with the "desired storms" of François-René; see my contribution, "Charles du Bos ou d'un romantism européen" in *Revue Générale Belge,* 88, (June 1953).

mutatis mutandis, "Biblical man."[77] So the personages of the Old Testament are not described with any help from the psychology of character; to put it better, the characteristics that individualize them – for example, Sara's laugh, Moses' stammering, the rather artful transparency of David, the noble power of Isaias' word, the quivering sensitiveness of Jeremias – are at every moment, as it were, swept away by the visitations of the Word of God.

The men of the Old Testament suffer from weakness and fragility, but they are continually raised to a level of sovereign greatness when the hand of the Lord transports them. They realize the paradox of being at the same time quite different from one another – it is impossible to confuse Amos with Osee, Ruben with Joseph, Samuel with David, etc.– and profoundly akin, communicating on the heights each time that the Spirit makes use of them: from Abraham to Jesus a continuity thus becomes visible through an incredible diversity of "characters."

In the same way, the humanity of the Savior is marked by a range of characteristics that make Him concrete, recognizable among all others: a kind of unsparing gentleness, a sensibility extraordinarily perceptive of the humblest realities, giving place to outbursts of indignation. At the

[77] What classical wisdom calls "character," therefore, made up of a series of meaningful characteristics of the social or individual order which particularize and distinguish such and such a "character" in a comedy or a tragedy or in a silhouette of La Bruyère's, easily becomes petrified. If such "characters" pretend to represent the whole truth about man, they quickly take on a fixed grimace or "stoic cramp," according to the phrase of Bernanos, or manifest that love typical of "classic" souls which Sartre made fun of in *Qu'est-ce que la littérature.* By contrast, when the bond, at least the potential bond, is re-established between this behavior according to character and a profound availability to calls from without, whether they be of the poetic or mystical orders—and frequently they are both at once—the human person recovers all his dimensions and his flexibility.

An example can be found in Claudel's works in the person of the young woman in *Tobie et Sara.* It shows very clearly this transition from the level of "character" to that of the poetic and mystical call.

Now and again, Sara is swept through by a breath from on high; then she becomes a kind of young prophetess; she is open to the Spirit come from God; she perceives the future—and here we think of the scene that Sainte-Beuve calls the Sinai of French tragedy, the vision of Joad in the third act of *Athalie*—she breaks out in rejoicing over that child still unknown, who is the child of Tobias, over that young life not yet seen, which is an image of the life of God, over that germination of the birth which is growing in her womb; she is all ecstasy, supple, radiant, indwelt and acted on by the breath that suffuses her. And then she becomes once more the young woman, hardly grown out of the mutinous candor of a little girl, still mocking and coaxing her mother-in-law, the old woman who is a little difficult, but with a courageous silence.

The two aspects complete one another, for this "character" is without any inflexibility, precisely because we feel it to be secretly open to poetic or prophetic calls, its roots bathed in that profound water over which the Spirit hovers as on the first day of creation. On the other hand, the states of "supraconsciousness," those during which the personality expands in the hearing of the voices from on high and thus attains to a jubilant and ecstatic humanity, these moments are not lost in some indistinct and chaotic world, but are bound up with that clearly defined "character."

J. P. Sartre in *Qu'est-ce que la littérature, Situations,* II, (Paris, 1948) has made a critique of the "classical" soul, showing how it has become hardened and factitious because it is cut off from its concrete situation in the world; unfortunately, this critique is incomplete, for it does not integrate the values of poetry, Sartre rejecting everything that can be truly received.

same time, the man Jesus passed whole nights in prayer; He called Himself the Son of God; He was, even He, subject to disturbance of spirit, for example at the tomb of Lazarus, or at the time of His great thanksgiving to the Father for having "revealed His mysteries to little ones." And, finally, His humanity was transfigured before the eyes of the apostles, and His human nature, at the resurrection, seemed to escape from the laws of space and time.

In other words, Jesus realized this paradox of being continually "acted upon," driven, led by the Holy Spirit, the power of God which anointed His humanity, and also of imposing Himself by a gift of presence on daily realities, in a tranquil transparency, *nettezza,* as Grandmaison calls it, a clarity, calm at its very source.[78] All this was achieved because His humanity is "substantially" consecrated by its unutterable union ("hypostasis," as theology calls it) with the second Person of the Trinity. In other words, His human nature is integrally true, because it is indwelt by, because it subsists in a living union with, the all powerful torrent of life of the *Logos.*[79]

5) Finally, the fifth stepping-stone is the return to the values of *symbolism* by certain contemporary humanists. Works such as those of Rimbaud, Larbaud, Péguy, Claudel, Saint-John Perse, Eluard, Supervielle, Eliot, Faulkner, Kafka, make use of concrete symbols, meant to make perceptible the bond between man and nature, between nature and man; the cultures most foreign to our own in space and time, the colors and scents of continents and even the gravitational pull of the stars, appear in a cosmic vision at once shimmering with light and echoing with music, and also mysteriously in harmony with "what is not seen." Since the famous sonnet of Baudelaire's:

> Nature is a temple, and its living pillars
> From time to time give forth obscure words,

these hidden "correspondences" have been rediscovered, for "perfumes, colors and sounds re-echo one another." *Amers,* by Saint-John Perse, is one of the most recent examples of this sacral poetry which, going beyond the consecrated lyricism of Baudelaire, is akin to the cosmic lyricism of certain psalms.[80]

An approach to symbolism may be found in the more and more marked interest of the man of the twentieth century in conventionalized forms of art: Byzantine art, for example, with its slightly barbaric quality, now attracts visitors to Ravenna, to Palermo; sculpture of the Roman, hieratic kind is now gaining in the public taste over that Gothic imagery which we find too close to common daily humanity, not sufficiently charged

[78] We must not forget that, although the human nature of Jesus is not a person in the ontological sense of the word, this does not mean that it is *abstract;* it is concrete.

[79] The human nature of Jesus possesses a series of characteristics that allow us to say that He was, in the *psychological* sense of the word, what we call a "personality"; but these concrete traits subsist in the second Person of the Trinity.

[80] Surrealism represents an unsuccessful attempt along these lines, because it was paralyzed from the start by a concern for systematic revolt which dried up the sources of true poetic lyricism.

with that meaning which carries the glance of the spirit beyond appearances; modern painting inspires us by its capacity to suggest "a beyond, present" in colors and lines – for example, the embracing flames of the landscapes by Van Gogh of Saint-Rémy in Provence, or the architecture of Mt. Sainte-Victoire in the canvasses of Cézanne.[81]

In a more general way, "existentialist" thought, of which we have already spoken, seeks in events themselves a significance more important than any possible speculations about them. The interest of ethnologists in religious symbols and myths should be noted: the "*cahier posthume*" of Lévy-Bruhl shows that philosophy has rediscovered in primitive "myths" one of those "stages" of which I spoke earlier, following Alain, and not at all a "prelogical" type of thought; the works of Mircea Eliade have succeeded in unveiling in the religious "myth" one of the necessary incarnations of human consciousness.[82]

FROM THE EARTHLY ADAM TO THE NEW ADAM

May we now be allowed to sketch out an answer to the three questions posed at the beginning of this essay as examples of some of the major difficulties facing modern man in the Bible.

The First Adam

Concerning the state of Adam in paradise, the first chapters of Genesis contain essential truths, but these are exclusively of the religious order. Paradise, the garden in which God loved to walk in the cool of the evening, helps us to understand how, before sin, man lived in familiarity with God. Since sin came into the world, however, "to see God is to die"; this is why Adam hid himself; this is why the Cherubim were stationed at the gate of the blessed garden; this is why, finally, from Genesis to the Apocalypse, God is at once concealed and revealed by the cloud; in the same way, the humanity of Jesus, the mysterious and substantial sign of His divinity, both hides it and manifests it.

Furthermore, while we should look neither for antinomies nor harmonies between science and Genesis, the problem still remains of the

[81] In music, the search for new sounds to render perceptible some invisible architecture is found, for example, in O. Messiaen; the general public, unfortunately, balks at all this; yet the success of the harmonizations of the psalms made by Fr. Gelineau and Fr. Deiss is a good sign. This music speaks only to those who grasp the meaning of the text; and this, in the psalms, is often symbolic.

[82] This last stepping-stone, in which we can see an expansion of contemporary anthropology toward cosmology, prepares the way especially for a rediscovery of "vertical" symbolism, which discovers in things below the shadow of things on high. Biblical symbolism is, above all, "horizontal," since it is founded on the typology of past events as being heralds of events in the future. Consonance with the Bible is here most remote.

We must not be astonished at this, for here we have originality closely allied with the paradox of revelation itself; the actions of God to save His people in the past manifest the same power of re-creation of what was dead, of resurrection of what was annihilated. No natural symbol can give the idea of this pedagogy, the cycle of the seasons being an apparent image, certainly, but an ambiguous one. Yet the fact remains that, in a general way at any rate, the modern return to symbolism prepares men's minds for the perception of a hidden significance in events.

co-existence of two schemes, that of an ascent, on the one hand, that of an initial fall on the other. First of all, we must abandon the idea of infused knowledge as proper to the first man; this is only an opinion of the Middle Ages which has no necessary connection with revelation.

And then in connection with the "perfection" of Adam, the idea of "the childhood of a royal humanity" will be found very enlightening—on condition, obviously, of taking away from the idea of childhood any connotations of infantilism. This remark of Fr. Labourdette, who proposed the comparison in question,[83] can be illustrated by the precociousness of certain children in the order of art or in that of holiness. While sexual precocity is always monstrous, that of the moral faculties is not; on the contrary, there is in the precocious moral purity of a child an inexhaustible wealth which represents in its own order a singular perfection. But this perfection is that of first fruits, the starting-point of a growth in profundity, through an indispensable trial, which is essential to all spiritual life.

The Adamic state of perfection, then, may be thought of as an enormous progress over what had gone before, as it were, a sort of leap into a new state; but, in comparison with what should have come after, it had within itself the promise of further development. We find here again, therefore, a law of Biblical pedagogy: the attainment of full growth in one stage is at the same time the starting-point of a new one; thus, Abraham, Moses, David, are at once climaxes and foundation-stones. Whatever the degree of technical development that Adam might have reached, he had in the gift of God a fullness belonging to the moral order.

But, just as the holiness of a child is not recognized by the Church unless she can prove its heroic character by the victory it has won over an inevitable trial,[84] so the perfection of Adam had to be tried; the stabilization of the primitive gift of holiness and integrity had to depend on the way in which he underwent the trial. Alas, *adolescendo peccavit*: these words of St. Irenaeus tell us how, in the process of growing, the first man could not stand the trial of his freedom; he then had to begin again, from zero, as it were, the ascent toward moral perfection.[85]

Satan

In the fall of man, in the infidelities of the people of God, the devil was at work. Here again, without attempting to fathom the mystery, we can try to bring to light the correspondences between the devil "of psychology" and the devil "of theology." Satan always works by exer-

[83] M.-M. Labourdette, *Le péché originel et les origines de l'homme,* (Paris, 1953), and the very valuable review by J. Daniélou in *Dieu vivant,* n. 26, pp. 146-147.

[84] An interesting problem for theologians would be that of the "canonization of children"; I believe that there has to be some trial which allows for the heroism of the person's virtues (as, for example, in the case of St. Maria Goretti); without this, canonization would certainly be impossible.

[85] I must admit that this hypothesis is not explicitly Biblical, but the patronage of St. Irenaeus is a valuable guarantee.

cising a kind of fascination over the sensible powers of man; he cannot reach the spiritual faculty properly so called, but yet, indirectly, he tries to overthrow it by disturbing the sensible instrument which it must use – for example, by calling up strange phenomena or dreams which upset man's sensitive nature, or by making use of the disorders of society, above all those which are multiplied by war, sickness, destitution or those "works of the devil," concentration camps.

When the human will lets itself be captured by this fascination; when it yields to the vertigo that says that "the die is cast," that life is absurd; when it abandons itself to fear or anguish in the face of death, chaos, the threats of war; when the intelligence affirms that life is hopeless and irremediably so, then we are playing the devil's game. At the very moment in which we affirm that the situation is "demoniacal," at the precise second in which we believe that we are discharging our responsibility by throwing it back onto those satanic forces which, we think, are too great for us – then we are granting to Satan a power which he does not have, for it is we ourselves alone who yield, it is our own will that capitulates.

At the instant in which we yield to the prince of this world, our weakness, our weariness, our despair in the face of "fatalism" in some way become separate entities from ourselves; they grow, they become personified and return, like a boomerang, to destroy us; we have the impression that events are set against us and have become the accomplices of our despair. Yet, for the spell to be broken it is enough for us to know that the devil exists, certainly, but that "the power of darkness can accomplish nothing" against us, as Jesus said on the eve of His passion; it is enough at such a moment that we hear a friendly word, which is then the reflection of the Word of God, for us to be freed from the madness of fascination.[86]

We can now certainly understand better the passage in Hebrews 2:14-15; the text speaks of Jesus, our High Priest, who "shared equally in our flesh and blood so as, by His death, to break the power of him who had the empire of death, that is, the devil, and to deliver those whom the fear of death had kept in servitude all their lives." This passage shows that the resurrection of Jesus is a victory over the devil; it was by reading this passage to the students whom I mentioned earlier – after having opened their minds to the "tactics of the devil" – that I was able to introduce them progressively to an understanding of the victorious passion.

Along the same lines, we might give an "explanation" of the anointing of the sick. In the hour in which death menaces the organism, fascination grows in the face of the apparent victory of chaos, in the face of the collapse of all that we are and have loved into the abyss of "nothingness"; the temptation to despair or to final unbelief is then terrible.

[86] See, along these lines, my analysis of J. Green, *Le malfaiteur,* in *La Revue Nouvelle,* 25, (1957), pp. 779-884, and also the article mentioned in note 8 of this chapter.

If the anointing often accomplishes the healing of the sick person and very frequently a sensible amelioration of his physical condition, this is doubtless because grace saves the whole man, but it is also because our organism (that is to say, we repeat, the sensible instrument used by our spiritual freedom) needs to have restored to it the equilibrium which will facilitate that act of love which is especially demanded of us on the threshold of the great journey. In other words, the amelioration of the health of the sick person aids him to make the gesture of spiritual self-commitment in our final "pasch," our passing-over.

For the rest, our sensible organism needs to be wholly evangelized by grace so that the terrain of Satan may be as small as possible, so that he can make no use of those deep troubles that escape the conscious will to lead us into sin.[87] Though here below the satanic "platform of operations" in us cannot be completely destroyed – this would be to anticipate our stabilization in glory – we should yet make use of all means, both those that are called "natural" and those that are supernatural, to reduce it to a minimum. The Church gives this anointing to the sick, but she does not dispense us from taking care of them; she carries out exorcisms, but she also sees that a doctor is consulted.[88]

We can understand now why the liturgy has us invoke the Lord so that the devil will not soil our bodies. Our instincts (our passions, as St. Thomas says) must be evangelized from within so that even their reflex motions become moral. Psychological education alone could not have made Francis de Sales, whose temperament was that of a violent man, into that model of gentleness who made people believe that he was such by instinct. In the same way, the involuntary phenomena of our sensibility, which are often the most upsetting, are to be made supple, disciplined, "moralized" from within; only the grace of the Holy Spirit can penetrate sufficiently into these depths of our instinctive life.[89]

More generally, along these same lines we can see how the exorcisms of baptism effect a liberation from the sensible world, deliver us from that ambiguity which fascinates and disturbs us. The material universe is given back to us in its lustral purity, like that so well depicted by Walter Pater's hero, Marius the Epicurean, when he speaks of a dedicated, unworldly life; man is then delivered from all complicity with "that deaf and dumb part" of himself which Satan strives to utilize.[90] The lyricism of Easter is made up of the certitude that the most desperate situations, those which are death and annihilation, are precisely those from which the power of the Spirit delivers us. The resurrection is victory over the power of darkness.

[87] Hence all the efforts of medicine, hygiene, social legislation, etc., which contribute to lessening sickness and unhealthful conditions, contribute also to diminishing Satan's "base of operations"; this is a beautiful justification of "humanism." But we must not confuse a "minimum" of well-being with a "maximum."

[88] Cf. *Satan,* (New York: Sheed & Ward, 1952).

[89] There are other aspects of "satanism," for example, its connection with everything of a magical and idolatrous order; I have only given one example here.

[90] I take my inspiration here from a beautiful passage from Claudel's *Tobie et Sara.*

The Resurrection of the New Adam

The resurrection is victory over Satan; it is also entrance into a new life. The glorified Lord realized in His humanity the most perfect mode of presence to the world. His body is no more than the sign of the coming of divine love amongst us; His humanity, become "subtle," gives itself to us as He wills and when He wills; it is *transparence and presence.* Just as love tends "to multiply itself" so as to be everywhere that its help is called for, so the risen Jesus, become "the Son of God in power, by the Holy Spirit, in virtue of the resurrection of the dead," comes wherever His bride the Church calls Him; this is the Eucharist.[91]

This transparency of the risen Christ is bound up with His victory over sin. We can perceive something of this connection between the communicability of a being, its profound availability and moral purity, in our experience of the virtuous life. As Bernanos has seen, the expression of the man who desires impurely becomes fixed, like a mask, in a kind of mysterious and restless sleep; egoistic love is allied to a kind of withered opacity, which can be discerned in the face and even in the bearing of such a man, who seems to be silently becoming duller and heavier.

But to give welcome to others, to forget oneself, above all to accept death, gives back to the human being both his flexibility and his availability; a kind of restrained impetus then marks his bearing; the joy of expressing his love to everyone is evident; it continually renews him. It is because Jesus has conquered sin, because sin has never had power over Him, it is because He accepted death and its terrors that He could manifest in His human nature — which is also ours — that indescribable paschal liberty, that abounding joy, that transparency which makes Him present wherever He is called on, which revealed Him to the disciples at Emmaus at the moment of breaking bread.[92]

Furthermore, this transparency and this communicability are allied to the *gift of childhood.* Of himself the child is all sympathy, welcome, rebounding, springing up. When the Lord told us that we must "become like a little child, for the kingdom belongs to such," this means that something of the transparency and availability of childhood is restored to us. Beyond our "wisdoms," which are often only obstinacy in clinging to our disillusionments and bitternesses, beyond our prudence, our scleroses and hardening, beyond that shell of ourselves which at each moment tends to close up and shrink in on itself, beyond that growing dullness of physical old age and psychological old age, beyond that ineluctable weight, that quasi-immobility, like a stone or mineral, which already weighs on us and stifles us, the grace of Jesus gives back to us the unfailing freshness of our early years.

[91] See J. Guitton, *The Problem of Jesus,* (New York: Kenedy, 1955); R. Guardini, *The Last Things,* (New York: Pantheon, 1954); R. Tresfontaines, "Death: A Test for Love, a Condition of Liberty," *Cross Currents,* VII, (Summer, 1957), pp. 201-212.

[92] C. du Bos, *Journal,* Vol. II, (Paris, 1948), p. 200, shows the connection between imperviousness and desire, between transparency and the moral sense that causes us to obey our conscience (in connection with Walter Pater).

This "God who renews our youth" is He of Easter, "He who died on Friday and rose again on Sunday," as Apollinaris says. It is Jesus who gives back to us that "childhood of a royal humanity" which should never have been lost, but rather deepened, stabilized, ripened, as St. Genevieve of Paris died at "eighty years old, a young and clear-eyed old woman." The risen Jesus restores to us that true childhood of which the Introit of Low Sunday sings: "Like children new born you eagerly desire the pure spiritual milk, so that it may make you grow, for salvation, if you have tasted how good is the Lord." This "childhood" which is welcome, transparency, love (do we not say that lovers regain their lost childhood?), this desire "to be with" has nothing infantile about it, nothing in common with "the elements of this world" under which we were held captive.

And further, the resurrection of Christ manifests the passage from "flesh" to "spirit." This does not mean some passage from an "incarnate" state to one of disincarnation in which the humanity of the Savior would have been dissolved, but from a state of weakness (at least according to "the economy")[93] to a state of power, of "catholicity," of communicability of the humanity of the Lord, of which the Eucharist is the efficacious sign, the sacrament.[94]

A mysterious link is thus revealed between the risen state and the perfection of *agape;* more profoundly still, the transparency of the divine Persons among Themselves and the communication of the life of the incarnate Logos to the world, in a humanity become perfectly permeable by it (always according to the "economy"), are providentially allied: the redeeming work of Christ is to render "present" to the world this mutual presence of the Persons of the Trinity.

This profound link between passion-resurrection, on the one hand, and the communion of the divine Persons among Themselves and with men, on the other, is found in almost every line of the discourse after the Last Supper. It can be read also in the third chapter of the Epistle to the Colossians, in the Latin Breviary on Low Sunday. In the same context, the Apostle speaks of those who are risen with Jesus, the baptized, who should think of the things above; but he speaks also of perfect charity in daily life. The risen Christ realizes in His humanity the perfection of this being "with us" which He promised to His disciples.[95]

[93] The word "economy" is used here in the patristic sense, which distinguishes the order of the incarnation from the revelation of the life of the Trinity (which is, in the strict sense, "theology").

[94] The error to be avoided here is that of ubiquitism, which maintains that the human nature of Jesus has of its own power, since the resurrection, the same gift of omnipresence as has His divinity; we are speaking here of His *Eucharistic* presence only. It should be clearly understood and never forgotten that it is quite as much Christ who unites us to Himself as it is He who communicates Himself to us; moreover, the Eucharistic species have a connection with the heavenly Christ, but according to His humanity. The theory of P. Billot is well-known; cf. J. Coppens, *Miscellanées Bibliques,* XXIV, *Mysterium fidei,* in *Ephemerides Théol. Lovaniensis,* 33 (1957), pp. 482-506.

[95] I believe that this idea of "with us," coming close to the "being with" of modern phenomenology, could be a valuable stepping-stone in the modern mentality. In other words, *economy* introduces us to *theology.*

This is why the theological *locus* in which the Bible, the liturgy, and the man of the twentieth century can meet and unite with one another is the account of the pilgrims at Emmaus. The two disciples are men like ourselves: "But we were hoping — *nos autem sperabamus* — that in Jesus the salvation of Israel would be accomplished"; they are on the edge of that despair by which Satan triumphs. A mysterious passer-by joins them; He explains the Scriptures to them, shows them that the Messiah must suffer and so enter into His glory. Then, during this "liturgy of the Word," the hearts of the travellers begin to burn within them; they do not know Him as yet; they have not yet recognized Him who is speaking with them; they have not yet become aware, explicitly, of the victory of Jesus over the devil and over sin.

When the Visitor makes the gesture of breaking bread, then their eyes are opened; they recognize what they knew already, and at once Jesus disappears. The pilgrims of Emmaus understand then that the resurrection is henceforth present to the world, in the power of the Spirit, in that Eucharist of the Body of Jesus who draws all men to Himself.[96]

CONCLUSION

The man of the twentieth century must be converted into the man of the Bible. This conversion can (and should) be made less difficult by taking the measures that I have suggested or, perhaps, by some entirely different methods; but it finds a foothold in us that I have not as yet brought out.

One theme that dominates both the Biblical and liturgical movement is that expressed in the word "today," *hodie*. The man of the Bible is of "today"; he is always "of the present time," he is always close to us, because he is always close to God, created according to God, and the "today" of the Bible opens on eternity. It is enough to penetrate into the soul of twentieth-century man in order to cause that deep water to spring forth from which will be reborn, recreated by grace, the man of the Bible, the new and eternal man, in Jesus.[97]

Hodie: the man of the Bible is of today because God, "as young as He is eternal," has so completely entered into the temporal, has become so "internal" to him that He continually recreates him, raises him from death. He gives us back our youth and that of the world. He renews it "like that of the eagle."

[96] Cf. J. Guitton, *Jesus*, pp. 433-439

[97] This "deep water" is placed in us by God Himself: it is grace.

Rev. Joseph Lecuyer, C.S.Sp.

CHAPTER 9

"HAPPY ARE THEY WHO HEAR THE WORD OF GOD AND PUT IT INTO PRACTICE"

Bible and liturgy, liturgy and the Word of God: the essays in this book have spoken frequently of the close and essential union between these two realities, and also of the necessity for not dissociating them in the work of Christian formation and catechesis.

But a problem still remains to be studied: the Word of God is meant for all men, while its official proclamation in the liturgy reaches directly only believers, and, among them, only practicing Catholics. What about the others: first, the Christians who do not practice their religion, who may still be believers, but in any case are outside the reach of the Word proclaimed by the ministry of the Church in the liturgical assembly? What about the vast number of members of Protestant denominations, adherents of various cults? What about complete unbelievers? None of these take part in the liturgical assembly.

As Father Bouyer wrote not long ago, "The liturgy is not a direct means of the apostolate to the people nor can it become so, since this apostolate, *by its very nature,* is addressed to those who are outside the Church, and since the liturgy, *by its nature,* is addressed to those within the Church.... The liturgy belongs to the sanctuary in the most precise sense of the term. It is not in any way made for the non-Christian who is to be converted."[1]

Does this mean that the Word of God which resounds in the sanctuary is not to go beyond these limits? The source of living water issuing from the sanctuary described by Ezechiel (47:1) which, as the liturgy for Eastertide tells us, saves all those whom it reaches (Ant. *Vidi Aquam*), is not this the same river which, as the Apocalypse tells us, waters the tree of life whose leaves are "for the healing of the nations" (Apoc. 22:1-2)? Is the Biblical and liturgical movement to be concerned only with a more or less limited group of initiates? Or should we think that the Word of God is to reach all those who do not practice or believe in Christianity only by means that have nothing to do with the liturgy – conferences, study-clubs, distribution of pamphlets, books and Bibles?

There should be no question of underestimating the usefulness of these means nor the merit of those who make use of them. But then another inevitable difficulty presents itself: in giving the Bible directly to those who do not believe in or have only superficially entered into the Christian mystery, we run into the obvious opposition between the Biblical mentality and, on the one hand, the pagan mentality which exists in every age, and, on the other, the special modern mentality which is often materialistic and positivistic. If the Bible is presented directly to many of our contemporaries, it can arouse reactions similar to those of a Celsus or a Lucian of Samosota in the second century: it seems to be a tissue of fables that are good, at best, only for the ignorant and for children, even when the grandeur of some of the ideas it proposes is vaguely recognized.

The difficulty is no less great if we imagine an unbeliever of today assisting at one of our liturgical ceremonies and there listening to the proclamation of the Word of God. Canon Bardy, proposing this hypothesis about a pagan of the first centuries, describes his reactions in terms that apply equally to pagans of today:

What would he have heard that was calculated to awaken his enthusiasm or even to engage his curiosity?... He would have listened to the readings of the Old and New Testaments, and, if he had any degree of culture, he would have been struck above all by the popular character of these books, by their poor style, their grammatical incorrectness; he would certainly not have got very much out of the prophecies; he would have been greatly amused by Noe's ark, Balaam's ass, and Jonas' whale. After this he would have had to hear a sermon, most frequently an allegorical or moral commentary on one of these readings, and he would have been quick to criticize in his own mind a method so well calculated to remove, as if by a juggler's trick, the difficulties of the story.[2]

[1] *Études de Pastorale Liturgique, Lex Orandi,* 1, p. 380.
[2] *La conversion au christianisme durant les premiers siècles,* (Paris, 1949), p. 284.

Some page of Celsus denaturing and ridiculing the teachings of the Gospel would not seem out of place in the best anthologies of free thought;[3] and, at the beginning of the fourth century, Lactantius preserved for us the reflections of the cultivated pagans of his time concerning the Christian Books, as written in an uncouth language, filled with solecisms and barbarisms, a tissue of lies and contradictions.[4]

These difficulties can be felt all the more vividly and universally in our own time because of the extension of culture, and of a culture that is more and more oriented toward the study of the positive sciences, of the controllable fact, of technology. And even though in our times certain men who keep up with the discoveries of archeology or the history of religions have been able to go beyond the difficulties inherent in the material presentation of the Word of God, the fact still remains that the Wisdom of the Cross appears as folly to the wisdom of this world; here is a difficulty of every age which can be removed by no modernization of vocabulary or of style.

In a society in which everything seems to be organized in function of earthly well-being to be preserved, acquired or developed, how can a Word which preaches a crucified God whom we must follow by carrying our own cross not appear unbearably anachronistic?

And yet, we know that the Word of God still retains in our time its power to convince, and this even for those outside the Church. What I wish to show is precisely that its proclamation in the liturgy is of invaluable importance in this regard. We shall ask ourselves first, therefore, how the Word of God received in the liturgical celebration tends by its very nature to go beyond the material limits of this celebration to make itself heard everywhere, in all human activities, to reach all those for whom it is destined; this will be the subject of the first part of this chapter. And then we shall see how this Word of God, proclaimed in the life and the witness of Christians and thus placed within the reach of all, only obtains its full effect when it leads men to the liturgical community, to the Christian assembly gathered for the Eucharist; this will be our second topic.

FROM LITURGICAL PROCLAMATION TO PROCLAMATION IN DAILY LIFE

It will appear clearly that the proclamation of the Bible in the liturgy has its necessary prolongation in the life of each Christian if we recall (a) that this proclamation is part of a covenant-rite; (b) that this rite is not simply any kind of rite, but an efficacious one.

The Proclamation of the Bible in the Liturgy is Part of a Covenant-Rite

The liturgical life of the Church is centered in her sacramental life and especially in the Eucharistic sacrifice. Now, as the encyclical

[3] Cf. Origen, *Contra Celsum,* VII, 9.
[4] *Divin. Instit.,* V, 1 and 2.

Mystici Corporis teaches, all the sacraments have as their end and effect to establish or to draw closer the bonds between the Christian and the Church, the Body of Christ and the people of the New Covenant. By baptism, by confirmation, by the Eucharist, the Christian is constituted a member of the new people of God, and becomes, in his own way, responsible for the mission of this people in the world, a depository of and witness to the covenant proposed by God and the Law in which His requirements are expressed. This point is easily understood when we consider an aspect of the Sacrifice of the Mass which is solemnly stated by Christ Himself: the Eucharist is *the Sacrifice of the New Covenant.* What does this mean?

We can understand the significance of this *New* Covenant only in reference to the covenant it replaces, since it concerns the same sacred history and the realization of its figures. What, then, did the Old Covenant mean to the Jewish people? In spite of the confusion of traditions concerning the covenant of Sinai, the following elements may be considered certain: (1) at the beginning there was a divine choice, an *election,* expressed to men by the *Word of God,* which proposed to the people the acceptance of this choice with *the Law* which expressed its conditions. (2) The offer of God was answered by the acceptance of the people, manifesting their will to obey the Law proposed to them. (3) Hence there arose a new bond between God and His people, and a new *order of worship*: "I will take you as a kingdom of priests and a consecrated nation . . . if you obey Me and respect My covenant" (Ex. 19:5-6).

The rite of the conclusion of the covenant, then, included essentially, as the 24th chapter of Exodus tells us, the solemn reading to the people of the laws promulgated by God and written down by Moses; the acceptance and promise of the people: "Everything that Yahweh has said, we will put it into practice and obey it"; a sacrifice symbolically uniting God with His people by the sprinkling of blood on the people and the altar and by a communion meal.

In this complex rite, the reading of the Word of God and the sacrificial action were closely united, and this union was not accidental, but required by the very nature of the act of alliance concluded between God who proposed a law and the people who accepted it. The participation of a man in the cult had no meaning unless he had given his personal response to the Word, unless he had accepted the will of God as manifested in the book of the Law; without this acceptance the liturgical rite lost all its value: "You required neither holocaust nor victim, then I said, Behold, I come. At the head of the book it is prescribed that I should do Thy will" (Ps. 40:7-9).

To participate in the sacrifice of the Old Covenant was, therefore, to pledge oneself to enter into the people of God in order there to assume one's personal part in the mission of this people in the history of salvation, according to the conditions expressed by the Word of God.

This Word came again and again to remind the people of the demands of their mission and of the true meaning of their participation in worship. To those who had allowed themselves to be drawn into a wholly material "religion of the Book" or into a kind of worship separated from life, the voice of the prophets proclaimed the authentic dimensions of the covenant; these protestations found their most wonderful expression in the second part of the Book of Isaias and especially in the Servant Songs.

To a people who had a tendency to isolate themselves in a narrow consciousness of their privileges, the inspired Word came to remind them of the universal meaning of their mission (Is. 66:18-25). To those pious observers of the Law who forgot the true meaning of their acts of worship and practices of fasting, the Word protested that true fasting and true worship could not exist without justice and charity (Is. 58). In the same way, at the door of the temple Jeremias inveighed against those who had made it a den of thieves, that is to say, who dared to present themselves for prayer and sacrifice without first ordering their lives in accord with the requirements of the covenant (Jer. 7).

If such is the import of the worship and sacrifice of the Old Covenant, we cannot doubt that the Sacrifice of the New Covenant must be understood along the same lines. We have, furthermore, the explicit affirmation of this in the Epistle to the Hebrews (19:19-21), which applies to the Sacrifice of Christ the details of the sacrifice which sealed the covenant of Sinai. What was effected at the conclusion of this covenant was reproduced, but in an infinitely more perfect way, in the Sacrifice of Jesus and is renewed each day in the Eucharistic liturgy: the Christian who participates in it engages himself in a covenant, that is to say, he makes his own, he undertakes the universal mission of the people of God.

In the Mass, therefore, are to be found the essential elements of the rite which concluded the first covenant: the presentation of the Word of God to the people by those who have received the mission to do so; acceptance by the believer engaging to obey the Law with his whole life; the sacrificial rite sealing the covenant in Christ's Blood.

We can see from this first aspect how great is the significance for the whole of Christian life of the proclamation of the Bible in the liturgy: by its union with a covenant-sacrifice, it requires of him who accepts it a personal commitment to prolong the echo of this Word in his whole life.

The Rite of the New Covenant Is An Efficacious Rite

This necessary prolongation in daily life of the Word of God proclaimed in the liturgy appears still more clearly when we recall the fact that the rite of which this proclamation is a part is not any kind of rite, but an *efficacious* one. The Sacrifice in which we participate does not only signify the covenant exteriorly, it inscribes it in the believer's heart, in the most intimate essence of his being, by infusing into him the grace and the charity of Christ.

Such is the superiority of the New Covenant over the Old. In the face of the continually recurring temptation to consider the book of the Law as nothing more than an external code, we see in the prophets from the period of the Exile on, the appearance of a nostalgic desire for a Law, for a Word of God, which would be inscribed directly in the thought and the heart of the chosen people. This is the New Covenant announced by Jeremias (31:31ff.) and by Ezechiel (36:25ff.), the concluding of which by the Sacrifice of Christ is proclaimed in the Epistle to the Hebrews: "I will place My laws in their thought, I will engrave them in their heart" (Hebr. 8:8-12).

Henceforth the Word of God, His law, is no longer written only on tablets of stone, or in a book which remains exterior to man; by the liturgical proclamation, by the interior adherence of the believer, by the efficacious rite this Word of God is inscribed in the deepest essence of man, there to become living and incarnate. As St. Paul says to the Corinthians, "Clearly you are a letter of Christ's, inscribed by our efforts, written not with ink but with the Spirit of the living God, not on tablets of stone, but on tablets of flesh, on your hearts" (2 Cor. 3:3).

Thus Bible and liturgy unite to produce the same wonderful effect: the Word of God proposed in the first, present and active in the second, transforms and vivifies the believer: "If the hierarchy communicates by the liturgy the truth and grace of Christ, it is for the faithful, on their part, to accept these wholeheartedly and to transform them into living realities" (Pius XII).[5]

The hierarchy is, therefore, not content with exteriorly presenting the truth; by the sacraments, it transforms the believer interiorly through infusing into him the life that animates the Body of Christ, the grace of the Holy Spirit. Now, we know from the teaching of St. Paul that what constitutes the New Law in its essence is, precisely, grace with the interior dynamism of charity which sums up *the Law and the Prophets*, that is to say, which sums up the whole Bible. The Word of God, of course, continues to be that written in a book, to be proclaimed exteriorly, but it depends only on the good will of the hearer for it to become also, in the most intimate part of himself, a living and divine force. As St. Paul said to the Romans: "The Word is near you, in your mouth and in your heart, that is, the word of faith, which we preach" (Rom. 10:8).

Such is the wonderful efficacy of the Christian ministry: the bishops, aided by their collaborators, the priests, are the "ministers of a New

[5] Allocution at the Assisi Congress, *The Assisi Papers* (Collegeville, Minn.: Liturgical Press, 1957), p. 226.

Covenant, not of the letter, but of the Spirit" (2 Cor. 3:3), having received the power not only externally to present the letter of the Word of God, but still more to inscribe this Word in the hearts of those who welcome its message; and these can then leave the liturgical celebration as bearers of this Word, to render it present in all human activities.

Whenever the Christian, then, comes again to take his part in the liturgy, the Word of God is presented to him afresh, both in the Biblical readings and in the official preaching. He is thus invited to compare his own life with the law which has been written in his heart, the requirements of which are expressed objectively in the external proclamation and preaching of it. However little he may be receptive to this proclamation of the Word, he will be judged by it; he will be led to an authentic revision of his life in the face of this mirror which is presented to him (cf. James 1:22-23). The constant reminder which the Church gives us of the requirements of the New Covenant is a perpetual invitation to him to take his part in the mission of the people of God, to become "not a forgetful hearer but a true doer" (James 1:15).

Furthermore, to him who has become aware of this pressing invitation, the liturgical proclamation of the Word of God will not run the risk of seeming to resemble simply, in the phrase of Ezechiel, "a song of love, pleasantly sung, to the accompaniment of music" (Ezech. 33:32), like an aesthetic entertainment. "For the Word of God is living and effective, more penetrating than any two-edged sword; it penetrates even to the point of division between soul and spirit, between the joints and the marrow of the bones, it can *judge* the feelings and the thoughts of the heart" (Hebr. 4:12).

It judges, first, the very way in which we take part in worship, especially in the Sacrifice of the New Covenant; for a man to bring his offering to the altar, to approach it himself, without having made the decision to bring about in his life what is signified by this eternal action, without being reconciled with his brother (Matt. 5:24), without seeking to overcome the egoisms of family, of country, of race, of social class (*cf.* James 2:2ff.) and sordid concerns (*ibid.*, 4:13ff.) is to deny interiorly the law of charity that he professes exteriorly in the Eucharistic assembly.

The Word of God also judges the whole life of the Christian. By its very nature it tends to grow, to produce fruits of justice and holiness, not only in the individual life of him who receives it but in his whole activity; it is a talent that he must multiply, the seed of the parable which only needs good soil in order to produce fruit a hundredfold.

As bearers of this Word, Christians are, therefore, also responsible for the mission of salvation of the people of the covenant. St. John Chrysostom insistently reminds his hearers of this duty to communicate to others the Word heard in the liturgical assembly, "each to take his part in my own ministry as bishop."[6] No personal holiness is possible without this concern for others; the Word of God become the law of charity in the Christian's heart is a force within him that tends to expand, a leaven that is to cause the whole mass of dough to rise, a light that cannot be left covered up.

But how is this diffusion of the Word to be brought about? We think first, obviously, of all the forms of individual or family apostolate, for which we find many practical counsels in the Epistles of St. Peter and St. Paul (1 Pet. 3:1-2; Col. 4:5-6). We think also of all the other forms of direct or indirect action on human societies. The Word of God is a leaven that is to penetrate everywhere as an invincible demand for justice and charity.

But the very nature of the New Law, which is above all *interior*, and its intimate association with a liturgy which is essentially *communal* should make us think also, and perhaps primarily, not so much of the external activities of charity, of social action or of instruction, as of action on the various kinds of mentality which are obstacles to the formation of a truly Christian community. As Pius XII said, the question is that of bringing the Word of God to others "so that they will live by it . . . to transform them, not from without by some superficial activity, but from within, so that they too will begin to see . . . and to conceive the desire, at first hesitating, then more assured, of changing themselves, and of becoming in their turn, in their own surroundings, centers of Christian life."[7]

Any activity that would transform social structures externally, without transforming the underlying ways of thinking of the various human groups, would not succeed in making the people of God into the true community of life and charity which the Eucharist signifies and requires. The Word, in judging the "feelings and thoughts of the heart" judges also, in and through each hearer, the mentality of his society with its more or less conscious resistances to the leaven of the Gospel; it imposes on him the duty to bring everything that is in himself first of all, and then in others, within the reach of its transforming power.

Many other prolongations of the Word of God in the life of Christians could certainly be indicated; it would be impossible to mention them all. But what we must still consider is the course which this Word should take from the moment when, in some fashion, it has reached the non-practicing Catholic or the non-Christian.

FROM PROCLAMATION IN LIFE TO THE LITURGICAL CELEBRATION

As we said at the beginning of this essay, the Word of God proclaimed in the liturgy reaches directly practicing Catholics only. Yet

[6] *P.G.*, 62:499.

[7] Discourse to the *Rinascita Cristiana, Osserv. Rom.*, 7 Nov. 1956.

this proclamation in the liturgy, by its very nature, demands extension into every human activity in which Christians engage; in this way it is to come into contact with all those engaged in the same activities.

But there remains the other difficulty which we have already pointed out – the opposition between the message of the Bible and the mentality of the modern world, or, simply, of the pagan world in general, whether it is a question of the difficulties due to the material presentation of the sacred Books, or of those more profound ones due to the nature of the message itself, the scandal of the Cross.

As we saw in the first part of our discussion, the Word of God is not only an external message but a living force, a law written in the hearts of Christians, one which should vivify their whole life; understood in this way, it is clear that the terms of the problem are profoundly altered. We are led to consider the problem of the position of the unbeliever in relation to the Biblical message as translated into the life of Christians. What might be the advance of the Word of God in a listener of good will from the very first contacts until the day when he is finally led to take part himself in the liturgical assembly gathered for the Eucharist?

Doubtless there is a real danger here – that of *a priorism* which does not take into account either the mystery or personal liberty, nor, above all, the infinitely varied activity of God's grace. Yet even here, the teaching of the Bible and of tradition does not leave us without some elements of a solution, and it may be useful to mention them briefly.

The Presentation of the Message of the Bible

To begin with, taking into account the conclusions of the first part of this essay, how would the message of the Bible ordinarily be presented to the unbeliever?

There are, certainly, cases in which a direct presentation of the Word, written or preached, to men of good will obtains at once its full effect; in our day there are still men who are seeking God and whom an apostolic word reaches with no effort, with the all-powerful aid of grace; so the eunuch from Ethiopia needed only Philip's explanations to come to the faith; similarly, the centurion Cornelius.

Ordinary believers also can carry the Word directly to their unbelieving brothers. After the martyrdom of Stephen, "all, except the apostles, were scattered abroad throughout the land of Judea and Samaria . . . now those who were scattered abroad went about preaching the Word" (Acts 8:1-4). Soon the same scattered believers "went all the way to Phoenicia and Cyprus and Antioch, speaking the Word to none but Jews only. But some of them were Cyprians and Cyreneans, who on reaching Antioch began to speak to the Greeks also, preaching the Lord Jesus. And the hand of the Lord was with them, and a great number believed and turned to the Lord" (Acts 11:19-21).

Yet the fact must always be emphasized that, even in such cases of a direct proclamation of the message, the question is not simply of contact with a written or spoken word; it is not a dead letter which is presented to the hearer; to this is added the living witness, the contact with a contemporary engaged in the same daily life and work and so witnessing to his certitude and his faith.

Frequently, moreover, and for innumerable reasons, any direct witness to the Word is impossible. St. Peter foresaw such cases when he wrote to Christian wives: "In like manner also let wives be subject to their husbands, so that even if any do not believe the Word, they may without the Word be won through the behavior of their wives, observing reverently your chaste behavior" (1 Pet. 3:1-2). And, in a more general way: "Behave yourselves honorably among the pagans; that, whereas they slander you as evildoers, they may, through observing your good works, glorify God in the day of visitation" (1 Pet. 2:12). In all such cases the question is one of the witness given by the whole of Christian life, a witness which is summed up in one word: *charity.*

Charity, first of all, among Christians themselves. We cannot insist too much on the importance of this witness, for Christ told us that this is the special sign of His own mission: "That all may be one, even as Thou, Father, in Me and I in Thee; that they also may be one in Us, that the world may believe that Thou hast sent Me . . . I in them and Thou in Me, that they may be perfected in unity, and that the world may know that Thou hast sent Me and that Thou hast loved them even as Thou hast loved Me" (John 17:21-23).

This unity of Christians in charity should, then, be such that it arouses the wonder of non-Christians, as being a real moral miracle which discloses the very presence of the power of God. Here again, we know that this should be a normal fruit of the Eucharistic liturgy, as the ceremony of Holy Thursday reminds us with such insistence.

Charity also to those outside the Church. The unbeliever ought to be able to see this love at work not only among Christians but in their attitude toward all mankind, and, here and now, toward himself.[8] Then the Word of God will cease to seem merely an old and venerable book, good at most for archeologists and Oriental scholars. He will hear this Word addressing him *personally,* as an *invitation* or a call. Every real love is an invitation to enter into communion with him who loves, to accept the *good* that he offers us; every love of true Christian charity should, then, appear as an invitation to participate in the truth and the blessings that give meaning to this charity "which sums up the Law and the Prophets," that is to say, as an invitation to enter into Biblical history itself.

[8] In this connection, cf. in H. U. von Balthasar, *Science, Religion and Christianity* (Westminster, Md.: Newman Press, 1959), the chapter on "The Sacrament of the Brother." (*Edit. note*)

For this is precisely the question – one of a history of salvation, a history not only of the past but of the present, always living, always active, tending toward the realization of the true welfare of all mankind, toward its salvation. The charity of Christians should be such as to manifest through their whole lives the infinite Love of which their own love is only a feeble echo, the Love that vivifies the whole history of salvation and continues to solicit the love of the human heart, as in the time of Abraham and of the prophets, and, above all, as it was manifested in Christ.

But this will not come about unless Christians themselves have truly made the Christian law the law of their deepest being; they must make it, not simply a code of morals, wholly external, a collection of observances or customs which have frequently lost their true significance, but the very love of Christ at work in them, which leads them in turn to sacrifice themselves for the salvation of the world.

If only Christians who approached an unbeliever were true Christians, engaged in their vocation with their whole soul, aware of their role in the continuing history of salvation, but also wholly present in the current history of the world, manifesting in all their actions the invisible power of the charity which is the soul and the summary of the whole history of salvation – could the unbeliever help being profoundly affected? The question is how to bring about a real contact with the Bible, with that wonderful history of the people of God, the great stages of which the Apocalypse describes in advance, which is, finally, the history of the initiatives taken by Love to save the world.

Thus the presentation of the Word of God, concretely, is infinitely diversified; each Christian is to translate it into the myriad forms of his own life. The workman ought to be able to perceive it in his companion at work, the intellectual in the behavior of his companions in study. This was the great intuition of Pius XI when he stated the necessity for the apostolate of "like by like."

And it is also by this means, not only that the Word of God will reach each man in his own language, but also that with the grace of God the scandal of the Cross can be surmounted. It is only love that can make attractive and desirable what is so repugnant to our nature; sacrifice, mortification, and such requirements can only seem legitimate if they are understood to be a requirement of saving love.

It is the task of each Christian to make comprehensible to the world by his own life that when he refuses impurity, egoism or hatred, he does not do so out of a kind of superstitious respect for an external law or out of fear of some punishment, but because he has chosen freely, following his Master, to be led by love alone and so to refuse everything that is incompatible with that love: "The children of God," St. Thomas writes, "are led by the Holy Spirit freely, under the impulse of love, and not as slaves are, by fear. . . . That man acts like a slave who, from fear of the law only, abstains from doing what he continues to desire to do . . . he is the slave of the law, not its friend."[9]

Catholic life should give the same impression of freedom that it produced on the Russian thinker Rozanov: "With them discipline is free: Brothers, you are called to heroism, to a most difficult life, but remain free. . . . Yes, we are going to carry out great and hard deeds, but we are going to do so freely. . . . This dialogue constitutes the soul of Catholicism."[10]

The Presentation of the Liturgy

We may hope that many men of good will, led in this way, if not to understand fully, at least to consider the Biblical message with esteem and sympathy, may be further led to question themselves. Here again the Word of God as it manifests itself in the life of their Christian brothers comes to judge them, to invite them to a revision of their lives. What would be the normal goal of this progress of the Word in such persons? Would it be enough if it led them to repent, to change their lives, or even personally to read and meditate on the Bible? In other words, would it be enough to lead them, by example or by the Word, to lead a moral life, to pray, to carry out to the greatest possible extent the spiritual worship of a virtuous life, of doing good, or even of personal prayer in the Name of Christ and through Christ?

All this would certainly constitute a most important step, but we know that it is not enough; the Acts of the Apostles indicate this on every page. The Ethiopian who was returning from Jerusalem was a religious man who made pilgrimages and read the prophet Isaias; but he still needed to hear the teaching of Philip the deacon and to receive baptism at his hand. The preaching of the Bible carried out by the Church leads to the liturgical celebration, to baptism.

Nor is baptism the final goal. A number of Samaritans had already been baptized in the Name of the Lord Jesus. But then Peter and John "laid their hands upon them that they might receive the Holy Spirit" (Acts 8:17). There is no need to mention more examples. We all know that a conversion is complete only when a man has fully entered into the people of God which is the Church. And the Church is not simply an invisible society of just or predestined men, but the very Body of Christ, prolonging here below, by human actions that are the bearers of truth and grace, the life-giving presence of the incarnate Word.

To accept the Bible for what it truly is means to accept it as God's invitation to enter into the history of salvation, the great stages of which it describes. And each man who enters into the Church must relive in his personal life these decisive stages in the life of God's people, in the mystery of a communal liturgy.

[9] *Contra Gent.,* IV, 22.
[10] Quoted by S. Tyszkiewicz in *Nouv. Rev. Théol.* (Dec., 1952), p. 1071.

Like the people of God held captive in Egypt, he must agree to enter into the mystery of the Pasch, of deliverance from sin, to hear the call that God transmits to him by His official representatives and, passing through the water of baptism, be united to those who on the banks of the Jordan sing the canticle of Moses and the canticle of the Lamb (Apoc. 15:3).

Then, with the people on pilgrimage he must agree to enter into the mystery of Pentecost, to approach, not to Sinai, "a mountain that may be touched, and a burning fire, and whirlwind and darkness and storm, and sound of trumpet . . . but to Jesus, Mediator of a New Covenant" (Heb. 12:18ff.), to engage personally in this covenant and to become the witness of the law of the Spirit by the sacrament of confirmation.

And, finally, he must seal this covenant and renew it periodically by participation in the Eucharistic sacrifice and nourish himself during his pilgrimage toward the true Land of Promise with the true Bread of Heaven, of which the manna was only an image.

In a word, the only real acceptance of the message of the Bible is that which leads a man to enter into Biblical history itself, continued in the life of the Church and especially in its liturgy. The Epistle to the Hebrews says: "not forsaking our assembly" (10:28), and these words are to be understood above all, as F. J. Schierse[11] has recently shown, of the liturgical assembly.

It is here that every convert must finally be united with the whole Christian people to hear the Word of God proclaimed officially by those who have received the charge of doing so: "In the liturgical function," said A. Bea, S.J., speaking to the Assisi Congress, "the shepherd of souls speaks not as the president of an association or director of a club or professor in a scholastic chair. Here the priest speaks as a priest, as teacher and guide of the souls entrusted to him, deputy of God, appointed and sent by the bishop, successor of the apostles."[12] And the Epistle to the Hebrews, again, says of the rebellious Jews: "But the word that was heard did not profit them, since they did not remain in communion with those who heard" (4:2).

And it is not only to hear the proclamation of the Word of God that one must come to the liturgy. Since, as we have said, the sacraments cause us to enter into the people of God, each of the members of this people must be united in the community prayer which is, according to the expression of Pius XII, "the worship of the whole Mystical Body." And we cannot doubt that this prayer, itself wholly inspired by the Bible, is the truest means of rendering us capable of hearing the Word of God as God wishes it to be heard. For if it is true that "no prophecy of Scripture is made by private interpretation" (Rom. 8:27) and only the Holy Spirit can cause us to enter into

[11] *Verheissung und Heilsollendung,* (Munich, 1955).
[12] *The Assisi Papers,* (Collegeville, Minn.: Liturgical Press, 1957), p. 84.

the true thought of the Bible, it is also certain that only an interior attitude of docility can give us habitual entrance to the school of the Spirit: "Take heed, therefore, how you hear," warns our Lord (Luke 8:18).

Now this attitude of interior docility is the fruit of prayer, and of a prayer which is "according to God" (Rom. 8:27); there is no more certain guarantee of true prayer than to unite oneself with the official prayer of the Church, for of ourselves "we do not know what we should pray for as we ought" (Rom. 8:26). In this way the liturgy little by little forms the Christian character, according to the desire of Solomon for "a heart that knows how to listen" (1 Kings 3:9). The Word of God, falling onto good ground, produces fruit "in one case a hundredfold, in another sixtyfold, and in another thirtyfold" (Matt. 13:23).

Here again, to bring the non-Christian to desire and to accept this participation in the liturgical life of the Church, how important is the witness of those already participating! How can he understand that the liturgy is the concrete means of entering into the people of the New Covenant if he does not see us practice in our whole lives the charity which the covenant should have inscribed in our hearts? How can the Eucharistic assembly appear to those outside the Church as being the *sign* and the *source* of Christian love if we do not manifest this love outside the limits of the sanctuary, if we do not go out determined to live up to its requirements? The recent studies of Bo Reicke and certain of the papers given at the national Eucharistic Congress at Barcelona have strongly insisted on this essential bond between the Eucharist and charity: if this bond is not visible, the Christian liturgy will not show its true face to the world.

And, finally, if Christians seem to have little affection for the liturgy, if they participate in it only to the extent to which they are obliged to do so by an external law, what a sad idea they give of it! If, as the Epistle to the Hebrews says, the people freed from Egypt approached Sinai in an atmosphere of fear and trembling to receive the first covenant, the new people of God should approach the Sacrifice of the New Covenant and all the other rites connected with it in quite a different disposition. This is a Eucharist, a thanksgiving which we celebrate, united to "the heavenly Jerusalem, and to the company of many thousands of angels, and to the Church of the first-born who are enrolled in the heavens" (Heb. 12:22-23).

How can anyone believe that we are risen with Christ, "reborn, not from corruptible seed, but from incorruptible, through the Word of God" (1 Pet. 1:23), if we do not show in our liturgical assemblies and in our eagerness to participate in them that atmosphere of paschal joy which befits the Eucharist? In a word, the liturgy of the Church can only show its true face to those outside the Church if Christians practice in their life what the liturgical mysteries signify.

CONCLUSION

It has often been remarked that in the New Testament the technical terms designating worship, liturgy, sacrifices, and even the priesthood, are almost always used to mean the Christian life or the apostolate; the fact is so striking that certain exegetes and non-Catholic theologians have tried to conclude from it to a lack of all external liturgical worship, or at least of any real sacrifice. While, of course, we cannot accept this conclusion, the usage of the New Testament nonetheless remains extremely significant, for it reminds us that each liturgical celebration has meaning and value only to the extent to which it is bound up with the *life* of Christians united to their Head in carrying out the same work of the salvation of the world.

If the Word of God has been made flesh, it is to bring back to the Father, in the unique Sacrifice that gives meaning to our liturgy, the whole of redeemed mankind. If the Word of God is still addressed to us today in the liturgy, it is to continue this work of the Word incarnate, so that we may make up in our own flesh what is wanting to the sufferings of Christ.

Here we must beware of a certain misunderstanding. It is rightly said that the purpose of the liturgy is to procure the glory of God. Nothing could be more exactly true. But there is a tendency to forget that this glory of God is, according to the expression of theologians, His extrinsic glory, that is to say, the knowledge that men may have of Him and His wonderful works, a knowledge such that it expands in praise: *clara cum laude notitia.* Recent studies have reminded us of this: no worship, no liturgy, however splendid or solemn, procures the glory of God except to the extent to which it leads men better to know and to serve their God. As St. Irenaeus said long ago and as St. Thomas repeated after him, it is for the good of men, and only for this good, that God requires liturgical worship; to lose sight of this purpose would be to take away from our liturgy all its meaning.

The day will come when the sacramental cult will cease and the Word of God will make itself heard with no intermediary in the inmost depths of our hearts. In the heavenly Jerusalem there will no longer be any external temple, for the "the Lord God almighty and the Lamb are the temple thereof" (Apoc. 21:22). There will no longer be in it any intermediary to proclaim the Word of God: "The city has no need of sun or moon to shine upon it, for the glory of God lights it up and the Lamb is the lamp thereof" (Apoc. 21:23).

But, here and now, our Christian worship, by inscribing in our hearts the Word of the covenant, renders us capable of preparing by all our good works for the nuptial liturgy of heaven: "For the marriage of the Lamb has come, and His spouse has prepared herself. And she has been permitted to clothe herself in fine linen, shining, bright. For the fine linen is the *just deeds of the saints*" (Apoc. 19:7-8).

Most Rev. Otto Spuelbeck

CHAPTER 10

THE LITURGY AND THE WORD OF GOD IN PARISH LIFE IN THE GERMAN DIASPORO

SINCE I WAS INVITED to discuss the Bible and the liturgy as realities in parish life, I am taking the liberty of handling this subject, not from the viewpoint of an ordinary German parish, but of those in the great cities of the "diaspora," that is to say, the dispersion of a weak Catholic minority among the whole population. This diaspora in the great cities presents at once special difficulties and special possibilities, and the exposition of these will, I trust, help to shed light on our subject.

In the great city of Leipzig, of which I am going to speak and in which I have exercised the ministry for twenty years, the number of Catholics is a "negligible quantity," hardly 6% of the population. A parish in this great city takes on the aspect of a *paroikia*, leading a life apart, alongside of the political community, in which each person individually has the feeling of being a *paroikos*, that is, a stranger, in the sense that the word is used in St. Peter's First Epistle (2:11). The city of Leipzig is part of the diocese of Meissen, which includes the ancient land of Saxony and has some 7-8% Catholics in a population of six million. This diocese is almost as large as the dioceses of Strasbourg, Nancy and Metz put together.

The situation of the diaspora in such a large city was aggravated by the attacks of the Nazis; it is characterized today in a special way by the militant atheism to which the political situation exposes us. The Soviet occupation forces give complete freedom of action to Marxist atheism. Our Catholics are a minority as compared to the Protestants, and their faith is exposed to the permanent menace of Soviet atheism as taught in all the schools, universities and professional schools and dominating all the newspapers. Private or Catholic schools are forbidden.

How, in such a situation, can the life of faith of a parish community be developed? It is with profound gratitude to God that we say: Catholic life does indeed flourish, and the tried fidelity of our Catholics enjoys a special blessing.

To explain this, I will first give an analysis of our religious situation. Protestantism in central Germany has turned away from church. In this country, which counts 90% of the population as baptized evangelical Christians, only 1% in the country and, at most, 2% in the cities attend Sunday worship. In addition to the Protestants who do attend their churches, there are some 8% convinced Christians who take the Biblical Word of God seriously and call themselves evangelicals even though they do not attend any church.

As to the religious activity of our Catholics, the situation is numerically more favorable. At Leipzig we have more than 33% as participants in Sunday worship. In spite of the great distances involved, Catholics do attend holy Mass. But what does this mean in the normal life of Leipzig? Out of every hundred people, only four at the most, Catholics and Protestants included, go to church; 96% have become strangers, if not actually hostile, to any church. In the consciousness of the man on the street the Church plays no part.

At Leipzig, this alienation from the Protestant Church has gone so far that, according to the superintendent of the Protestant Church, in the past twenty-five years more than a hundred thousand children have not been baptized; in other words, within this great city another great city has been formed no longer having any contact with religion, Christianity, or the Church. The latter has become a foreign body, a relic of times gone by. And this is especially true of the Catholic Church. The question of the truth of the Christian message no longer even arises. Places of work – the factory, the office and public life – are strangers to everything religious.

To this is added the massive attack of political atheism. Whoever desires advancement must declare himself to have no connections with any church. On one's identification card is noted the fact of not belonging to any church. Since the Church does not exercise any attraction on people, nobody hesitates thus to separate himself from it definitively.

According to Marx, "religion is the opium of the people"; and this is proclaimed everywhere by propaganda. Buildings of worship are called "places to meet the fumes of opium" (Boukharine). Cartloads of mud gathered up in anti-clerical publications are thrown at the Church. We have neither the right to defend ourselves nor the possibility of doing so. True, we have a Catholic publishing house and a weekly religious paper, *The Day of the Lord,* of which we print some 125,000 copies. But the total number of the faithful who attend church in the Democratic Republic of Germany is 600,000. All discussion with Marxism is made impossible. So the environment in which our Catholics live is wholly poisoned, either by a liberal Protestantism turned away from the Church, or by a militant atheism of Soviet manufacture.

Up to the end of the last war, our diocese counted 190,000 Catholics, who even then were insufficiently served by the existing ecclesiastical organization. By the evacuations of the East, of Silesia, of East Prussia, of Czechoslovakia, and Hungary, 290,000 more Catholics have been added, so that today the number of Catholics is two and a half times greater than before the war. These people are scattered throughout the whole country; worship is celebrated once a month, sometimes in the dance-hall of a hotel, sometimes in the Protestant church or a school hall.

How can the life of faith expand in such poverty and in this poisoned atmosphere? Is it not condemned to perish? Everything is lacking that might support faith: the living, praying community, the beautiful church of one's own, the experience of feasts and celebrations, religious environment, Catholic books, chant books, prayer books, religious publications. And we live in surroundings that are foreign and even hostile to the Church.

And yet, certain conditions, certain favorable antecedents have allowed us to accomplish something in this desperate situation.

1) *The Catholics of the diaspora before the war remained faithful.* Our parishes were established from fifty to a hundred years ago and were composed of fervent believers, originally from Catholic regions, from Bavaria, the Rhineland, Westphalia, Silesia. Coming into a Protestant society, formerly they preserved their faith. Since that time many apostatized; a certain number still remained faithful. Thus years ago a selection had already been made of those who with unshakable fidelity gathered around their Church and their pastors. This remnant of some 25-30% had preserved their faith at the price of many struggles and controversies. They still bore the scars of the wounds sustained in this combat. It was an élite – of men, it is true, not of saints – but of tried Catholic fidelity, filled with an apostolic and missionary spirit.

2) *There was the trial of the Nazi era.* These Catholics were once more hardened and tried in the times of Hitler; the chaff was separated from the good grain. Many weakened; others, however, went from an indifferent to an active religious life. The trial was severe but it was salutary. Almost every parish community had a martyr, men who compromised themselves for the Jews or for the workers for a foreign power, and because of this they were shut up in concentration camps and died there. The sufferings of these valiant men and women bore fruit. Their suffering and their death drew down God's blessing on our sadly isolated diaspora.

3) *Now we are suffering the trial by Marxism.* We were prepared for it by the two previous ones. If we may make any such summary judgment, we might even say that the Marxist ideology has gained no ground in the sphere of the Catholic Church. On the contrary, magnificent examples give witness to an unshakable perseverance in the faith. The massive attacks against the faith have forced our Catholics to thought and to discussion, and many have thus come to know their faith more profoundly, to love it and to practice it.

Under these circumstances, one might think that our Christian life must have been reduced to a kind of catacomb existence, in which nothing could be kept but the minimum necessary for administering the sacraments and teaching doctrine, as if we had to live on "iron rations." But actually things have turned out differently. In this hard dialectic and this incessant trial imposed by the atheistic atmosphere, our faithful have gained a more perceptive regard for what is essential and fundamental. Our religious life in the diaspora does not have at its disposal many rich and varied forms from which one may choose according to one's taste and for enjoyment. All the same, our faithful demand religious forms and celebrations; but they want those which will sustain them and help them to carry the day's burden.

We were all in agreement on the fact that the Sunday Mass is the decisive function of our pastoral ministry. Its celebration should be at the same time a fitting form of worship, a school of prayer, a catechesis in the faith, and a radiant center of life. This is why our first pastoral task is and always will be the proper carrying out of the sacred liturgy, but in a way adapted to the parish. What is primary should also call for the most joyful and intense effort.

To this end, we all took the resolution not to refuse any amount of work and not to be afraid of any loss of time. Conscious of our responsibility, we prepared with great care for the celebrations in our parishes, so threatened in their faith; we were especially heedful of the choice of hymns, of the selection of readers and prayer-leaders, of the formation of servers. And in addition to the servers, very vital groups of young people have been formed, the choir of readers and prayer-leaders, who became indispensable to us for a worthy celebration of Sunday Mass.

In this way we succeeded in founding, in the midst of this otherwise disastrous dispersion, ardent centers of true liturgical prayer. The work of the Oratorians of Leipzig, who for many years have carried on the work of the liturgical education and formation of the Christian people, is well known. Our people must be able to live from the celebration and the preaching given at it. This is the "iron ration" that we have to dispense, and this must suffice for a whole week. There is no room for any accessory religious decoration nor for any refinements; here the kind of bread offered must be substantial, a nourishment that will vivify, fortify and strengthen souls.

We asked ourselves, also, whether we should not first of all defend the faith against these many attacks. But we refused any cheap apologetics. The Word of the Lord in St. John's Gospel was our guide: "If anyone desires to do the will of God, he will know whether my teaching comes from God, or whether I speak on my own authority" (John 7:17). Unbelief that is tired, desperate or skeptical will not let itself be overcome by arguments but only by actions. We must practice the faith, and then the heart will be inflamed. Unbelief that is aggressive and enthusiastic, such as is preached by the Marxists, can only be conquered by a faith that is more enthusiastic. A heart filled with love and ardor kindles others also and conquers everything. What is decisive is to have a heart filled with Christ, full of burning love for Christ.

It was evident, then, that an immediate contact with Christ was essential and, consequently, that the Eucharistic celebration must be our first concern, and not didactic and explanatory sermons.

The parish community lives from the Eucharist. We have often experienced this fact. When we tried to assemble the faithful for works of charity or for meetings of parish groups, or to gather the children together for religious instruction, we would never reach more than a part of the faithful each time. But when holy Mass was celebrated, and this often in poor and primitive localities, the faithful came from all sides. We did not know them as yet; but they knew Christ and let themselves be gathered together by Him. The Eucharist has the power to build communities. We have living examples of this fact.

Thus the Eucharistic celebration became of itself the rallying point for the diaspora. It was necessary for us, then, to arrange this celebration in such a way that modern man, so active, might himself be active in it. He must be concerned in the celebration of the Mass and stimulated to active participation. The man of today is disposed to assume some responsibility in his social group and to take part in activity. If this is refused him, he becomes uninterested and soon is lost in the passive crowd.

There could be no question, therefore, of devoting our effort to liturgical refinements or to any formalism; the question was to create a living community, ready to participate actively, not remaining silent as at a play or spectacle. The parish must grow in vigor – then it would be capable of missionary action and by its vitality reanimate dead members. As in certain German dioceses the Reform was checked by allowing the Latin high Mass to be celebrated with hymns in the German language, in a similar way the faith has been saved among us. And the familiarity of the priests with the faithful people of our diaspora has greatly facilitated the work.

The custom of the parishioners' taking part in the prayers, the hymns and the acclamations, the alternation between the prayer-leader, the reader, the choir are so well established that there are no more private or low Masses. Even the *Gloria,* for instance, is taken up, when an organist is lacking, in a German hymn which the priest at the altar frequently has to intone himself; but the community sings, sings a hymn of God's glory. Or else the parts proper to the people are prayed together aloud.

How often have I celebrated Mass during these last ten years in prisons, under the most difficult circumstances, with no organist, no server, no sacristan! And with what intensity have the men and women present celebrated the Mass with me, praying and singing together. Only a few words are needed to explain its structure, so understandable and natural are the dialogue prayers of the liturgy. It is most important, then, to emphasize the value of this kind of dialogue.

I experienced this afresh a few weeks ago when at Neue-Zelle, near Frankfurt-on-the-Oder, I conferred priestly ordination on three deacons. A great cross, placed on the altar in the open air, saluted, as it were, the country of Silesia across the Oder, which now belongs to Poland. Around the altar some 2,500 people were assembled to assist for the first time at an ordination. All of them had been driven out of that country, their homeland, beyond the Oder. There I experienced the profound meaning of the sacred dialogue when the bishop, facing that country that they had left with so much suffering and addressing these young people with no homeland, gave the acclamation: *Pax vobis,* and they all replied courageously: *Et cum spiritu tuo.* It is this dialogue form, this living acclamation, the singing and prayer of the people that have welded together the community of our faithful.

What always matters is the Sacrifice of the Lord. This Christ who offers Himself – I must see Him, I must feel Him present, meet Him and wholly unite myself with Him. To meet the violent attacks of unbelief requires valiant hearts filled with the love of Christ. Without Him we cannot withstand the enemy. Our own miseries and cares, our own sufferings must be poured into the Sacrifice of the Lord, and this needs to be expressed in a visible way. It is not enough to explain this and to cause people to realize it interiorly. It is not enough spiritually to place one's own offering on the paten of the priest.

Each of the faithful, therefore, without any commotion places in the cup a little host which represents his own poverty and weakness; then after the *Credo* the subdeacon, or the servers at a recited Mass, carry this cup in procession to the altar in the name and in the place of the faithful.

This Offertory procession has come to be of capital importance to us. At the entrance of the church are placed the table of offerings, a cup with the hosts, a silver spoon to place the hosts on the paten, which in this case is a ciborium. No great explanation is needed. The faithful understand its significance at once. Whoever wishes to communicate places his host in the ciborium on entering the church, and at the moment of the Offertory procession everyone present spontaneously stands up, without needing any command, and thus associates himself visibly with the rite. The offering is consecrated and changed into the Body of Christ and distributed at Communion: *ex hac altaris participatione.* Then we can sing the song of triumph: *Christus vincit! Christus regnat! Christus imperat!*

I consider this Offertory procession, carried out by the ministers or servers in the name and in the place of the whole community, as being a decisive act in the Mass. In the principal church of Leipzig, where I exercised the ministry for a long time, some 4,000 of the faithful come to Mass, and each Mass has this Offertory procession.

I deny the objection that such a procession is not possible in a big city parish where the congregation is constantly changing. I have tried it out during periods of continual change in membership, when Sunday after Sunday many strangers took part in the celebration. The regularity of the Offertory procession formed the community to such a point that even at the solemn high Mass on feastdays, which could not begin before 11:30, we distributed hundreds of Communions. To become integrated in Christ and His Sacrifice — this is what matters; but this must be brought about in a living way with rites and gestures that are expressive and dynamic.

When the love of Christ inflames the heart of a Christian, then he is also capable of defending his faith and of perceiving what is essential. Here are two examples: in the time of the Nazis, when the Church was being severely oppressed, a young man, about nineteen years old, came to hunt me up. It was certainly a moment of grace when he confessed to me, "I am not good. My father and mother are not happy about me, nor am I about myself. But I know one thing: I love Christ our Lord."

Another quite recent example, again of a young man about twenty years old. The Communist organization "Free German Youth," as well as his comrades at work, had been trying to force him to leave the Catholic Youth organization and to enroll in the people's police. For three days he had to keep on answering his seven questioners:

"Come with us. What have you got to do with priests? It is we who have science; the future is ours. With us you can get somewhere." At the end he did not know what to say, but he answered them spontaneously: "Among the Catholic Youth I find what you do not have and cannot give me: I find Christ, and He is what I want." After this frank profession of his attachment to Christ they left him alone.

It is Christ whom we must have. To have recognized this fact in our desperate situation, does not this justify the course on which we have embarked? Does this not bring back every kind of teaching of the faith to the simplest and most direct path? What is the essence of Christianity? Here is the answer: *Christianity is Christ.* The liturgy, when it is dynamic, that is to say, set in action and clearly dialogued, is the power of the Christian of the diaspora in his life-and-death struggle for his faith. What we experience on Palm Sunday during the acclamations to Christ, on Good Friday during the adoration of the Cross, on the night of Easter during the acclamation to the new light: *Lumen Christi! Deo Gratias!*, only the further confirms us in our convictions. This confidence in the sacred efficacy of the liturgy sustains, nourishes and strengthens our faith.

But participation in the sacred action is still not all that is needed to enter into union with Christ; for faith comes from hearing. We must, therefore, break the bread of the Word. The mind also needs to be nourished in the way that is proper to it. It is necessary not only to receive the bread of life in the holy Eucharist, but also the bread of the Word in preaching and prayer. At each Sunday Mass throughout the whole year we have preaching, although this preaching must always be brief. (Longer didactic sermons are given only in the afternoon or evening at special services.) Such continual proclamation of the Word gives it the weight and the penetrating quality that come from something carried out regularly. This breaking of the bread of the Word Sunday after Sunday, and again during the week in Masses for young people, for women, has opened out hearts and nourished minds.

In our region the Bible has retained to the present day, thanks to Protestantism, a high degree of prestige. Even those who have given up the articles of faith greatly esteem the Bible, if only as the book of a sublime way of living, full of wisdom and deep reflection. Thus our faithful are naturally open to the Biblical Word. There are many people who, while turning away from the churches, find inspiration in and live by the Biblical sayings for each day of the year published by the Fraternal Union of the Free Church of the Moravian Brothers, called the *Herrnhut.* For such people each day is to be inspired by a word from the Bible. In the same way, our faithful are open to the words of the Introits, Graduals, Offertories and Communions, understanding that the Church in celebrating the Eucharist does not formulate her own prayers, but gives us the words of the Bible.

Thus they learn to make use of the Biblical Word for their own prayer. Our book of diocesan prayer, *Laudate,* contains for the Introit and Gradual of each Mass extra psalm verses for use in community Masses; in the same way, for the Communion chant, the antiphon alternates with several verses of the psalm proper to the Sunday. The faithful are glad to be able to use the divine Word to express the joy or the anguish of their own hearts. It is by this means that the psalms and the sapiential Books of the Old Testament have entered into our hearts. With great fervor our faithful read beforehand the texts of the Sunday Mass.

Our diocesan prayer book contains the Propers of all the Sunday and feastday Masses of the liturgical year. Many are the people who have found that in praying these texts they have heard the pressing call of God which accompanied them all through the day and even through the following week. In former times our faithful used at Mass some book of devotions containing exercises composed by a pious author. Today they love the texts of the Mass itself. Among our parishioners everywhere there are groups for the study and reading of the Bible. The majority of the faithful do not take part in such groups, yet all love their missal, which is their familiar companion.

Thus the greatness and majesty of the divine Word of the Old Testament are revealed to us. We have learned to know God the all holy, all powerful, God the eternal and infinite. We understand what it means to fear His justice, to await His judgment, to hope in His providence. The great personages of the Old Covenant, the prophets, the just men, stand before us in their austerity as well as in their intimacy with God.

We have done everything possible to bring alive to our people the imposing and venerable image of the God of the Old Covenant. The liberal tendency of Protestantism in our land has spoiled and enfeebled the image of God; this is why we need to bring out the true majesty and grandeur of God, of God who causes the mountains to tremble and shatters the forests, who raises up the waves of the sea and calms its billows, who in our worst distresses demands of us an unreserved confidence in His fatherly goodness. We have seen Christians weeping when the Nazis set fire to synagogues, because a place that was God's had been destroyed, and we thought of the verse of the psalm: "Tears flow in rivers from my eyes, because men do not keep Your law" (*Ps.* 118).

In such surroundings there is nothing to do but to place oneself completely on the side of God and His commandments. Our faithful understand quite well those other words of the psalmist when Marxism openly scoffs at God's commandments and opposes a Communist ethic to Christian morality: "Your decrees have become my songs, in the place where I abide" (*Ps.* 118:54). Or another verse of the same psalm: "Just wrath lays hold of me because of sinners who forsake Your law." "The law of God is in his heart" (*Ps.* 86:31). Confidence in God and His protecting hand permeates the psalms and takes hold of the faithful, who so often lack consolation and feel themselves so forsaken. In the words of the Mass they learn that "the Lord is near to all who call upon Him" (*Ps.* 144:18), and they say: "Lord, into Your hands I commend my spirit" (*Ps.* 30:6; Luke 23:45).

The so-called *positive Christianity* of Hitler revealed to us the malice of Satan. Since that time we know how to pray the psalms containing maledictions, and we would not do without them – not that we wish to curse other men, but we have seen Satan at work and we know that one can make no agreements with the devil. There is only an unequivocal "No" to oppose him with, and an absolute "Yes" to say to God. These psalms repeat to us that in our days also the devil "goes about like a roaring lion, seeking whom he may devour" (1 Pet. 5:8). To resist him, we cannot remain hesitant, unwilling to commit ourselves. We must call him by his name. To protect ourselves against the demon we must frankly protest against his machinations in everyday life.

Our times minimize too much the work of the Evil One; they lack discernment of spirits. This is why we pray the psalms of malediction and learn afresh to range ourselves with intensity and passion on God's side. A heart that trembles but that is entirely on God's side, taken hold of by God, turned to God, is expressed in this prayer. One must have seen the malice of Satan actually at work to realize the degree to which our present world is threatened, and how supremely important it is to devote ourselves passionately to God.

This is exactly what has happened amongst us with regard to Soviet Marxism. Unceasingly it tries to conquer our faithful by flattery. It says: "Religion is a private affair." We answer: "God is not a private individual. God is the supreme, most serious reality. God is the Lord." And when the saying of Karl Marx echoes continually in our ears: "Religion is the opium of the people, it stupefies men's minds," we can only protest against it passionately and confess God with an ardent heart. For us, the Old Testament, with its obvious struggle for the true God against the pagan divinities, has become a book of vital importance. In our editions of the New Testament we give as a supplement a choice of psalms; our faithful make use of them gladly. And thus we know to what a point the image of the God of the Old Covenant and an attachment to Him that is filled with love is essential to us and helps us.

If the prayer texts of the Mass are food for the soul, if they guarantee to us the presence and help of God and enable us to keep our heads in a life filled with cares, troubles and difficulties, the Gospel is in a special way a meeting with Christ. His Word resounds. We must reawaken the love of His Word. It is now, at the present time, that we hear Him, and here and now the question is: "What would He say today if He were in my place, what would He do? What would He answer?"

We remind ourselves of the beautiful sentence of Adam Moehler which he said about a century ago at Tuebingen: "Without holy Scripture, we should be deprived of the original and special form of Jesus' discourse; we should not know how the Man-God actually spoke; and it seems to me that I would not wish to go on living if I could not hear Him speak." But he added: "Without tradition, we should not know who He is who spoke and what He proclaimed, and the joy of knowing His manner of speaking would disappear."[1] We hear the Word of the Lord which is addressed not to a bygone age, but to us. He converses with us, and we wish to answer Him.

This interior dialogue engenders in us an ardent love for Christ. We reach out to Him, it is He whom we must never abandon! To possess Him, that is what matters. In the discussions that take place among us everything has an existential value and is permeated with a warm breath, that of an impassioned love for Christ. Christ today! This is the perpetually recurring theme of our brief sermons: The Lord is our salvation!

Our parishioners insistently ask for books about Christ. The work of Romano Guardini, although it demands a great effort from the reader, has gone through many editions. Under our circumstances, it is all the more necessary that the series of Sunday pericopes be augmented, so that the image of the Lord may shine out in new ways in our Sunday celebrations also.

What we have just said might perhaps induce our readers to believe that our services are frequented by congregations entirely made up of profound and ardent believers. No, our parishioners have their faults and imperfections like other people. But in our poverty we have the wealth offered to us by the liturgy and the Biblical Word. We have tried to arouse in our faithful the joy of possessing such riches. Our people know what they have to defend.

The massive attacks of militant atheism create clear and precise lines of battle and fix our attention on the bridgehead to be defended. This is the Lord Jesus Christ. In the language of the Bible, He is the Keystone. Everything depends on Him. If, then, not only our young people but also our adults wear a small silver cross on their lapels, it is not as the insignia of some large organization, but a clear and frank profession of faith in Jesus Christ crucified and risen again. With humble gratitude we dare confess that this love of Christ has grown among us and that it does not cease to manifest itself.

Two recent experiences confirm this. First, the pilgrimage to Rosenthal of our diocesan youth in May 1957. On trucks, bicycles, on foot these young people came together from the whole diocese, to the number of 10,000. The pontifical Mass was celebrated in the open air, 6,000 communicated, and in the afternoon we went in pilgrimage,

[1] Moehler, *L'Unité dans l'Église,* p. 53.

singing and praying under a burning sun, to the old convent of the Cistercians of Marienstern, some seven kilometers away. All this cost many sacrifices both of time and money. But: *Christus vincit! Christus regnat! Christus imperat!*

Then the celebration of Corpus Christi at Leipzig in 1957, a feast which in our country does not fall on a holiday. Each of the participants in the procession had to ask his employer for a day off, the children for a holiday from school. Some 12,000 to 15,000 persons came together on this workday morning to assist at the pontifical high Mass, to communicate and to pay homage to the Lord by the procession.

What is it that gives us fortitude in such circumstances? It is the Lord who lives amongst us and whom we meet continually in the holy liturgy and in His revealing Word.

To Him be glory for ever and ever!